APUK
A STATE IN WAITING

Professor Madhel Malek Agei BA, Msc, PhD

A Note from the Publisher

The publisher wishes to acknowledge and thank Dr Douglas H. Johnson for his invaluable help and support for Africa World Books and its mission of preserving and promoting African cultural and literary traditions and history. Dr Johnson and fellow historians have been instrumental in ensuring that African people remain connected to their past and their identity. Africa World Books is proud to carry on this mission.

ISBN 978-0-6487937-8-6
© Professor Madhel Malek Agei

All rights reserved. No part of this publication may be reproduced, stored in a retrieval system, or transmitted, in any form, or by any means, electronic, mechanical, photocopying, recording or otherwise, without the prior permission of the publishers.
This book is sold subject to the conditions that it shall not, by way of trade or otherwise, be lent, re-sold, hired out or otherwise circulated without the publisher's prior consent in any form of binding or cover other than in which it is published and without a similar condition including the condition being imposed on the subsequent purchaser.
Africa World Books Pty. Ltd.
Editors: Nathan Ellis, Larry Ellis

*This book is dedicated to my parents, Ajok and Malek
who have departed from this world.
The pain from these losses cemented a way.*

About the Author

Wherever people have experienced poverty or severe life trauma, it is not rare for their lives to atrophy. Endemic poverty decreases the ability of people to combat its causes. Thusly, they continue to be disabled and unable to sustain themselves.

My great passion is resurrecting such people. I wish to help my people who include traumatized children and the disabled, to find healthy perceptions of themselves, improve relationships and to know themselves as peaceful, complete, whole and safe.

I know that no single approach is the right one for every person, and so I have been trained in a range of modalities including historical development on sovereign clan nations in antiquity, core values, cultural identity, divinity, and helping to attune to development goals.

I was born 1954 in Chueibet Malek Village, Jak Apuk County. I have trained teachers and taught business policy and strategic planning at the Catholic University of South Sudan. I also served in public services and as a Minister in the Public Services, and Education ministries.

My educational background includes a Doctorate of Philosophy in Business Administration for Development Planning, a MSC in Regional Planning from Graduate School of the University of Liberia in Liberia, a BA in Political Science from Cuttington University, a Divinity College in Liberia.

Acknowledgements

I am grateful to the Nhialic-God, Deng-Mayual, the Creator of the Universe, the Heavenly, and the Most-High, whose faithfulness has been my strength. How awesome!

I would be failing in my duty if I do not recognize, with deep appreciation, all the people who provided invaluable financial assistance towards the publication of this book. Their unwavering support has made it all a reality.

I am deeply indebted to James Maruon Agolong Bol, my promoter, for his valuable guidance, influence, critical comments, insight, constant encouragement, supportive attitude and patience during the difficult time of writing this book.

I must thank Miss Aguer Ngor Athian who was always ready to help whenever I approached. She is indeed a wonderful person whom I can never forget.

I wish to express my great debt to John Ashworth for his time and willingness to share his experiences, perceptions, opinions, scholastic materials. He has been a continual source of personal friendship and intellectual stimulation. Thank you for being the greatest of friends!

I have also to thank Dr Corby at the Department of Social Sciences, Cuttington University in Liberia for his scholarly spirit and his continued willingness to share his wealth of knowledge.

I am also deeply grateful to my beloved daughter Achan Agei. Although she is young and knows little of issues that I am writing about, she encouraged and inspired me to write this history of our heritage. Also, to my nephew Chan Ngor Bak Matik, who tirelessly helped me to travel home and took photos of the Unknown Sacred Spear and The House of Spirit Powers.

To Mador Malek Agei known as Mador Kuen-yom, Aguelet Agei Aguelet Agei known as Aguelet Lonh-toch, Maruop Atany Adiar Agei and others, thank you for the interest you have shown in this book and for your valuable input.

To my wife, the Honourable Ayak Ngor Agei, thank you for believing in me always and for your unwavering support. You are indeed an unwavering pillar of strength!

To my children, Achan Agei, Deng Agei, Ajok Amuor Agei, Malek Agei, Agei Adam Agei and Angou Charity Agei, who wanted me to write the history of their grandparents and beyond to know and be with them. You have been the driving force behind the achievement of this book. Thank you for being the greatest of colleagues!

To my late parents, Ajok and Malek Agei and my late parents-in-law, Achol and Ngor Athian. May your souls rest in peace in the world of spirit!

Many thanks to my brothers, sisters, nephews and nieces, my sisters-in-law, brothers-in-law, uncles, aunts, indeed all my relatives and those supported me in any respect during the journey of writing this book.

My thanks also go to those who provided some photos, such as Peter Lual Reech Deng and Agei Deng Malek.

I should also mention and acknowledge the wounded hero soldiers of the Bride Start Campaign, Operation Jungle Storm, and the Division Koryom colleagues in the National Parliament of South Sudan who from time to time would lament the fact that the history of our people was written by the same people who colonized the country (Apuk state included). That situation led to glorification of the colonial conquerors. Those who collaborated with them were sometimes perceived to be freedom fighters, thus distorting the historical facts. This, I must acknowledge, influenced and inspired me to write this book, with the goal to reveal the true nature of what happened in the past. They are many and I must say their concerns made political and historical sense. My acknowledgement goes to them.

One more person that I am indebted to is Tinega George Ong'ondi, who tirelessly contributed to the typing of the book. He freely gave me office space, computer and printing equipment, and he assisted despite the heavy duties entrusted to him by International

Acknowledgements

and National Organizations. His assistance contributed a great deal towards shaping the book into sensible and prudent material. All despite me being ambitious, hardworking, and jobless in my beloved country.

Finally, but not least, I am greatly indebted to Peter Lual Reech Deng the CEO and founder of Africa World Books including the entire team there, and to the editors; Nathan Ellis and Larry Ellis, whose intellectual and wonderful timely input contributed to making this book a sound and sensible publication. You indeed made very important corrections, suggestions, and extremely useful comments regarding the issues dealt with in the book.

Special acknowledgements to Michael Mahoney for the brilliant design and artwork on the cover.

Sections

Why did I write this book?	13
Overview	19
The Dinka Apuk and South Sudan	23
Culture and Religion	30
Rum, Aleek, and the Sausage Tree	65
Bol	68
Rum the Stranger	69
"Apuk" Defined	78
Deng Mabuoch. Spiritual Priest or an Impostor?	99
Customary Law in the Modern Era	104
Apuk Cultural Curses	128
A Very Fishy Tale	158
The Dinka Apuk People	170
Symbols and Rituals	203
Apuk Life	213
Traditional Mourning for a High Priest Chief	215
Politics and History	232
Fighting Corruption	248
The Problem with Judiciary Revenues	252
Geographics and Boundaries	266
Social and Economic Development	293
The Dynasty Founded by Rum	308
Appendix 1 - Mourning Rituals and Practices for the Burial of a Priest Chief	375
Appendix 2 - The Reunion with Body Spirits after the Burial of a Priest Chief	360
Appendix 3 - Erection of a Shrine to Deng Enactments of Warfare from the Past	383

Why did I write this book?

Whoever does not inform his children of his grandparents has destroyed his child, marred his descendants, and injured his offspring the day he dies. Whoever does not make use of his ancestry, has muddled his reason. Whoever is unconcerned with his lineage, has lost his mind. Whoever neglects his origin, his stupidity has become critical. Whoever is unaware of his ancestry, his incompetence has become immense. Whoever is ignorant of his roots, his intellect has vanished. Whoever does not know his place of origin, his honour has collapsed.

Quote from a Timbuktu scholar in the 14th century

I am not writing about the clans of the Apuk of the Nilotic speaking peoples to glorify or praise them in anyway whatsoever. I simply want people to appreciate where today's Apuk clan historically came from, what they went through, and the meaning behind the word *apuk* as it is essentially a state of mind and spirit.

I have in my very respectful approach attempted to record some events that happened during my lifetime that I have witnessed and experienced. I have also written about what ancient sources said about our ancestors during the dynasty eras. I have provided the explanation about *apuk*, reconciliation, prayer, ritual, sacrifice, homicide, crime, and the Law of *apuk* penalties, forgiveness, clan-divinity and their relationship to *apuk* itself. In achieving this I am driven by the principles of pure honesty, openness and respect for all those who I have mentioned regarding the history, identity, and culture of the Apuk. If what I have written is painful to some it is without intent or malice. What I wrote are reflections of the true facts of what actually took place. And if some appear glorified it is because those mentioned did exactly what was transcribed.

1 The intention is to quote the historical reality and the truth of what happened during the ancient dynasty eras under discussion for present and future generations.
2 To the best of my recall and understanding, it is very painful that the history of our clan, sub-clan and clan-divinities has not been recorded properly. Often, it has been written by outsiders who did not experience the events themselves and have ended up distorting the facts.
3 To write a history book on clan-divinity, culture, clan and language of identity like this can sometimes generate negativity in some while being admired by others.
4 For every written event, you may find those who will be irritated by the truth and would rather like or prefer the facts to be swept under the carpet, while others might like the truth to be told as is. Therefore, it is necessary that I wrote largely only about those things that ancient sources said and issues that I personally observed and witnessed.
5 As we are all aware, much of the history in this world has been written by the 'victors' and all else ends up destroyed. I can only transcribe what I have managed to unearth.

When I grew up in the Apuk homeland in Machuet area at Chueibet Malek village, a number of the things I have written about took place. During this time, I was associated with high priest chief Malek Agei in the Traditional Appeals Court. I was recording cases on trial sentences there after school holidays from 1962 to 1969.

The journey I travelled in my lifetime was extraordinary, difficult and unpredictable.

To have grown up and escaped from our beloved country because of diabolic and barbaric treatment to which we were subjected by

Why did I write this book?

the Colonial regime; to have fought for the independence of the motherland and finally to have returned alive to our country in the manner I did, was indeed equivalent to coming back to enjoy normal life in my beloved country that was unlike the one I left before.

My Inherent Bias

In all writing there is always the flaw of inherent bias, and no person can claim to be truly independent in that regard. The strength of debate is in the ability to discern and be open to constructive critiques. The writer has refined his position by placing material in the public domain where it was reviewed and interrogated. Mistakes were referred to the sources for correction. I come to this study of the history of the Apuk clans with prior clan divinity, culture, social and other convictions which define my scope of interest, interaction and prejudices regarding assorted topics. I am charged with providing a truthful history of the Apuk Clans overlapped by the history of South Sudan so as to pursue honest discourse. I dealt with the historical facts as they appear, not how I wanted them to appear. I am fully aware that it is usually natural to defend what one believes in. However, if the material is adjusted to suit those persuasions, it becomes dishonest. The whole lot of this is easier said than done, but my integrity as a person is on the line. The stink of natural bias, specifically extreme bias, pollutes everything it touches, thus annulling the quality of knowledge and betrays its greater pursuit to seek the truth.

The writer views the science of disagreement as more important than the process of agreeing. Biased arguments are not constructive, and arguments of opinion where the facts are not provided correctly are destructive. I do not seek any converts whatsoever but hope for intellectual discourse that lends its intelligence to the development of humankind in South Sudan. Debate is critical in this pursuit and I encourage constructive discourse that will benefit South Sudanese unity and diversity. The goal is the cream of logic, and not the simply letting the loudest voice dominate.

Disagreeing with someone does not automatically invalidate their sincerity or their broader work outside the area under debate. If an argument is valid it will always focus on the area under discussion. If the logic presented is invalid people must speak to that specific thing as opposed to making wide-ranging statements. I attempted to address the following issues:

1. The origin of the culture, clans, history, people, names and South Sudan itself.
2. The identity of the people of South Sudan, and its clans.
3. A history of the Apuk clans, South Sudan, state positions, dirty money, and the dishonest use of public funds.
4. Geographical location, boundaries, demarcation and definitions.
5. Advantages, disadvantages and consequences of the old colonial boundaries between South Sudan and Sudan.

I came to write this history of the Apuk because I am part of it. I am possessed of clan divinity and social conviction. They define my scope of interest, my interactions and my prejudices.

The ideological foundation of the history of Apuk culture and civilization is created through the knowledge of the philosophers and great minds of the past and building upon that foundational knowledge.

For instance, according to some academicians, it is not that truly educated people know a lot, it is their ability to process and correctly apply the information they receive. They understand complex hypotheses and the consequences created. One tool that truly conscious, sensible and aware people use are debates to chase down truths and find optimal solutions. They are mature enough to deal with goals objectively and do not see informed disagreement as a disaster.

Every aspect of our history is ours to claim as tribes or clans. All our clans or tribes were part of Sudan, and now South Sudan. It is a history of diversity. If the world is not in isolation, then neither are the clans or the country.

Why did I write this book?

The history of the major religions of Egypt and Sudan did not occur in an ethnic vacuum, with clans and divinities on the outside. The constant victim even then was South Sudan. All this is part of the South Sudanese journey.

The history of South Sudan and the overlapping history of the Jieng-Dinka clans shows trade with the Arabs and even the Far East going back to antiquity. The history of the South Sudanese people must include the past and present contributions to be a true history and must include the good and the bad.

This history must conform to the clan cultural model-standard while at the same time meeting the highest threshold of truthful knowledge. This, however, is separate from viewing history through a political or tribal lens. History must be viewed in connection with the social dynamics of the contemporary day, but it must also be weighted within its timeframe. People must not superimpose contemporary views onto ancient history.

It is factual that there is a natural bias, inborn in all interpretations of historical events. However, the crucial goals still must be to seek the truth, learn from the past, absorb the spirit of human possibility, and honour our moral obligation to remember.

I am not presenting the history of the Apuk clans to make South Sudan more divided. I am seeking to express commonalities and linkages that might unite South Sudan in its diversity. I am fully aware that every reader of history has a motive for why they want to discover or clarify a truth. Every writer of history always has an agenda, hidden or expressed.

For some, it is ethnic pride. For others, it is the justification of their claim to the spoils of inequity. To others still, it is a way to blame the past for their current failures. Often, it is a way to make themselves heard for future political gain on tribalism notions and is a way to draw attention to national cohesion mechanisms.

For the history of the Apuk clans, I attempted to promote the good habits for national cohesion and national values. I hope to remove the bad habits that lead to failure, and inequity. I truly wish for us that we will reclaim our pride in our ethnicities and identities.

APUK : A STATE IN WAITING

I am writing this to be a symbol of qualitative work. It entails the ability and willingness of many contributors and investigators. They acknowledge and take account of the myriad ways they may influence findings that become accepted as knowledge.

I will explain the ability to reflect inward towards oneself as an inquirer. Outwards to the cultural, historical, linguistic, political, and other forces that shape everything about the inquiry. I came to this as a writer of history, sponsor, and participant regarding the social interactions we all share.

Overview

This book is mainly about the Dinka Apuk of South Sudan; its land, people, divinities, culture, authority, hegemony. I will attempt to address the challenges facing the southwest Dinka Rek clan, particularly in the Apuk area of Tonj state.

I will write the little I know about their historical beliefs and animal sacrifices. The implications of traditionalism, divinity penalties, and clan spirit roles will also be a discussion. I welcome those having an interest to write on the subject and look forward to more research being done regarding the vast issues besetting the region.

The term *apuk* originated from a punishment or penalty blood fine. Although just one word, it conveys an entire concept. Loosely, it is the method whereby homicides or serious breaches committed by clansmen or clanswomen, with or without implied consent from clan members, are resolved and ultimately forgiven.

In the Dinka language, *Juwiir* is the combination of *ju* and *wiir*.

Ju is the name of the savannah shrub tree that grows by the shore.

Wiir[1] refers to more than something that holds water. Rivers, wells, lakes, pools, and reservoirs, for example. The name literally describes an 'interior side, or a ring'.

Juwiir today means The Dinka Rek people.[2] or Homeland of the Dinka Rek clans.

---

1   Word –*wiir* describes a falling object inside a well, or pool, river by saying that a ring has fallen inside the well or river. In the Dinka Rek language, you say: "Aci lony wiir" – a ring felt inside a well or river water.

2   Encyclopedia Britannia "Sudan"

APUK : A STATE IN WAITING

I will focus on those who occupy the Savannah Valley[3] region, found in the southwest of the Apuk homeland in order to preserve its history in writing.

The Dinka Apuk clans are derived from the Muonyjang or Jang Rek nationalities. The Dinka Rek clan is the original stem from which other clans branched off during migration periods. These clans separated and settled in the Juwiir territory in the middle of the Bahr El Ghazal Region.

These people call themselves "Eagle", after the most powerful and impressive raptor bird of prey in Africa. It is embodied in many ways in their cultural symbols. The Apuk Eagle land of the Dinka Rek is bordered by the Kuanythii, Nyang and Kuach sub-clans in the north, Jurchol-Luo of the Nilotic stock of Wau State in the west, Muok sub-clans in the extreme south, and Yar sub-clans in the south, Thony sub-clans are in the southeast across the Wanhalel River on the eastern bank. The Thony are also in the swampy wetland to the extreme the east, far beyond the Mading and Akarap Apuk Juwiir at the Toch wetland, and of the Luanykoth sub-clans in the east. The Apuk clan is the largest in Southern Tonj State.

Nowhere in the Apuk clans is there spirituality outside of the culture that holds it and governs its practices as a community. Most use symbolic art for institutionalizing beliefs for posterity. The key religion is usually ethno-specific which generally share elements in common with Abrahamic faiths and other indigenous belief practices around the country.

It is similar to Judaism, as they are not involved in proselytizing when compared to Islam and Christianity. The many religions of the Dinka Apuk clans are inseparable from ethnic culture and their symbols of identification.

For example, the religion of the Pabuor, Parum, Padiangbaar and Patiir clans are historically part of their cultural identity.

The spiritual fabric is for subjective discourse. The rituals of the

---

[3] Department of Arts of Africa, Oceania, and the Americas. Trade and the Spread of Islam in Africa. In Heilbrunn Timeline of Art History. New York: The Metropolitan Museum of Art, 2000- (October 2001)

Overview

priests/chiefs when invoking prayers in each clan are all highly organized. Without exception, they function and are practised in a communal setting. The clans all have various degrees of a priest class for ceremonies, sacrifices, libations, religious holidays, creation stories, saints, and the divine principles of punishment and reward. There is one creator in clan belief principles. It is infused with different energies that are valued as aspects of the 'divine forces' found in nature. Not so different from Allah, who is said to have various attributes embodied in one God.

The transformation of the dynasty era of the Apuk began in the 19th century. Contemporary chiefdom changed to Apuk traditional chieftaincy.

It was recognized in 1893[4] as home to numerous ancient civilizations, such as the Kingdom of Kush. Most of them flourished and simultaneously evolved systems of kingship along the Nile valley[5]. The early history is interweaved with the history of ancient Sudan and ancient Kush.

Through trade and military expeditions, the Nilotic people contributed to the inclusive history of the Nile Valley in the Savannah region. It was Christianised in the 19th century AD[6], and remains primarily so in conjunction with traditional beliefs[7].

The ancient Savannah valley language stands as the oldest recorded Nilotic language (Nilo-Saharan language) with records dating to the 9th century AD. Christians promoted the written Apuk language through the Dinka Rek clans, and it stands as one of the few recorded Nilotic Languages in the region.

The traditional mourning ritual and practices after the burial of a priest/chief is a popular ceremony among Apuk clans in South Sudan. By using a phenomenological approach, the Parum clan experiences,

---

4 AbbasAbbas, Mekki. The Sudan question: the dispute over the Anglo-Egyptian condominium, 1884- 1951 (1952)
5 Warburg, Gabriel. Sudan Under Wingate: Administration in the Anglo-Egyptian Sudan (1899-1916) (1971)
6 Ibb
7 Holt, P.M., and M.W. Daly. History of the Sudan: From the Coming of Islam to the Present Day (6th es. 2011)

and the meaning of the after-burial shrine ceremony for a priest/chief were studied. The available literature outlined the rituals and practices of various sub-clans and clans of the Apuk and the Jieng of Tonj State, that were performed. They included the slaughtering of bulls and sheep with specific colours, the celebration style, the mourning period, and the cleansing ceremonies.

Some of the death rituals and practices are still adhered to in the contemporary villages of Apuk. Others are adapted, and new practices have emerged. One is the use of the coffin. While popular, it has not fully replaced the practices of readily available cowhides in the communities. Within an Apuk context, the dead are regarded as ancestors, while spiritual priests are agents for prosperity and continued descended lineage within families.

They are treated with great respect as they are believed to have a special relationship with the living, raw life spirit, the body spirit, and the world spirit. Proper rites and ceremonies performed following the death of a priest-chief in the community reflect this belief. Any deviation from the above might be alleged as a sign of disrespect for the ancestors, or the various spirits. Bad luck from spiritual powers could befall a clan or an heir to the family member who does not adhere to the stipulated practices.

The shrine rituals and practices of raising a shrine on the tomb after the burial of the current priest-chief in the Parum clan highlight the significant perceptions, meanings, and feelings about the "after burial shrine ceremonies". While it is perceived as a celebration, the important functions of this ceremony were connected to the comforting and supporting of the bereaved and helping them to cope with the impact of the loss of a high priest/chief in the spiritual clan.

Neglecting the rituals hurts the bereaved community and the family. This also delays the chances of recovery from grief. The afterburial shrine ceremony can be an effective coping strategy because of the nature of the way it is conducted, and types of donations collected for ceremonies. The experiences of this writer regarding the "afterburial shrine" ceremony and the meaning attached to it might serve as guiding principles for interested researchers to explore regarding the psychological needs of the bereaved in the Apuk communities.

The Dinka Apuk and South Sudan

The Dinka Apuk clans are the largest clans of the Dinka Rek (known as Jaang or Jieng) ethnic groups in the southern Tonj State. They belong to a group of cultures known as the Nilotic, inhabiting southern Tonj. They are located along the small rivers, streams, and small seasonal lakes in the savannah region.

The Apuk is an alliance of tribes (or clans). Each section is a separate political entity with established clan-based rights to well defined territories. The main Apuk sections and sub-sections include the Machuet Apuk, Maluil Apuk, Malony Apuk, and Aliai Apuk.

The people have no centralized political authority. As a substitute, they are an alliance of many independent states united by security threats, socioeconomic interests, symbols of divinities and the religious spirituality of Jok and Yath, and the interlinked sub-clans. The spiritual beings worshipped have numerous names such as: Yath, Jak, Agoloong, Atiip. Deng, Deng Kur, Dengdit, Deng Mayual, Deng Piol, Macar, Machar, Machardit, Abuk, and Garang. However, Nhialic towers above all others.

Divine clans traditionally have ritual chiefs, known as the masters of the fishing spear or *beny bith*, who have two separate lines of authority. They control of both the priesthood (*beny bith*) and lead the fighters in times of war. They have powers providing divine unity, reconciliation, peace, body spirits, human life, clan spiritual prayers, sacrifices, mediation, invocations, and leadership. This goes all the way back to the development era of the ancient dynasties.

They are an agro-pastoral people, relying on cattle herding near lake and river banks and swampy wetland camps in the dry season. They are adept at growing millet (*awuou*), groundnuts (*miguang*), sorghum (*rap*), beans (*akuem*), and other varieties of grains at their homesteads during the rainy season. The Apuk population constitutes about 48% of the population of Tonj South.

They speak a Rek language called *thuongmuonyjang* and are a branch of the Rek clan that refer to themselves as *Muonyjang* (singular) and *Muonyjieng* (plural). The name means "people" in the Dinka language. It refers to one of the branches of the Nile River near Lake Nilotes and derives mainly from the sedentary agro-pastoral peoples of the Nile Valley and African Great Lakes region who speak Nilotic languages, including the Luo.

The meaning of the word *apuk* is compensation for forgiveness re clan crimes when leading a sorrowful life. This will be explained later in the book. The understanding of *apuk* is vital for the salvation of everyone from the damage or wrongdoings in a person's life.

Later, I will write about the historical development of *apuk*, most especially how it evolved into its basic rules of laws regarding traditional clan practices. I will elaborate upon the eagle identity genesis. My wish is to enlighten you, the reader, of its history, identity, nationality, reparations, customary laws, and bany bith power. Through these lies the spirit and power of its people.

I write about forgiveness to enlighten people regarding our history. It is as much about facts as feeling and way of life. Much of it is unwritten history passed along by word of mouth. This and future generations should be aware of the inexorable Apuk Law of Compensation. I wish to explain Apuk history to say that when adversaries commenced twisting the pride of Apuk national identity, they have no way of escaping the law unless they explain themselves and atone. This atonement removes these memories and satisfies the laws of the clan spirit dating back to antiquity.

Concerning those people who do not acknowledge that *apuk* is the best path to reconciliation, and when this is brought to the attention of the clan, the traditional rules of law to enforce reparation penalties or punishments for the forgiveness of clan crimes such as homicide, are channelled through the ritual priest/chief. He will declare to the victimised clans the best way in which the clan spirit may be obtained to punish guilty clans and reimburse victim clans in order to reconcile them. This provides clan-wide recognition where it applies to learning the divine truths made visible by the divine minister or the divine master of the fishing spear. The spear houses spiritual powers replicated through descended heirs of the divine clan divinities. The Parum, Pabuor and Pagong clans possess divine spiritual powers as reputable masters of the fishing spear through which the powers of the clan divinity spears may be exercised for the benefit of the Apuk people.

History is the grandfather clock that the people of Apuk clans use to tell their social, political and cultural time of day. It is a compass they use to find themselves on the map of human geography. It tells them where they are, but more importantly, what they must be. The eagle symbol tells them where people, divinities, customary rules of laws, culture, and values are. It tells them what their past, present and future looks like. What they have done, and what they must not do.

Identity should be of paramount consideration. Without it, life would not be grounded. History is our clarifier and our memory. Every person and every struggle that forgets history repeats it.

Clan Apukism is all about the indigenous clans and the people who live it. This is the sole ideology proven capable of protecting and sustaining the gains of the people against the new scramble for our Apuk homeland. This is an immensely important statement at a time where our land is being handed over on a silver platter to any and all bidders. Those criminals who are using our people, lands, and natural resources for their own self-serving, foolish purposes.

A Dinka Apuk transformation should begin with a realization of what Apuk means by Apuk clans, for Apuk clans. We must see our specific identity, historic identity, cultural identity, our conception of life, and our political and social associations. The Apuk clan consciousness must be aware of its obligations, duties, and responsibilities to the truth. It must be faithful in its allegiance to kin and in its respect for human dignity, freedom, and self-reliance in the Apuk homeland.

This study of the Apuk clans is dedicated to providing comprehensive, reliable, and accurate information concerning their history in South Sudan. I have attempted to provide insight into its culture including those Apuk people caught in the dispersion of the communities and those living outside either the present day Apuk region or the ancient Apuk homeland.

In past times many were horrifically kidnapped and carried off into servitude, never to be returned. Pro-Apukism was and remains the only proven ideology that can rescue and resolve the conditions of our people. Specifically, those in Southern Apuk, Northern Apuk Toch, and Eastern Apuk Padoch. We must rescue them from the present-day predators that came, stole, robbed, raped, looted, mis-educated, misled, destroyed them and plundered their resources. This abomination turned the Apuk people into beggars and dependent on others. It is the goal of this writer and the sponsors to nurture understanding through knowledge in order to generate constructive change in South Sudanese society.

Serudi Ta of Ancient Egypt was quoted as saying:

"Repair the damaged, re-join the separated, replenish the depleted, set right the wrong, strengthen the weak and weakened, and make to flourish the fragile and undeveloped!"

Society is owned by everyone who chooses to contribute. People pool intelligence and hard work to deliver a lifestyle reflecting an authentic perspective on the people. The people are the key, and consistent good work determines everything. It is up to the people to decide their future. There are no great names, only great works.

The Apuk Lith symbol of an eagle is an Apuk ethos representing the fundamental coming together of their most cherished ideas and ideals. These serve as the basis for a broad people-based accord for progressive growth. Understanding the genesis of one's historical identity is the task embodied in the word Apuk. It is defined as a social justice, a rule of customary law, a name, a clan divinity, a culture, and the power of freedom arising up for peace. Just like an eagle. The king of birds.

The Jieng language definition explains *apuk* as a punishment or penalty blood fine of customary court for killing, or for inflicting serious wounds executed with the full knowledge and understanding of those actions by the clansmen or clanswomen found guilty.

The word eagle is translated as *lith*. The name Apuk Lith or *clan lith* identifies them.

Apuk Lith itself has three identical branches. There is the Southern Apuk Juwiir Eagle, the Eastern Apuk Padoch Eagle and the Northern Apuk Toch Eagle. They have had identical cultures and rules of law since antiquity. I will explain the little that I may know about Southern Apuk Eagle and will provide an explanation on what Apuk means in *thong muonyjang*, or *thuongjang*.

The three branches of people of the clan Apuk Lith and their geographical locations are described below:

The Northern Apuk Lith

The Northern Apuk Lith inhabit the Jur River swampland territory in the northeast Gogrial State. This covers both sides to the northwest and northeast of Dinka Rek. Their clans moved towards the north-eastern Rek Dinka and settled along the vast eastern Jur River banks and along the western Jur River in the enclaves of Dinka Rek. It borders the Jurchol-Luo Nilotic ethnic groups in the south and east, and the Waw clans and Kuac clans of the Dinka Rek in the southwest. It also borders the Aguok clans in the west, and the Twic clans in the north, as well as the Nuer of the Nilotic ethnic groups of the Western White Nile River in the east stretching into Toch wetland swamps, and the Kongor clans in the south. It also borders the Abiem clans in the extreme south in the Savannah region.

The Northeastern Apuk Lith

The north-eastern Apuk Lith settled in Padoch on the western shores of the Machar Rek River. These clans occupy both sides of the river stretching to the Apuk swampland territory to the northeast of the Dinka Rek clans.

The Southern Apuk Lith

The Southern Apuk Lith inhabit the banks on the western Wanhalel River in southwestern Dinka Rek of Tonj State. In this study, I focus on Southern Apuk and its people. I do so primarily regarding the historical development eras, and how Apuk history formed the basic rules of law and traditional clan practices. I will elaborate a little on what clan Apuk is all about regarding homicide, and on what the *apuk* tradition entails regarding court penalties for the guilty. I will cover clan divinities and eagle identification symbolism, what made it so important regarding clan homicide penalties, and how Apuk history evolved into the basic rules of laws for traditional clan practices.

About the Region

- Apuk is located approximately 19.4 km (12 mi) north of the Tonj capital of the state, and 64.37 km (40 mi) from the eastern border of Wau state.
- Area: approximately 430 sq. km (166 sq. mi).
- Population: approximately 60,000 (2016 census).
- Population density: 50 to 100 inhabitants per sq. km.
- Economy: Agro-pastoralist, with livestock accounting for 85 percent of the community's per capita income.
- Endowed with rich natural resource deposits of oil and gas. Can also be developed, for tourism although the two are not generally compatible.

The Dinka Apuk and South Sudan

- Apuk controls 70 percent of the money markets in the southern Tonj region.
- The first Conference regarding Dinka Customary Laws was held in the town of Wanhalel of the Dinka Apuk in 1927. It marked the birth of the written Jieng Traditional Customary Laws, Traditional Chiefs Courts and Traditional Appeal Courts. They were all adopted into laws. It was a cultural victory.
- Thiet Town of Apuk was captured on August 22, 1984 by the SPLA forces under the command of George Kuach, a son of the Malual Rek clan in the northern Bahr El Ghazal Region.
- After he captured Thiet Town, Mayom Mission School became the main Military Headquarters for the SPLA and SPLM operations in the whole of the Bahr El Ghazal Region and remained there until the CPA was ratified.
- The base of the Sudan People's Liberation in Army (SPLA) was established in the Apuk area in 1984, immediately after the movement's inception in 1983. However, military operations initially began in 1981 when they started attacking traders, military forces, military convoys and security agents.
- Banking institutions are keen to locate there, and the process is underway to have branches in Thiet Town.
- A social insurance firm has identified Thiet Town as suitable for a branch.
- There is a Kurlueth Teachers Training Institute and campus for students.
- The first SPLM Regional Conference was held in the Kurlueth Institute of Education (KIE) and the Mayom Mission School and was chaired by the late Dr John Garang De Mabior, in 2000 for Bahr El Ghazal Region.
- All major traders in Tonj region have small branches operating in the area.

Culture and Religion

Like other Dinka nationalities, the Apuk are an alliance and a cultural federation of sub-nationalities rather than a political federation. The concept of state and hence political institution, structure, and consequently authority does not exist among the Southern Apuk clans. Each Apuk nationality is a section in an autonomous political entity.

Chieftainship is ritualized in the lineage of a clan. It is hereditary and holds the title of *beny baai* or *beny bith* for one person. In plural, *bany baai* refers to traditional chiefs, or *bany biith* referring to masters of the fishing spear or *bany* referring to both traditional chiefs and masters of the fishing spear. This translates into different things such as chief, divine priest chief, knowledgeable, skilful or military officer. There has always been the dual control title for military leaders and ritual priest chiefs. The title always has an attribute attached to indicate the office. For example, *beny ring* or *beny rim* (or *riem*), *beny bith* or *beny aciek* and *bany baai*, means chieftainship of the clan people or sub-clan people.

The word *ring* (or *rem* or *riem*) refers to the supernatural powers of the chief or his spirit powers and is also referred to as *jak* or *jok*, *yath* or *yieth*. *Bith*, on the other hand, refers to the sacred fishing-spear (un-barbed or un-serrated) as a symbol of office and the power of clan divinities and clan spirits.

The divine priests who are also leaders (masters of the fishing spear, medicine women/men, and clan chiefs) exert great influence.

Culture and Religion

Except in a few cases, the spiritual leaders more often reject secular authority, but not in the same manner that fundamental Islamic leaders reject secular state authority. The Apuk traditional chiefs exercise republican authority by persuasion but not through any known instruments of coercion and force. Divinity authority can only be exercised effectively in the family, particularly the clan Parum or clan Wundior lineages while being adherent strictly to the values and practices of Rum Wenkook, the first founding father of the clan Parum and father of Ateny Wundior and the Apuk dynasty.

The Apuk in Tonj State

According to anthropologists, the Apuk is a sub-clan of the main Dinka Rek clan known as the Muonyjang or Jaang. Jaang defines "tribe or clan" as a state or a nation (wut or wuonda, meaning "our nation" or "our country" or "our state").

However, many writers define a "clan" as a "tribe". The history of the Apuk state, its conquests, and the centralized worship of the one true God, yath, or jok or jak, figure prominently in the history of the Dinka Rek culture through the supreme, creator god which is Nhialic the god of the sky and rain, and the ruler of all the spirits.

The associations of nationalities of sub-clans, about a dozen in all, call themselves Raan de Jieng or Kooch de Jieng. That is, Jieng clansmen and clanswomen or Jieng states or nations or countries.[8]

The ancient Sudanese people are the source of the Jaang people. The Jaang Rek branch may have been the original stem of the Dinka Apuk, in the habitat of southern Tonj State and other Jaang Rek states. But this may be questioned considering that all Jaang or Jieng states, also known as Jaang clans, speak very similar languages and share the common marks of clans made differently between clansmen. They speak the language of the Apuk clans of southern

---

8 Nebel, Arthur, *The Dinka Dictionary*, published by Veronica Father, Wau, 1954

Tonj that belong to the Rek national languages of southwestern Rek Jieng in South Sudan.

It is possible that the Jaang nation-states descend from a people whose original language, habitat and migrations through many centuries can no longer be traced.

Therefore, the Apuk clan state developed mostly in seclusion when determining how to respond to the unique cultural, historical, and divinity challenges it faced. One of these challenges was confronting the fundamental aspects of reality that are the grounds and influences of its history, culture, and nationality.

Cultural and Religious History

The moment you have a religion you have organization. Two inseparable concepts, as one creates the other. Organized rituals make culture. Organized spirituality makes a religion. It is believed it was ancient native religion, and not agriculture, that gave rise to Apuk. This was followed by centralized political and military organizations, economies, and identities. Created thusly were centralized values and divine laws for what would have been otherwise disparate peoples. The commonalities allow for greater cooperation and collective objectives.

During the reign of the Christian reformers from the early medieval or feudal periods down to the 1900s, missionaries came to convert the Nilotic clans in the Apuk homelands in South Sudan.

The earliest historical records come from Anglo-Egyptian Sudan sources, which describe the land upstream towards the south as "wretched."[9] The Apuk is part of the territories of the Ancient Kush King, Meroe and the Rek Dinka state of Nilotic descendants which is older than Ancient Egypt or Sudan. It had a dominating political structure and a significant influence over its neighbours for centuries. Even today, the legacy of the Apuk and

---

9   S. O. Y. Keita (1993). "Studies and Comments on Ancient Egyptian Biological Relationships". History in Africa (JSTOR) 20: 129- 154. Retrieved 2015-04-11.

Culture and Religion

their cultural and traditional religious practices remain important ancient studies.

Dinka Apuk mythology refers to the culture and folk tales of those people. Spirituality is the fundamental culture of the divine connection that the people have as a diverse group. It is just as varied from Agar Jieng to Bor Jieng, to the Azande in East Africa. There is no genetic connection that binds all Apuk religions. No unique exclusive religious approval that puts 'Apuk spirituality' into one empirically definable block. That religious experience is locked into the culture, and the culture is locked into identity. Where one varies, so too does the other.

One persistent misconception is that the native faiths are all polytheistic. That the religions of the clans of southwestern Apuk may be henotheistic, or monotheistic. This blunder is mocking since the concept of monotheism had its genesis in early clan divinity. In many belief systems, there is still one creator with different energies that are valued and are aspects of the divine forces found in culture or nature.

There is no genetic material, which can create uniformity in belief and religions all over Apuk that are unvaryingly tied to lifestyle. The people range from the nomadic to sedentary, from dynastic chiefdoms to town dwellers, from hunters to herders and farmers.

Religion evolves to suit society. And because there is language variation, plus deep cultural and genetic diversity, there is not any process to make entire clans and sub-clans share one religion. For at least the last 700 years, these people shared the same problems in the same area. For millennia, most people of them did not know of anyone beyond 1000 km (620 miles) away. Military expeditions for territorial expansionism was uncommon.

The clan divinity or religion of the Apuk, as with everywhere else, has a profound connection to culture. Often, those cultures are not destroyed by new faiths but modified to accommodate the lessees of the new religion. This has happened in Judaism, Christianity and Islam. The greater the cultural ethos of the group, the more they traditionalize the incoming faiths into their poli-cultural domain.

APUK : A STATE IN WAITING

Divinity, Spirits, and the Clans

Like all clans of the Rek Jieng in the west, the Apuk clans call the Divinity *Nhialic ee tok*. The Christians know it as 'God', the Muslims as 'Allah'[10], the Jews by several names, and the list goes on. Nonetheless, divinity is also a widespread term for multiple conceptions that differ significantly from one another. The powers of divine clan spirits and the clan divinities are distinct from one another, although most simply say *ee Nhialic*, "it is Divinity"[11] in southwestern Apuk. Multiple gods cause no problem in the context of clan language and life. Nevertheless, it is impossible to completely avoid the problems when statements bearing upon the subject are translated into other languages.

The Apuk have a circular temple of deities and of course, Nhialic[12] who controls the destiny of every human, plant and animal on Earth. *Atiep* or *Atiip, Jok* or *Jaak* or *Jak, Yath* or *Yieth*, and *agolong* or *agoloong* are all associated with the gods of ancestors. Throughout the clan's history, Nhialic has been a central aspect of identity, a symbol of power, authority and unity. There is no concept of a clansperson as an atheist in antiquity. There is only the concept of the antique native spirituality; *yath dhieeth*.

The name Yahweh, the god of the later Israelites, may indicate connections with *yath* or *yieth* or *yanhwah, yanhda, yanhwei, yath dhieeth, yanh dhieeth* etc. These are the gods of the ancestors of the southwestern Apuk clans. The prevailing opinion today is that those who eventually evolved into the modern Jews, are an outgrowth of the indigenous clans from the Jieng Rek to Apuk cultures that emerged in the vicinity eons ago.

This belief in Nhialic is a key aspect of the clans that separated

---

10   Lienhard, Godfrey, "Divinity and Experience: The Religion of the Dinka", Oxford University Press (1961)

11   Lienhard, Godfrey, "Divinity and Experience: The Religion of the Dinka", Oxford University Press (1961)

12   Lienhardt, Godfrey, "Divinity and Experience: The Religion of the Dinka", Oxford University Press (1988)

from the original ancestors, probably before reaching southwestern Apuk.

The diversity of sub-clans or clan faiths do share some common features:
- A belief in a supreme deity above a host of lesser gods, or semi-divine figures.
- A belief in the superior spiritual powers of the divine priest 'the master of the fishing spear' who is tasked to give life, make prayers, invocations, and to make sacrifices for the cure of the sick.
- A belief in the power and mediation of lineage spirits.
- An idea of sacrifice and libation to ensure divine protection, rainmaking, peace-making and generosity.
- A need to undergo rituals of passage to move on from different stages of life, such as childhood to adulthood, and from life to death.

Many clan religions have creation stories that speak of the structure for the self-identification of these clans in a universal context. The role of humanity is by and large seen as a harmonizing connection between nature and the supernatural forces. Ancestry worship is not a divinity. It is a scriptural feature of a divinity in as much as monotheism is not a divinity.

Politics and Clan Divinity Relationships

Long before any foreign conquests, slave traders, military conscriptions, or an indirect rule policy, the southwestern Apuk clans had trading relationships. Via these conduits, ideologies, names, divinities, politics, and cultures, were exchanged across ethnic lines, differing politics, and geographical boundaries. These relationships are evident in the sub-clans and their relationship with not only the different Rek clans in South Sudan but extended into the Nilotic stock clans in the southwestern Apuk region. The clan divinity emblems or symbols signify this. Clansmen are differentiated by generation, personality, or family and lineage. The emblems of the clan divinities formed a single undifferentiated group. The clan is a divided unity.

However, in relation to clan divinity and its emblem, the Apuk clans transcend the divisions and oppositions between them. For example, the clansmen are not only men or women, they are half-brothers of a common ancestor. All the clan ancestors become one ancestor in the clan divinity, and all the clansmen become equally 'half-brothers and sisters', socially. They were politically equivalent to one another in relation to the emblems of the divinity[13].

Most historical records are lost so the details of what is 'really' nativity, and what is introduced, is forgotten. In any event, 'purist history' is not history, but politics. New research portrays the Jieng clans as a diverse confederation that formed complex defences, relationships, alliances, and foes, for a multifaceted set of reasons.

These relationships encompass dual control of politics and clan divinity versus military, master of the fishing spear versus war leader, spiritual power clan versus commoner clan, or lower diviner clan versus newcomer clan.

The legendary ancestral fathers of the clans of Apuk guided wars with spiritual powers. They used the spear symbol to unite large clans occupying vast areas to put together the largest empire in Apuk history.

Specific interests, ideological interests and social organization policies of clans were formed along the line of their own political interests. Sometimes these ideologies clashed. The policies of the clans with the greatest religious spiritual powers, which were then the key to spear emblems of unity, became the dominant policies. The highest deity or priest provided blessing to a military campaign and gave an advantage because it was non-ethnocentric and had a sophisticated political creed. The spear of the high priest, however, was the only symbol of the power of authority and unity during this dynastic era. Clans with spiritual powers and traditional high priests had the advantage of greater political and military partnerships with commoner or *kiic* clans and common people or lower diviners bearing faith. These included the Rek, Apuk and Jieng, clans.

---

13   Lienhard, Godfrey, "Divinity and Experience: The Religion of the Dinka", Oxford University Press (1961)

Culture and Religion

Apuk Clans and Sub-clans
(kiic = common)

Clan/Sub-clan	Category	Historic Figures
Pabuor	Divine	Bol Mel (Bol Chiirial)
Patiir	kiic	Aguet Lokbaithok
Padiangbaar	kiic	Bek Amuuk
Parum	Divine	Rum (Rum Wen Kook), Ateny (Ateny Wun Dior)
Pakuieth	kiic	
Pakot	kiic	
Pagong	Divine	Jiel, Longar
Payuom	kiic	
Paluet	kiic	
Patiop	kiic	
Pagun	kiic	
Panyier	kiic	
Padolmuot	kiic	
Pagoor	kiic	
Pagor	kiic	
Paliei	Kiic	
Paguar	kiic	
Payat	kiic	
Pakueny	kiic	
Pabiel	kiic	
Payii	kiic	
Pajiing	kiic	
Panon	kiic	
Pagak	kiic	
Papaach	kiic	
Pangok	kiic	
Pawet	Kiic	
Pachol	kiic	
Pangueet	kiic	

APUK : A STATE IN WAITING

Clan/Sub-clan	Category	Historic Figures
Pageu	kiic	
Pagou	kiic	
Padeel	kiic	
Paker	kiic	
Palet	kiic	

The relationships between clans, deities, and cultures, modulated customs, culture and how they functioned. For every step the deities made, dynastic chiefdom development also took place. Cultures merged, and where the culture of the old ways joined with deity precepts, new spiritual ministers or priests emerged. This is where the sub-clan war leaderships transferred to the concept of the more common *kiic* (*kiich*), militarism increased among clansmen.

There is a belief that what lineage 'did' makes something valid and desirable. Divine clan descendants Bol Mel, Jiel, Ayuel, Longar, Rum Wenkook, and Ateny Wundior, were deities and high priests. In the Apuk, there was a practice of killing the high priest or priest chief while still alive if he was gravely ill or when he expressed the desire to appease the clan spirit for supplication to the people he guides and gives life so they may prosper in good health. By doing so he could leave behind spiritual prayers for his clan divinity and for descended spiritual powers to continue to guide his people after he had gone to his ancestors. However, his life and body spirits survive and invisibly guide society.

The culture of Apuk clans and sub-clans has also created ills, such as when Lwalla predators kidnapped the Deity Rum (as told in a different chapter). This was not to justify every high priest's work, which often used the occurrence of evil dualists to demonize commoners (*kiic* clans), common people and strangers. All this despite evil dualists being very rare in the region. The aim here is to warn people that not everything in everyone's culture is valid just because it has a history.

Culture and Religion

Divine Clan	Supreme Deity	Location
Parum (Symbol is rual, Sausage Tree)	Rum (Rum Wenkook)	Machuet, Maluach, Aliai, and Maluil in Apuk, Agar, Rek, and all Jieng in South Sudan.
	Ateny (Ateny Wun Dior or Ateny Wundior)	Machuet, Maluach, Aliai, and Maluil in Apuk, Agar, all Rek and other Jieng in South Sudan
	Aleek Jiel (Aleek is said to be the mother of Ateny Wun Dior or Wundior, not a deity but respected by the lineage)	Machuet, Maluach, Aliai, Maluil in Apuk, part Rek and Agar Clans in South Sudan
Pagong (Emblem is Awar)	Jiel	Malony, Machuet, Aliai in Apuk, Rek, Agar and parts of Jieng in South Sudan
	Ayuel and or Longar	Machar village of Malony, Machuet in Apuk, Rek, Agar, Luachjak, and parts of Jieng in South Sudan
Pabuor	Bol (Bol Ciirial)	Maluach, Machuet, Madhol in Mauil in Apuk. Little is known in parts of Jieng in South Sudan.
Machuet Apuk, all over Rek in the southwest of Jieng		
Aliai subclans in Apuk		
Ju, Wun Ngap, Angol and part Maluil in Apuk		
Agar, Malual Giernyang, Twic, Aguok, Laucjang, Lou-chol/Lou Ariik, Luanykoth, Thiik, Jalwau and other Jieng clans in South Sudan.		
All over Jieng territories in South Sudan		

The Supreme Deities

Deng, a Supreme Deity known as Deng Mayual or Dengdit, is the god of rain and fertility and empowered by Nhialic. He traced to the union of Garang and Abuk. Abuk is then traced to the Earth. The mother of Abuk is commonly addressed as Abuk Apiny Ayak. The earth is called Apiny or Apiny Ayak.

Deng is a Supreme Deity who does not have the lustre of Rum, Jiel, Bol, Ateny. Atang or other supreme Deties. Deng and Macardit are general or common or free spirits celebrated outside in the yard, where cooking ash is kept. When thunder and lightning occur in the rainy season, it means Deng Mayual or Deng Kur is angry and behind it. Rituals are performed, and animal sacrifices are made on top of ash. Animal skin is cut to be tied on shrines erected there.

Abuk is the patron goddess of gardening and all women. She drowned when crossing a river that her son Deng Mayual flew over safely.

Garang and Abuk are said to be the first human beings created, much like Adam and Eve. Garang is a deity believed to have been surpassed by Deng. Garang's spirits are described as being the primary cause for women, and some men to scream.

Deng Mayual is described in artistically woven stories and analysis. His symbol became a model and the basis of general religions in the region.

The clans have their stories to describe Deng Mayual and link him with Rum Wenkook, who was begotten not from man but from the sacred cave of the sausage tree, *rual mangok*.

Some clans regard themselves as the children of Deng. All have their variations of stories describing him. Garang is often linked with him and is often reported to be quite different.

Deng's influence on religious authority persisted via a line of clan chieftains. The deity told the spiritual priest chiefs to record their reigns and to erect temples to contain sacred tombs. These, and the ruins of military camps, cattle camps, cattle byres, temples, and burial places, attest to a decentralized political system that employed skills and commanded the labour of large military forces comprised of commoner, or *kiic* clans and sub-clans.

The use of symbols and traditional writings gave way to an ancestral script that adapted its writing system to the indigenous, clan related language spoken by the people of the eagle identity in the region. The clan succession system involved inheritance. The matriarch who holds a position of dominance, authority, or respect is deemed as the worthiest option to be the new leader.

The role of a woman who is recognized as being the head of a family or a community in the selection process is crucial to smooth succession in spiritual clans. Rule appears to have passed from divine priest chief as brother to brother. Only when no priest chief brothers remained, or from father to son or to sister's son was the chain broken. Traditionally, women have had great ability to mobilize their communities and exert influence regarding patriarchal lineage.

The Pagong and their Deities

Little is known about the clan Pagong and its deity Jiel. Pagong is defined as the *pan-gong* or descendants of *gong* and commonly known as Clan Pagong. Jiel is the highest deity, and Logar is the first son and second deity in their clan tradition. They are nicknamed Aluong.

Jiel performed his first and most popular miracles in the early period, when his caravans travelled deep into savannah land severely devastated by a drought that had wiped out every living thing. When people ran out of water and were dying, Jiel ordered his caravans to converge. He looked around and made green grass grow on top of the soil.

Jiel pulled out the green grass bundle from the dry ground and clean water came out abundantly from the deep hole. In the accounts, the event was part of the second miracle whereas cow dung was spread out on top of the water to dry out there. Once dried they were collected and safely burnt in the middle of cattle byres and cattle camps to drive away the mosquitoes and insects that attack cows at swampy areas.

The relationship between Rum and Jiel is linked to water and water-grass or cow-grass called *awar* or *Awar Mangok*. It was reportedly issued to the Jiel Deity by Rum as a dowry for Aleek, the daughter of Jiel and sister to Longar Jiel. The union of Rum and Aleek brought forth Ateny-Wundior, Wol, Akuien, and the child who was said to have been taken to the sky as the last child. Nhialic took Deng Garang from Garang and Abuk Apiny-Ayak and took Rum Wenkook and Aleek Jiel to the sky. Clans believe in this mythology up to the present day.

It is the legend that Parum clan members believe to be their source of spiritual powers possessed by the descended high priests or masters of the fishing spear from the Rum lineage. Jiel and his son Longar are believed to be the protectors of the people from the evil spirits responsible for death, miseries, sicknesses, and so on.

The Pabuor and their Supreme Deity

Bol Mel, the High Priest Chief, was born to the family of the spiritual Pabuor clan, inherited their identity and emerged as the priest chief and military campaign leader. It is also believed that the clan originated from the family name of Abuor Mel Madut Anei, brother to Bol Mel Madut Anei himself. Pabuor equally refers to the lineage family, jointly called the Pabuor clan in Clan Divinity.

The Dinka Apuk country is an alliance or association which was first established in the section of Machuet located in Wunriir and expanded to areas of "Bur Apuuk" (plural) or "Bur Apuk" (singular) in the dynasty era by high priest chief rulers. This was well known due to the high occurrence of divinity plays in ordinary life. Oral traditional accounts speak of the shared responsibility in the association between Bol Mel, the priest chief of clan Pabuor divinity, Aguet Lokbaithok of the ordinary clan Patiir, and Bek Amuuk of ordinary clan Padiangbaar.

Bol Mel, Aguet Lokbaithok and Bek Amuuk were the first three rulers of three Apuk clans. The clan traditional accounts mention Apuk of Bol Mel (or Apuk of Bol Chiirial), Tony (Toch) Bol Chiirial and Tony (Toch) Aguet Lokbaithok.

Aguet Lokbaythok, descended from the Patiir, might have been the first deputy and Bek Amuuk from the Padiangbaar might have been the second deputy to Bol Chiirial. Even Bek Amuuk and Aguet Lokbaithok described Bol as being out of the ordinary, as he was a spiritual master and not an ordinary man, or an ordinary fisherman for that matter.

Although Bol Chiirial was known as a fisherman on Aguudi Island, the early details of his career are obscure. However, his descendants to this day were made masters of the fishing spear. He established Madhol village next to Ju village at the triangle of wetland shorelines on western Aguudi Island, close to fishing grounds and forests teeming with game. A fragmentary inscription refers to the Pabuor clan divinity. Bol could have changed through religious, political, social, and ideological and clan traditional administrative positions open to a member of the Pabuor clan during the reign of Rum.

In the spring, Bol was usually crowned chief priest for religious rituals and libation, most likely with the help of his kin, or a senior uncle or mother.

The Parum and the Supreme Deity

The primary emblems or symbols of clan Parum founded by Rum Wenkook and Atany Wundior are the sausage tree (*rual*) and the winnowing tray (*atac*). There have been many challenges of explanations and analysis regarding them both. There are mixed messages regarding the knowledge of the Apuk about Rum. It presents us, particularly the writer, with a complicated picture as compared with other general divinities like Garang and Deng. The name Rum, which was given to the man adopted from the sacred cave of the sausage tree is usually associated with the sky god. The belief is that

that he had fallen from above, *Rum ee lony nhial*. However, often other reports could be quite different. So, Rum could, on certain occasions be associated with a clansman named after Rum, and the clan links, or does not link, the history of those given the same name in different circumstances. Thusly it is difficult to distinguish between the various 'Rums'.

The Parum clan regard themselves as the children of Rum, or Rum Wenkook. Many of those have named male children after him. There are a few among the Rek clans, which relate the masters of the fishing spear to the clans Parum, Padior, Pakuin or Wundior. They claim themselves be ultimately descended from a 'Parum' that became a common man's name among them. Descended members of these clans are clear about the relationship of their ancestor Rum, with the divinity. The other Southern Apuk clans do not make a similar claim.

Clan Parum Origins

Rum founded the clan Parum in his name. The translation of Parum is simply *pan-rum*. Pan means 'a family of'. Deities of the clan are Rum and Ateny. However, Deng, Garang and Abuk are shared deities because they are freely or commonly claimed by different clans as father and mother.

Rum is believed to have spiritual powers to guard, protect, control clan spirits, and to fight against evil spirits, devils and bewitchings that bring suffering, sickness, and death to the people. The main power of Parum's spiritual leader is centred in worshipping Nhialic.

The following hymns are usually recited in the event of danger that demands ritual prayers appealing to ancestry spirits to intervene:

> *Rual Mangok and Atany Wun Dior, Flesh (ring) belongs to my Father in the past, Flesh Cave (ring kook), if you accept this, Flesh, (ring) belongs to my father when we were being created with people.*

Culture and Religion

Sausage Tree

Winnowing Tray

APUK : A STATE IN WAITING

> *Rual Mangok and Atany Wun Dior (Wundior), bull horns were sharpened, Flesh Cave (ring kook) if you accept this, Flesh (ring) belongs to my Father in the past, when we were being created with people (war cek hook keek jaang).*

When the time of animal sacrifice has come, the elders will give orders to sing songs slaughtering ritual bull as follows:

> *Even though Rek will reject me, and Atany will not reject me, you are Atany Wundior, even though Rek will reject me. You Jak, clan spirits, your cover is our cover, even though Rek will reject me. You Jak, clan spirits, your cover is our cover, You Jak, clan spirits, your cover is our cover.*

This is repeated until the bull is finally ritualized to death.

Rum means to adopt or to take by force. The story behind this and the sausage tree will come later. Rum, a deity of the Parum clan describes people as *acuuk* (single) or *acuok* (plural); especially at prayer time.

The sausage tree, *rual mangok* became the symbol or emblem of the clan. The symbol links the Padior, Pakuin, Wundior or Dedior into a single Parum clan together wherever they may be.

All accounts trace Rum back to the Divinity. For any member of Parum clan community, or any pregnant woman married to a Parum clansman, the cutting of a sausage tree, *rual* mangok is believed to be a bad prophecy and a direct attack or injury to "Rum the son adopted from cave rual". The assumption is that Rum's spirits may strike the cutter. When such an offense happened, sheep with grey or green colours were offered as a compensation sacrifice. But Rum differs almost completely between the Deng nicknamed Deng Mayual and the Rum, nicknamed Rum Wenkook. The tradition names Nhialic and the sausage tree and has Rum as Atany's father and Aleek as his mother.

Indeed, the dual control of politics, warfare, and a high priest leadership that claims membership in the tribe of Jacob and from

Culture and Religion

there to the Abrahamic faiths, emerged from the Parum, Pagong and Pabuor clans of Apuk chiefdom. Rum is the image spirit dropped from Heaven by the Holy Spirit to make a Nhialic blessing on Earth. Rum Wenkook, Deng Mayual, Garang, Abuk Apiny, Atany Wundior, Jiel, and Longar deities all belong to the clan.

Dengdit or Deng Mayual is the sky god of rain and fertility and empowered by Nhialic. Deng has a mother called Abuk, the patron goddess of gardening and all women. Deng Abuk is worshipped by Parum clan with the belief that Deng and Abuk were created and assigned to the garden by Nhialic.

There is Garang, who shares a description with Dengdit or Deng Abuk. There is regular mention of Deng Kur where Kur is described to be the shining stone that falls from the sky when the rain falls, looking like crystal or diamond and worshipped by the Parum clan as the guiding spirit. Attempts explaining the differences between the genealogies of Deng Abuk and Garang and Rum Wenkook in the context of Parum clan have become divergent.

As I have written previously, Rum who is also called Rum Wenkook, meaning Rum of the Cave. *Aci lony ee kong rual yic along thin* or *kong ee rual yich*, according to the Apuk language. Apuk believers and especially the Parum descents trace Deng Mayual and Rum Wenkook paternity to the world of heavenly spirits. But Deng who was begotten within the union of Garang and Rum remained the adopted messenger of Divinity that fell, *ee lony Nhial*, to the cave of sausage tree on earth to guide life and provide good health and prosperity to people and members of Parum clan that Rum founded on earth.

All accounts trace Rum back to the heavenly sky god, the Supreme Deity. Many accounts are identical between Garang and Dengdit, but some differ. It could be surmised here that Deity Deng was begotten through Nhialic who created the Rum Wenkook guardian, but remains an invisible spirit living inside the sacred cave of the sausage tree. Or, Deng Mayual may have been the son of Garang and Abuk. However, Rum came into humanity through Aleek Jiel who adopted Rum outside the sacred cave of sausage tree on the river shore. There is some similarity to the son of Joseph and Mary, and the Immaculate Conception.

The Apuk clan names Deng as father and has beliefs in Garang and Abuk. The Parum clan says Rum was from the cave, without clearly mentioning Deng Garang as the Father. The accounts of the Parum clan and the Apuk clan regarding the birth of Rum have a number of points in common. Both have Rum being befriended by Aleek on the river bank after he came out from the sacred cave of the sausage tree. Rum *ee dom Aleek agor nhom aheer kee ci ben bey ee Kong Rual* yic. Both the Apuk clan state and the Parum clan have offspring named after Rum. Both state one such son travelled to far away War-Nyang on a fortune-hunting and military expedition to the Ancient Apuk village claimed to be Wunriir in the Machuet Apuk region. There is War-Nyang at Aguot village located in the middle, between Pankiir Malony cattle camp in the west, Akuwei Machuet cattle camp in the north and Git Manging-Maluil cattle camp in the south. Yet, nobody knows which War-Nyang Rum travelled to for hunting or fishing within the present day Apuk state. There he made a triumphal entry and founded the ancient dynasty in Machuet along the lake banks and river banks. He then expanded to control wider territories for the Apuk clans of today.

Beginnings and Expansions

Spiritual masters were placed on various thrones, as vassals of the Nilotic clans. Successors to those thrones used spiritual powers together with heroic military assaults to fight the wars against clans of Bantustan stock, the Lwalla or Lueel. The spiritual master unified military organizations, alliances of sub-clans, and made significant gains by defeating the Lwalla in the battles that marked the beginnings of the expansion of the dynasty.

By the end of the wars, the spiritual masters remained popular on the political stage. This they controlled using spiritual powers to

Culture and Religion

maintain the dynasty occupying the Maluach, Akon Agiu, Bur Apuk and Wunriir in Machuet territories.

As well, the holy river at Madol Aliai in the Toch wetland, the clan burial tombs and holy shrines at Maluac and Jak in the Machuet Apuk section, at the Wun-Ngap and Ju villages in the Maluil Apuk section, at Panakdit in the Aliai Apuk section, and at Machar in the Malony Apuk section were transferred to the high priest chiefs, in the reign of priest chief Ateny to his son Rum to Malek Rum, then to Agei Malek Rum, the war leader of the Dinka Apuk alliance. Rapid migration and population growth brought over thirty different clans together that settled all over the eight sections where Kongdeer, Aguurping, Maluac, Aliai, Malony, Manging, Angol, and Tarweng villages are located in the savannah lands.

The experience gained from the wars led the dynastic authorities to begin expansion and transformation. The results of this transformation developed into the chiefdom-controlled concept with spiritual powers of bringing together the sub-clans and commoner clans seeking security, protection, spiritual psychotherapies for their sick and spiritual psychiatric therapy for their families.

Clans of the lower level, without spiritual power, would usually have to hire spiritual masters to perform rituals and sacrifice prayers to the clan spirits on their behalf, to provide life for their sick, and to make them prosperous. The change in the sphere of influence on the eastern frontier and southern frontier caused confrontation between adversaries and the alliances of the sub-clans which controlled vast sections of present-day Apuk.

Their successors subdued the northern wing and annexed any enclaves. This began the development era of chiefdoms under traditional chieftaincy in the 19th and 20th centuries AD. Chieftaincy was passed on along family lines as they held the supernatural powers of the Parum spiritual priests. The Clan and associations of different sub-clans that unite for security purposes, or for any other interests consider themselves as a "nation, state, or country". A country refers to a chiefdom, a motherland, or a fatherland according to the Apuk.

APUK : A STATE IN WAITING

The clan divinity is the very nature of an ancestor. The symbols or emblems are the very nature of the clansman. The people of the clans are differentiated from each other by generation, personality, or by family and lineage. The symbols which are the identities of the clan divinities are non-human like the sausage tree, the rain stone or animals. They can form a single undifferentiated alliance. The clan is a divided unity. But in relation to the clan divinity and its emblem, the clanspeople transcend the divisions and oppositions between them. This played a significant role in times of war and in other social upheavals throughout the dynastic development era.

The emblem identity of clans, divinity temples and tombs was first seen in the Maluac homesteads. Their war leader seized territories and transferred spiritual priests that were collectively appointed as guardians for the shrines, holy temples, tombs, sacred rivers and streams for fishing activities, and strategic areas linking both wetlands and main highlands.

The clan traditions show that even though the divine priests or masters of the fishing spear were often killed in the violent conflicts that erupted between the different sub-clans or died via misadventure in the country of Apuk clan territories, the shrine was never desecrated. This was the case even when the erected wooden shrines, oxen thong pegs, and tombs fell into rot and disrepair. The sacred shrines and priest tombs of the Parum, Pagong and Pabuor clans were and are still treated with great respect. No clansman could safely approach shrines such as the holy shrines and tombs erected in Wun-ngap sanctuary by the descended children of Mabuoch Mabior, and that of holy shrines and tombs erected in the Jak Holy Place Centre for Wundior lineages, without making some small offering. Usually, this was accomplished by throwing tobacco, coins, or placing rings or milk on thong pegs, then posting a spear on the shrine five times, and moving in an easterly circle thrice around them.

The shrines and tombs are frequented by persons suffering from domestic troubles, infant mortality, and sickness. Sacrifices are

Culture and Religion

frequently made. The method of sacrifices is quite the same as normal Jieng practice since the animal is cast, and its throat cut with a special ritual spear kept for this practice.

The founding ancestors such as Rum, Atany, Jiel, Bol or Parum-Wundior, as fathers of the clan, are made the head of all creatures by God or the clan-Divinity. All are living in a very hostile place covered completely with clouds. The version of the Apuk account of the founding ancestor of the clan Rum is given in a way well represented in the following hymn:

Father Dengdit you will help me in everything!
Deng Mayual, you will help me in everything, Deng Mayual
Father Dengdit you will help me in everything! (repeated four or more times)
Deng Mayual, you will help me in everything, Deng Mayual! (repeated five or more times)
Deng Mayual, Deng Kur give me, provide me.
I am begging you so that you give me and to provide me.
O Divinity, I beg, give me so that I beg you always.

The sanctuaries of the divine prophets of most of the powerful clan spirits contained no reference to the divine priests of the Padiangbaar and Patiir clans. This is because their clansmen were believers of free divinities or gods like Deng, Garang, Macardit, and Abuk. The Patiir clan divinity symbol is the hippopotamus (*rou*). The Padiangbaar clan divinity symbol is the balanites tree (*thou*). Deng, Garang and Macar are the most common names given to men and Abuk is the only name given for women in Rek clans. The Padiangbaar often name a clansman Thou. These are the free divinities known in the Jieng land including southwestern Rek of the Apuk.

The Apuk clans try to bring the parts of their world together during suffering from death, sickness, and sorrowful crimes because they see them as a result of separation from God or a divinity.

Proclamation of the Religious Freedom

Ages ago, a Rum Deity announced: "The Pabuor and all others should have the liberty to follow that mode of religion which to each of them appeared best, thereby granting tolerance to all religions, including Parum clan spirituality". The proclamation went a step further than the earlier Proclamation of Toleration by the Deity heir Atany Wundior in returning confiscated cattle and paying cattle in blood wealth for reparation of life lost to forgive and reverse curses. This proclamation made the nationalities officially neutral regarding traditional religious worship. It neither made the traditional religions illegal nor made clan divinity the state religion mandatory, as had occurred with Islam. The proclamation of Rum as a Deity did, however, raise the stock of traditional spirituality within the Apuk nation and it reaffirmed the importance of religious worship, ritual sacrifice prayers, and ritual libations for the welfare of the Apuk.

There are no details regarding the early life, career and spirituality of the priest chiefs Rum, his offspring Atany, and the successors that survived. The Pabuor clan priest Chief Bol Chiirial, and commoners from Bek Amuuk and Aguet Lokbaythok who argued in favour of the clan divinity of Rum and his son assumed that Rum had been a chief priest and spiritual high priest chief with a high reputation since his arrival. They argued, therefore, that there was no need to explain the absence of evidence regarding his early life, career and spirituality.

Cattle herders, fishers and hunters could have been spiritualized from the Ancient Wunriir Village equidistant from the River Ju Village in the War Ju triangle in the southwest, or the Madhol village and the Liet-Nhom camps located on gateways connecting the wetland areas from the east. They could have been spiritualized also from the ancient Wunriir, Maluach, Machuet and Pankiir villages which are in the middle connecting the Wanhalel River from the southeast with the Majok River of Dinka Apuk from the northwest and connecting the ancient Panakdit villages to the east. Even if successor Rum was not himself a chief priest or spear minister with supernatural power, he would probably have been familiar with divine chief priests on the Crocodile River (War-Nyang) shores before arriving in Wunriir, Ju, Madhol, Akuwei and the other nearby settlements of the Apuk villages.

A traditional scholar and historian arguing against accounts of spirituality allow that Rum's son, Atany Wundior, may have been curious about a spirituality religion which had its origin in his War-Nyang place of birth in the homeland.

At an eastern village near fish-bearing wetland rivers, priest chief Bol Mel may not have been so intense in his commitment to the traditional Pabuor clan religion that he could not keep an open mind regarding other religions. However, Rum arrived in the village and accepted that the Maluach to Chiir villages, the Madhol, Wun-Ngap, Jak on holy shrine ground in Machuet through to Machar and Panak, probably contained spiritual tomb temples. In the clan culture, the absence of evidence for an ancient spiritual tomb temple does not warrant the unmerited assumption that Rum or Atany Wundior was a chief priest from early childhood.

A Rum Descendant

If this Rum descendant had been a spiritual high priest chief during his military career, he would not have been a particularly unusual figure for his era. Rum arrived and joined the territorial defence forces at an age ranging between 20 years to 30 years old. This was an age where he would be prohibited from certain practices by some supreme temple priests. He demonstrated his military capability in ways that would have required participation in certain rituals that some spiritual chief priests might find sacrilegious (which was not uncommon among the spiritual laity). The main role of a military career was to command troops and win wars. However, Rum emerged a Deity, political leader, and military commander who officiated over public rites and led the religious ceremonies of the army, even in time of war. Oral traditional scripture contains explicit prohibitions on this sort of behaviour under certain age groups by military figures.

The people of the more tolerant divinity of the cattle herders under Rum's control would have been able to justify participation in neutral rituals through an invited elderly spiritual priest-chief. We know that these people existed. The historical record includes spiritual priest-chief army officers, who could have been regularly guilty of idolatry, and the military martyrs of the early centuries. Their animal sacrifice rituals excluded them from certain parts of the clans with spiritual powers; but Rum nonetheless was a Deity and a high priest-chief. As such, he was recognized by his captors and prosecutors (see Rum Descendant Kidnapped section) as possessing the natural powers to spiritually communicate with divinity gods on earth and in heaven.

A Concept of Dual Control

The Apuk clan is an association of sub-clans with independent authority for clan leaders. The main aim of the association was to protect life and have a domain of their own identity of which they could be proud. Practically, clans permit the dual control of war leader and high priest chief. The role of the priest chief (the master of fishing spear), is akin to that of the priest chief in the Apuk of Rek Jieng of Nilotic ethnic groups in the sub-Sahara. His duty is to give life. He is 'the holder of life' and his life is bound together with the vitality of his people.

Some of the main functions of priest chief are:
- Prayers and invocations.
- Sacrifices for the cure of the sick and rainmaking.
- In war, he is the guide of his people, as well as the mediator and peacemaker.

Wunriir was the oldest centre for the clans. It expanded on a wider scale through the help of divine priest chiefs, military leaders and members of clans of general divinities. Godfrey Lienhardt described

Culture and Religion

these as 'free divinities'[14] that may be present in individual clansmen to have appeared in forms that give individual clansmen a sort of definition associated with their presence regarding any particular free divinities possession. Godfrey singled out Machardit, Garang, Abuk, and Deng as the free divinities best known to the Western Dinka during his study. All of these divinities do not have the separate holy shrines like the clan spirits of *jok, jak* and *atiep* or *atiip*.

The divine priest chief was the mediator, peacemaker and guardian of the people in war and of the holy shrine. His spiritual powers promoted expansionism and militarism supported by the members of the commoner clans that built cattle byres in Manyiel, Paduer, Akuwei, Panak, Machar, Pankiir, Machar Arol, and Jak.

The founder of the new succession of the chiefdom in the Dinka Apuk clans blessed the chiefs in the Parum, Pagong and Pabuor clans with spiritual powers and assigned them according to their respective holy shrines, deity tombs, temples and burial ground sites.

The most common and noticeable holy shrines and tombs with spiritual powers are:

- Pabuor Clan: The holy shrines, deity tombs and temple sites are at the Malek, Adol, and Maluach villages in the Machuet section, and at Madhol in the Maluil section.
- Pagong Clan: The holy shrines, deity tombs, and temple sites are at Machar in the Malony section.
- Parum Clan: The holy shrines, deity tombs and temple sites are at Jak for the Machuet, Wun-Ngap and Ju for the Maluil sub-clans, and Panakdit for the Aliai subclans.

---

14 Lienhardt, Godfrey, Divinity and Experience, The Religion of the Dinka, Oxford University Press, (1961), page 81.
15 Deng is described by many as a free or common god or divinity for all the clans. But Wundior, Padior, Dedior and some Pakuin of the Parum clan founded by Rum and Atany added the word "Mayual" which reads as Deng Mayual. This makes it difficult to describe in one way, because "Deng" is a free or general divinity for other clans. A Parum spear master describes Deng Mayual as the messenger of spirits and terms it as akuic in the Apuk language, and which usually sends messages of danger in place of fear. They said that Deng Mayual is akuic which alerts a person on danger and uses ancestor spirit powers to repulse and guide you to the safe place. Like Deng, there are no holy shrines erected for Deng Mayual by Parum lineage lines.

During dry seasons there is a priest to guide the holy river of Madol Aliai in the Toch swampland for people and cattle. This is the priest's primary role.

Those priest chiefs were superior priest chiefs from the Pakuin sect. All are of the Parum clan. They shared similar functions that included prayers and invocations, sacrifices for the cure of the sick, and rainmaking.

The priest Mabuoc of Pakuin had spirit powers that told him to locate at the strategic Maluil Apuk homestead in the Wun-ngap area. He was there to guide and pray for people in times of military campaigns, hunting/fishing, and for forgiveness and peace-making for all the sub-clans in Maluil, Aliai, Toch, Malony, Maluach, Tarweng and the Machuet Apuk sub-clans.

Malek Rum ascended to the throne in the 1880's with dual control. He was among the first traditional native chieftains recognized to implement the indirect rule policies for the Colonial Administration established in the Tonj District in 1903 by Anglo-Egyptian Sudan.

A later chief, Agei believed that the Condominium Administration was dangerous and objected to the policies being implemented. He mobilized spiritual clan leaders, commoner clans and warriors for an all-out fight. To safeguard territorial integrity, he reorganized traditional structures by opening new centres and appointed key spear masters, military commanders, and political leaders in strategic places such as the Maluil Apuk shrine in Wun-ngap, the Madhol shrine, the Angol shrines, Lietnhom camp, Diang camp, the Panak shrines, the Pankiir shrine, the Ju shrines in Maluil Apuk and the Machuet Apuk shrines in Jak, Akuwey, Paduer, the Malou holy tombs shrines camp and Manyiel.

Shrines and Temples of the Maluil Apuk

Chieftain Agei wanted holy shrines to be established in Maluil Apuk at the Wun-ngap village for the ancestral spirits of Atany Wundior the first-born son of the Supreme Deity Rum and Aleek, the first-born daughter of Supreme Deity Jiel. He wanted them to be accessible to all the people passing in the midway near the confluence of hunting zones and the great river Wanhalel. This holy shrine is encircled by formidable swampy river tributaries and governed by a clan chief priest and spiritual master.

To ensure the safety of his men who passed through that holy temple, chieftain Agei and his priest chiefs invented a manoeuvre whereby the Apuk army would carry along with them through the sacred caves of the shrine, defensive shields of hide from buffalo skins for combat when they confronted enemies. Spirit worship in the Maluil holy shrines was thereby established at Wun-Ngap village. They eventually subdued their fortune hunting adversaries in the Dinka Apuk chiefdom after the Priest Chief from Pakuin had successfully settled there. Spiritual High Priest Chief Rum settled at Ju holy tombs centre as the spiritual priest chief protecting crops from insects and birds at the triangle encompassing Ju village in Maluil Apuk.

The importance of the holy shrine of the Parum Clan Spirits is that the Maluil Apuk location lies strategically midway between Toch on the eastern side bordering Luanykoth to the northeast and the far east to Thony in the southeast, the Wanhalel River bordering Thony across to the eastern River and Yar to the extreme south with Muok.

The Madhol Shrine

The Pabuor clans from Maluach in Machuet Apuk were persuaded by the priest chief to have their spiritual centre established at the old village of Madhol, next to Aguudi Island where a blend of cultures comes together. This would create an interesting site to wander around. The charm of the old village is in the clan traditional architecture and crumbling mud-buildings as well as the tombs and shrines of Bol Mel. Shrine temples and tombs for the descended spear masters of the Pabuor clan were the first of their kind to be built in the region.

Bol's tomb shrine is a beautiful place of worship built in the 1910's by the Pabuor clan high priest chiefs from Maluach village. It is an important place of worship and attracts visiting herders seeking spiritual blessing as they take in the beauty of the edifices.

The Lietnhom Camp

It was a boozy day, spent regaling friends with hopes, dreams and aspirations for the future, when the 1700's pioneer Malek Wol decided to expand the Lietnhom cattle camp they were staying at in the Apuk wetland zone. It was a place for vast numbers of wild animals before hunters, fishermen and cattle herders came and established their cattle byres and cattle camps. Visiting Lietnhom in the middle of a hunting expedition, this visionary descendant of the Parum Clan hatched a plan to turn this charming paradise located at the strategic roots of the river streams, into one of the most remarkable and exclusive cattle camps in the wetland region. It became the Machuet Apuk cattle camp.

It was simply called Liet Nhom, a reference to the sand dust that so often traverses the horizontals nearby.

Over the years, it developed into something of a legendary retreat for the cattle keepers of Machuet Apuk. It is covered by the savannah green forest along the wetland zones. With the increasing influx from its seasonal herders, the place flourished and comfortable new cottages were added. The area became home to more than 100,000 head of cattle. The green thick forest surrounding it was inhabited by countless wild animals like buffaloes, giraffes, gazelles, antelopes, deer, lions, hyenas, leopards, impalas, hyrax, elephants, and so on.

It is easy to see why this camp and its breathtaking location won the hearts of Wol Rum and his friends all those years ago. As visitors walked up towards the tributaries of the rivers, the snow-capped mountains, to the great rivers themselves, and to the swamps of the Apuk, it was impossible not to be swept away by the majesty and solemnity of the surroundings.

Culture and Religion

Nowadays, the camps established at Lietnhom are owned by the clan groups, and they are enticing in a stately, palatial sort of way. Efforts to hark back to the golden age of expedition exist throughout adding to the overall appeal of the place.

The camps were warm and welcoming, with bonfires, and a busy gateway leading out into the wilderness. It was a seasonal residence for those from nearby villages, for fishermen and was a source of grazing land during the dry season.

Sheep, goat and cow herds are a staple feature and are enhanced by both legend and humorous tales. It is an accepted wisdom by some that the white sheep there are the spirits of life and grace. Others recount tales of grey sheep reincarnating to return at the end of the sacrifices of the Parum clan. In the same vein, it is accepted wisdom that goats are the spirits of the evils. Others recount tales of goats flying across a river stream to escape the lions, only to fly back across to the villages and Liet-Nhom in the evening.

The Diang Camp

When the Diang camp was revamped, a new confidence from travellers was gained and that allowed for the exploration of the Apuk territories. In a heartbeat, Diang Camp became relevant again and brought with it the vibrant injection resulting from being an attraction. One major event is the 'death in beauty' contests for the Maluil Apuk clan members (and includes visiting clan members).

The contest promises an interesting experience, whether visiting for pasture or pleasure. The reception and attention to detail on arrival is impeccable. Indigenous artistically designed chairs are used to sit on during body decorations for the contestants and for guests to sit on. Lying on or sitting on sleeping mats was only for those people who do not have body decorations as they may be wiped off on a mat.

The highlight is the Beauty Death that occurs as beauty ages. It is made up of six young people from Angol who comprise the head cattle herders from each of their clans. They wear bronze on their wrists and waist, ivory on their upper arms, and decorated their bodies. They sat on their chairs, avoided drinking milk, eating meat, fish or any food which will increase body size. They wanted to avoid anything that marred the decorations. This would flaw their beauty.

Despite all the conflicts afflicting the people, the Dinka Apuk clan thinkers, theorists and clan deities envisioned a situation where the territory could become a torchbearer in the region.

A study of current regional political and social trends points not only to an economically better homeland for them in Apuk, but a peaceful one as well. It is the vision of most thinkers that what the clan needs are not ammunition and explosives. Its strength lies in harnessing its rich historical and traditional birthright to derive inspiration.

Historical tradition is the inspirational reference that has been seriously lacking among clans including the Dinka Apuk and Dinka Rek clans. Since Dinka Apuk was the crib of Muonyjang Rek in the savannah lands and the source of the earliest progress in beliefs, values, arts and technology, she is destined to lead the region once more.

These assertions are rooted in the firm belief and understanding that we can no longer forge ahead without the inspirational reference of all spheres of our traditional influences, as well as in spheres of human excellence.

If the earliest men were found in Apuk, the original home of the Dinka Rek clans, and if they were indeed considered the first inhabitants of this region, then it is common sense to conclude that the people of Apuk, were among the first to influence the civilization that flourished there.

Individual clansmen are differentiated from each other by generation, personality, family and lineage. The emblems of the clan divinities can be thought to form a single undifferentiated group. Each sausage tree, for example, is seen by people as the equivalent to every other sausage tree in space or in time and is to be treated in

Culture and Religion

the same way by all members of the Parum, Padior and Pakuin clans. In purely individual social relationships this supreme equivalence of individual clansmen is not fully realized, for they are individuals and members of families and lineages.

However, they are conspicuously different from each other in many ways. The clan is a divided unity; but in relation to the clan divinity or *ee Nhialic* and its emblem, the Apuk, Rek and entire Jieng transcend the divisions and oppositions between them. As clansmen, not simply as men, they are undifferentiated the half-brothers of an animal, a tree or species standing in the same relationship to all, and children of a common ancestor.

Those who were the architects of the ancestral civilization, including the first agricultural skills, had a clear vision of the value of culture but have not been recorded. In fact, the rich heritage and legacy of Dinka Rek culture was shamelessly destroyed by conquerors.

Its value as an element of resistance to foreign domination lies in the fact that it is the vigorous manifestation on the ideological and idealistic level of the physical and historical reality of the society that others attempt to dominate. Culture is simultaneously the fruit of a people's history and a determinant of that history. This occurs via the positive or negative influence which it exerts on the revolution of relationships between man and his environment, among man or groups of men within a society, as well as among different societies. Ignorance of this fact may explain the failure of several attempts at foreign domination as well as the failure of some national movements.

It is without a doubt that the solution to the Apuk's woes lies in the affirmation of its diverse cultural and traditional birthright. For it is through that process that truth is affirmed while falsehoods are diminished. By diminishing falsehoods, the people of Apuk will ultimately receive a new perspective of themselves and others.

APUK : A STATE IN WAITING

Resurrection Prevents a Culture from Dying

What Apuk needs is a resurrection. A rebirth from unbearable existence under bondage and interventionism. But for such a rebirth to take place it must first subvert the mental genocide inflicted on it during the past.

This would mean the uprooting and complete destruction of the systematic and ruthless mental murder sustained through and by the formation of historical denial which brainwashed and indoctrinated generations into thinking that the Apuk does not exist. That it must be disintegrated to return to separate clan entities of old and is incapable of progressing without the generosity of other civilizations and their political patronage.

It is true to say that the naïve assimilation of new influences would eventually strip the Apuk of its cultural eagle identity. This is precisely the reason why Apuk dreamers, thinkers, truth-seekers and theorists are now calling for an Apuk program to deal with, and ultimately overcome, the social, cultural, and political challenges confronting today's generations.

To prevent the future from dying in the present, an investigation must take place as to how the Apuk culture lost its identification symbols through a systematic depersonalization process.

Depersonalization of the Apuk clans began when with the massive kidnapping and looting of uncounted thousands of our most able, knowledgeable and skilled people from all walks of life.

It took place throughout the land. Some were butchered while others were thrown to the Machar Rek River crocodiles to feed upon or into fire pits normally used for the dead to burn to ashes in Chuei Ajai. Those of the kidnapped who became ill were thrown into the Mediterranean or the Red Sea and others amputated to their knees to die as destitute slaves in the houses of Arab merchants.

It began a long time ago when Dinka tribesmen were taken as nothing but trash, to fight wars for the Turks, Arabs, and later the Europeans. Others were sold to Arab slave traders never to be seen again. The colonizing Europeans or Arabs upheld their beliefs of

Culture and Religion

superiority which robbed the intellect and potential abilities of the Apuk of Rek people.

It is not surprising that even after the demise of colonialism, there are still some Dinka tribesmen who still believe that if not for the Arabs and Europeans, the Apuk would still be jumping from one tree to another.

It is regrettable that this state of mind is also rooted in some of the intellectuals of Rek. The very ones who should be leading the community into resurrection.

Most of them live a difficult life of denial of the Dinka in themselves. It is partly because of the biased colonial culture, which demonized the Dinka way of doing things that has shaped their way of thinking.

The knowledge of Dinka gained over centuries suddenly became obsolete. The Dinka religion became pagan.

The Dinka Rek way of doing things became taboo. The corrupted existence under the conquerors mutilated the Dinka Rek mind. It deprived the tribesman a sense of pride in himself. The dehumanization occurred everywhere in all facets of life.

Even the attainment of South Sudan's political independence in 2011 has not assisted much in the re-awakening of the Apuk tribesmen. They are still in their coma being inferior. Because most imported cultural principles are irrelevant to the Rek traditions, a vacuum has been left on the spiritual, social and cultural fronts.

People repeatedly listen to rhetoric such as South Sudan has core values and original spirituality.

But which South Sudan is this? Is it the South Sudan of the 1820s to 1900s, when the Arab-Muslims hunting slaves and ivory roamed into our villages?

Or is it the South Sudan of the Anya Nya movement when the first civil war in Sudanese history took place from 1955 to 1972? At the time Emperor Haile Selassie of Ethiopia had the power to influence the rebels under Joseph Lagu to negotiate with the Sudanese government of Jaafar Nimeri and Abel Alier. The Addis Ababa Peace Accord and ended the first civil war in Sudan in 1972.

APUK : A STATE IN WAITING

Or is it the South Sudan of the Sudanese People's Liberation Army (SPLA) of the Second civil war/Anya Nya II from 1983 to 2005 when Dr John Garang De Mabior's vision of a "New Sudan State Identity" brought the secession of South Sudan in July 2011?

Or is it South Sudan of the Bari Kokora when the Bari speaking clans expressed their "Real Bari Cultural Identity"?

Attaching the South Sudanese identity to dark skin colour was "denied" by the Bari Kokora 45 years ago. An open dialogue about Kokora and the lessons learned from it contribute to discussions about how the various clans wish to define themselves, and how the South Sudanese national identity can be promoted in the clan context. The expression of the Bari cultural identity; the Apuk pursuit of its historical identity, cultural identity, nationality identity, clan divinity identity and the behaviour of people of different clans, seems to suggest a continuous historical and cultural pillar that was reconciled and pure before the onset of conquests and incursions.

In what way is the cultural shift from Bari to Kuku homogeneous, whereas the cultures from the Bari in Jubek State to the Jieng-Dinka in Jonglei State are heterogeneous? Linguistic sovereignty speaks of a totally different historical link.

The first step in analysing anything clan related starts with evaluation education and hypotheses. Even the most progressive minds in South Sudan are still responding to and outlining the history of the people within that timeframe. They are examining theories invented during the conquest eras of the slave traders, the Anglo-Egyptian Sudanese Government and Arab fundamentalism.

All of this is based on the historical core values of clan culture studied by progressive people (for the most part). Based on a sovereign nation of old, like the Jieng, Bari, Nuer or Fartit that had no similarities to the nations of the Azandes, Lango, Kakwa, Shilluk-Luo, Jurchol-Luo or Ndogo. South Sudan does not have a concept of contemporary clan construction. None of them shared any striking similarities as to justify being born under these prevailing opinions. As a result, the decisions on South Sudan are still expressed in the language of those preyed upon, aliens and the conquered.

Rum, Aleek and the Sausage Tree

The love and subsequent union between Rum and Aleek mark the beginnings of Rum's public function as a supreme deity. This event is recorded in the spirituality of Jiel, Rum, and Ateny Wundior, Apuk and Rek. In the clan traditions, rather than as a direct narrative, Rum bears witness to the episode

Rum Wenkook is believed to have fallen from the heavens (*ee lony nhial*) to live in the cave of the sausage tree on earth. From there he could provide life and guide the people to respect and to follow the rules of divinities. The term Wenkook (son of cave) means that Rum was adopted from the cave of the Rual (sausage tree). *Rum ee rum bey kong rual yic.*

The clan of Parum emblems or symbols are *rual* and *kur*. Both the rual tree and kur stone are given locally made melted cheese and grey sheep as offerings. They are then tranquil until the next time comes to sacrifice sheep and a greyish bull-calf as an offering to Jaak under the rual and its cave. Cutting a rual branch or pulling out rual fruit out or breaking the kur stone is believed to be a bad omen for the Parum clan.

The *Rual Mangok* symbol links the Padior, Pakuin, Wundior or Dedior into a single Parum clan.

Rum had been instructed not to enter into any sort of human relationship, to the extent even of avoiding any open discussion with Aleek while they admired each other. He was not to let Aleek know that he was a spirit fallen from the sky. He was not to associate with or to receive anyone human. Apparently, he was not very good at following these rules.

Rum would come out from the cave and change himself into human form to be seen by Aleek while she was alone looking after the cows, fetching water at the riverside or cutting grass in the forest. Aleek treated Rum with love and respect but did not disclose his whereabouts.

He often spoke secretly to Aleek in isolated locations near the rual tree. Rum would disappear whenever he saw any people coming towards them. Aleek admired and loved Rum. When she was impregnated by him under rual tree, she told no one, except him.

Aleek was a daughter of Jiel from the divine clan Pagong. Jiel is a high deity. He was fearful for his daughter at the time as she was acting strangely. She was of age to marry but showed no interest. He suspected a secret lover. The chief clan priests decided to summon her to appear in front of the elders.

Then one of the clan chief priests and Aleek's brother Longar Jiel went to elders and asked, "What are you willing to offer to Aleek if she confesses?" So, they agreed to bless her by allowing the person she loves to marry her. However, they must see that person she loves before wedding arrangements are made.

She had confessed that Rum Wenkook was the only person she loves. The tale of the confession was a traditional episode connected to the life of Rum and to the divinity or spirituality of all the cultures of Jiel and Rum. It connects the chief priests that persuaded Aleek to confess.

From then on Aleek watched for an opportunity to hand over Rum.

Rum Captured

The chief priests and the elders of the clans were looking for some way to capture Rum. They thought a group of women might work. However, the women were afraid Rum might not show himself to Aleek if they were there. Then, one of the chief priests asked Jiel to make ritual invocation for the powers of spirits and lineage to ensure divine intervention and generosity of passage for the women's group, and to use spiritual power to neutralize Rum to stay calm so that Aleek could grab him easily. Longar and his sister went together to the chief priests, and the priests of the temple guard, and discussed how the women groups led by Aleek might attract Rum out from the sacred cave.

They were delighted and agreed to send Aleek in the company of the women. Aleek gave her consent, went to the river shore close to the rual to fetch drinking water, and watched for an opportunity.

Rum emerged to speak to Aleek. Instead, she embraced him as in an act of love. She enfolded him lovingly, intensely, passionately, and grabbed him firmly as she might when they were totally alone. With the help of the other women, she then managed to pass Rum over to the chief priests, elders, and others.

They then cut Rum's thighs as a sign to change to human form which prevented Rum from changing quickly to his invisible spirit form and returning to the sacred cave.

Love and Marriage?
There is some guesswork regarding oral traditional tales as to whether Rum and Aleek were truly in agreement with each other and in love. The purpose may have simply been marriage as Aleek was the daughter of the Pagong clan deity and Rum was the son of the Parum clan deity. Because the Clan Chief Priests successfully laid siege to Aleek, Rum was eventually subdued by his faithful love. The marriage episode is attested to by other sources of that era and is regarded as a historical event. Jiel emphasized that clan spirituality was interconnected by this historical marriage forever.

There is also in the traditional stories the mention of "The Kiss". Whereas, Rum felt the kiss of the morning breeze on his skin. This is described by spirituality as a famous kiss that Aleek gave him. The scene is nearly always included in tales as, either "The Kiss" itself, or the moment after, during the confession of Rum's existence by Aleek. This is found in stories of the cycles of the life of Rum in clan spiritual tales.

Bol

I have provided a bit of information regarding Bol here as he appears in the following story. He will be featured prominently in 'A Fishy tale' later in the book.

Bol Mel, was a descendant from the divinity of the Pabuor clan.

Nothing much besides his name is known, but Apuk of Bol Mel (or Bol Chiirial) indicates that he held administrative functions and so must have been a prominent priest-chief in his clan.

A war between the rival sub-clans and nomadic predators was likely real.

The Bek Amuuk clan of the Padiangbaar and the Aguet Lokbaithok clan of the Patiir emerged from sub-clans in the Machuet Apuk region as the oldest homeland and expanded to the Tarweng section at western bank of the Wanhalel River. They deputized Bol Chiirial, indicating that the sub-clans of Pabuor, Padiangbaar and Patiir were first occupying area, even before the arrival of the Parum clan of Rum Wenkook.

Rum the Stranger

In the accounts of centuries ago, Rum appeared to be a cheerful young deity, who made his historical missions and hunting trips along the lake banks near the War Nyang River. The region seems not to have a name then, and none has been found recorded in history. The name of 'Rum' was frequently used in the belief that a new son named as such may receive the qualities of the Rum begotten in the cave of sausage tree, *rual*.

The tale states that Rum was about 24 to 30 years of age at the start of his journey. This Rum appears to be from among the descended members of the actual Rum Wenkook. Other storytellers referred to him as Rum Ateny.

When he arrived at the ancient Dinka Apuk, fear from predatory nomads was on the increase. They were identified as the Lwalla of the Bantustan ethnic group.

Upon realizing who he was, the people in a village contacted the leaders from the Pabuor, Padiangbaar and Patiir clans. They decided to let Rum be captured by the predators as they reasoned that the Lwalla would slay him as a stranger and pour his blood on the soil as a sacrificial beast so that it would pour down on the land of ancestors and clan spirits. That blood would wash away sorrowful crimes, killings, sins, evil spirits and devils from the Apuk homeland for the benefit of the entire ancestry world of spirits. They believed that Rum's blood, flesh, life spirit and body spirit could curse the predatory Lwalla forever.

To accomplish this, they invited Rum to a feast so that he would sleep very deeply. Once he fell asleep the people would desert him and hide in the thick forests and in caves.

The villagers prepared gifts of beasts to sacrifice for clan spirits. They collected two bulls and tethered them to pegs under the supervision of the invited chief priests and members of the clans and sub-clans. Traditionally, the children of the daughters have special connections with spirits from the ancestors. They recited ritual prayers repeated after the high priest invoked them, offering sacrifices directing the predators to where Rum slept that night.

Soon after, a ritual libation was poured over the tethering pegs, and the animals were sacrificially slaughtered.

They meant to use Rum as a blood victim. This way the clan spirits and independent spirits would curse away his killers. It was the occasion for forgiveness of offence for the divine spirits to repulse the recurring abduction, torturing and massacring of the local people. They seemingly thought this might have been brought about by the curses of angry gods, wrongdoings, evil spirits, disobedience to divine spirits, or ancestors that had turned up in the homestead. Some believed a curse been left there by a witch.

They focused on Rum Atany's sacrifice as an element of their religious celebration rituals to call for peace, good health and prosperity. They wanted the predators to kill Rum because he came from an unknown place and this was an opportunity to reconcile with the angry divine spirits. They poured libation blood on the pegs, the shrine, living room doors, and the roadsides behind the mud-walls to communicate the special signals of sacrifices offered to ancestral spirits.

The curse of Rum offered to the predators to kill him for sacrificial blood was done in anger. They believed it is a criminal act to kill an alien and is punishable by the spirit, and that the creator and the blood, flesh and body spirit of Rum would revenge itself after death by cursing the predators to never come back to the Apuk state.

Stories of the Dinka Apuk and the Parum Clan mention the details of the cursing sacrifices when Rum was to be abandoned to the predators.

Rum the Stranger

The people ran away to the forests and caves immediately in fear of the approaching enemy. They left Rum at their mercy on the ground as if he was just an alien from an unknown place visiting them.

Nhialic condemned this evil plan and sent the curses away instantly. Then the divine spirit shifted the plan of the predators so that they kidnapped him instead.

Back in the village, the Lwalla appeared, carrying weapons. They arrived at the house where Rum was staying with the help of villagers left behind for that purpose. Even though Rum awoke and heard them, he was alone and outnumbered. Rum tried to stop them by appealing to his father in heaven and threatened them with his spear. However, he was overpowered, captured, then imprisoned.

Meanwhile, the entire population remained in hiding until every enemy went away. Rum was highly offended. Why would the people run for their lives without warning him? He did not know what they had done to him.

After the capture of Rum, he was taken to the predator's court, an ancient nomadic judicial body. Rum was tried by them, mocked, beaten, and condemned for making claims of being a stranger and newcomer. He claimed he was a hunter crossing from far away, who does not know what went wrong or why he was captured.

Rum realized the danger that had befallen on him and began to ask his father, the creator, for help. The elderly council members asked the predators to judge and condemn Rum by accusing him of claiming to be a descendant of the Deity begotten from the cave of the sausage tree. After some questions, with few replies provided by Rum, the members of the predator's prosecution counsel declared that they found Rum, to truly be a descendant of the deity and innocent, as he is a stranger in this location.

However, the ones that arrested him demanded punishment by hanging or to be sentenced to hard labour. The prosecutors led by their elderly council leader disagreed and ordered Rum to be set free. Even though the Apuk accounts vary with respect to various details, whether Rum might have escaped alone in the process or not, they agree on the general character and overall structure of the trials of Rum and his return to freedom.

When the trial of Rum was over he was then taken to a court in a Lualla location (not known to date).

The thing that makes Rum distinctively of the Parum clan is his religion or divinity. It was this centrality of worship for a higher deity that travelled with Rum to the prison, the courts, and that survived the long journey from the Crocodile River, in War Nyang a great distance away from where the kidnapping occurred, to the predator courts, and finally to the perpetrator courts.

The oldest Wunriir villages belonged to the predators, so the Lwalla decided to send Rum to a different group named in accounts as *the perpetrators*. These people had wanted to see Rum the stranger for weeks because they had been hoping to see the son descended from Rum that was begotten through falling from the heavenly father and the son of the *Rual*. However, it is reported that Rum said almost nothing in response to questions they asked.

The perpetrators and their soldiers mocked Rum the stranger, put a robe of arrest on his neck, tied his hands at the back and returned him to the predators. Soon after the third interrogation of Rum the stranger and after receiving few replies from Rum himself, the perpetrators saw Rum as no threat and returned him claiming he was a stranger in that locality. But others described the process that helped Rum to find his way out was prayer until he saved his life by running. However, the Apuk clansmen believed Rum was rescued through the spiritual powers of his father Ateny, the High Priest Deity to salvage the dehumanized Patiir, Padiangbaar and Pabuor clans frequently massacred and kidnapped.

After Rum's return from the court, the predator elder publicly declared that he found Rum to be innocent of the charges. However, the crowd again insisted on capital punishment. The rules governing the predator limited capital punishment sentencing strictly to the tribunal of the Nomadic rulers. The elder decided to publicly wash his hands of it all as to not be privy to Rum's, and possibly a deity's, death. Thusly he could present himself as a patron pleading Rum's case rather than as a judge in an official hearing. Finally, he ordered the release of Rum to go as a free man and an ally.

The kidnappers eventually returned Rum back to same village.

His return to his Apuk homeland was like he was a man resurrected. He was welcomed back as a hero and liberator. The villagers had come to the conclusion that Rum must be a true high priest chief and a descendant of his ancestral father Nhialic. They believed he possessed spiritual powers to be the guardian, rainmaker, and peacemaker so all the clans could have a safe life on earth. His life was bound together with the vitality of the people he guided.

The entire population of Bol Ciirial, Bek Amuuk, and Aguet Lokbaithok turned out in celebration of the release of their visitor. He was someone that the Apuk clans were proud of.

Priests, the elderly, and women came to adore him. Clan leaders travelled from afar, to bring animal sacrifices to Rum the stranger.

The clan spirit, ritual prayers and mediation protected Rum while in jail and saved his life. This was because he was the son of the Parum deity and high priest chief from the powerful spiritual Parum clan founded by the first Rum Wenkook (although not directly related as far as we know).

Bol Chiirial and his two deputies immediately recognized Rum's leadership and authority. They divided responsibilities between them. He was appointed to the fight the predators that captured him (even though he was released totally unharmed). Bol retained the Pabuor Clan priesthood during his reign.

Over time, traditionalists have attempted to reconcile this bit of history, while contemporary traditional research mostly views them as legendary, or mythical.

When Rum was returned to the Ancient Chiir homesteads, he was put in command and was secure in that title by late winter.

Rum took over the fight against the enemy and began the process of defeating them. The war intensified and he, and the participating clans, fought many adversaries over time including the Lwalla, slave raiders, and neighbouring enemies.

APUK : A STATE IN WAITING

Initially, the Lwalla began stirring things up at the eastern and southern borders. At the same time, grazing land and water source conflicts started a war in the Toch bordered by the Thony, Yar, Muok and Luanykoth clans. Rum faced a third war when the forces he had used in successful campaigns against the perpetrators and predators on the Toch or swamp frontier were savagely attacked. Rum then conquered several grazing territories together with water sources in Toch and proclaimed dual control of warfare and high priest leadership. He was confirmed as a reputable priest and commander of the Apuk clans.

Rum emerged a liberator and stationed warriors in the villages of Machuet in Jak centre, Bur Apuk on the banks of the Pagol River, Akon Agiu, and the Wunriir homesteads in the Machuet region. He organized warriors to fight against their many enemies. With dual control and holding the sacrosanct spear, he moved south and conquered the Lwalla of Bantustan. He annihilated the predator threats completely. This made the Apuk clans effectively independent of foreign domination. His brothers and their offspring spread across the Rek clans and became the protectors of the region.

To restore order after the defeat of the predators, Rum Atany gave deputyship to a clansman of the region, and command of a section of the Apuk clan armies. However, in late spring, the armies proclaimed Wol Rum, son of Rum as the commanding officer. The civil war that followed ended in a battle outside Apuk boundaries and Wol Rum emerged victorious. It appears Rum was killed in battle. Wol Rum began his reign by negotiating a peaceful end to his predecessor's war.

This son of Atany, referred to as 'Rum Atany' emerged as a warrior commander from the Parum spiritual clan and started an expedition northward along the Nile valley swamps and crossed to Apuk Bol Mel or a section of Apuk where Bol had settled. This is where the Lwalla raided villages, kidnapped or massacred men, women and children and had forced the rest of the population to flee. When they tried to hide in the trees they were attacked by wild animals and snakes at night. This had occurred against a backdrop of centuries.

Rum the Stranger

Just how precarious the life of the Apuk clans could be was revealed by the capture of Wol when he undertook expeditions to map out the savannah zones in Nile valley from the thick forests to the rivers that stretched to the swamplands. It was not only the swampy rivers whose course was largely unknown. The Apuk did not know much about the vast Nile valley extending westwards, northwards, and then eastwards at the relatively higher ground bordering the Jurchol-Luo in the green forest of Machuet.

Consequently, one of the goals of the early expedition was to find out how far the Nile valley territory extended, the type of animals to hunt, and where the Swamp Rivers came from. Earlier, Rum, Atany, and Wol led an expedition along the swampy river to its source and crossed it there (possibly the current Wanhalel River, or the Pagol river). It is not clear even today, where War Nyang is located, and it is difficult to say whether 'War Nyang' shares its name with Nyang or the lake of crocodile (*war nyang*) around Bur Apuk on the border with the Nyang clans (of the Rek clans).

After he escaped he made his way back the nearly 80 miles (129km) downstream to Toch Bol Ciirial, then returned to his Nile valley village. Back in the ancient village, Wol Rum narrated an account of this capture and imprisonment.

The capture of a son of the Parum spiritual clan was another instance of brutality marked by utter and unacceptable imprisonment of a guest, and lack of respect for the lives and dignity of the ancient clan civil population.

The journal of Rum Atany from the first part of his expedition was not published. But he had not reached the end of the Nile valley, so people still speculate about that. However, the name Rum has been around so long so that the history of the many descendants of Rum Wenkook and his son Ateny Wunior can be a bit confusing.

Did he keep on going east until he reached the end of Nile valley, as the clans had believed? Or, did he go into the large savannah in the Nile valley that contemporary clans called the Apuk Bol Ciirial? Did he meet Bol Mel, Aguet Lokbaithok and Bek Amuuk in Bur Apuuk and create his dynastic headquarters before the separation of the Apuk Lith sub-clans into three branches? Or did he start his reign in Akon-Agiu, where the offspring of Agei eventually ascended the throne? Did this son of the Parum clan participate in or lead the construction of Bur Apuuk that was talked about and established centuries ago on the River shore of Pagol bordering the Nyang sub-clans and the Apuk in the extreme northern region? Did the son of the Parum clan traverse the western part of the Wanhalel River through the Apuk to join the Jurchol-Luo clan bordering in the west and the Nyang clans bordering in the north? Or did he expand the homeland to eastern frontier, without reaching the far extreme eastern swamp borders at all? So much remains unknown.

Four subsequent expeditions to the Nile valley continued to trace the boundaries of the map of the Apuk clans. An expedition, led by either Malek Rum or Wol Rum, finally succeeded. Landing at the Pankiir base to the west, they moved further westwards towards the agricultural lands and conquered territories of the Malony Apuk where they settled along the borders with the Yar clan, Muok clan and Jurchol clan.

Malek grew up strong and was popular amongst the clansmen who admired his military skills. These include the influential Pabuor, Parum, Padiangbaar, Patiir, Pagong and Pakot clans. Here he found and appointed deputies for his expeditions. From Akuwei in Machuet, they marched due north until they reached the Maluach, Kongdeer, and Agurpiny clans bordering the territories of the Jurchol-Luo of the Nilotic group in the west, Nyang in the north, Kuach in the northeast, and Luanykoth clans in the east.

Epilogue

The descendants of Rum Wenkook and his son Ateny Wendior Rum left behind them a celebrated history. They came to liberate and save lives and souls in Apuk country and in other regions. Rum was a spiritual priest chief, a liberator, a founder of the Rum dynasty, and a nationalist that put the unity of the clans first and foremost.

Rum the Stranger

The dynasty reached its height of power and expansionism under Atany, Rum, Wol, Rum, Agei, and Malek. Later, there was an era marked by deadly wars during the period of the recycling names of Malek and Malek, Agei and Agei, or Malek, Malek, Agei, Malek, Agei, Agei and his son Aguelet Agei who all fought foreign enemies. Subsequent bloody inter-tribal and inter-cultural struggles were exploited by the foreign conquerors who established a foothold resulting from the wars of invasion by Arab traders.

Rum had united the clans and subclans into a single state of Dinka clans, established the independent Apuk homeland and repulsed invaders. His successors adhered to those powers of spirituality and militarism until they became tradition.

"Apuk" Defined

The following is an explanation about *apuk*. It is the term used for for reconciliation, prayer, ritual, sacrifice, homicide, crime, the law of penalty, forgiveness, divinity and the people's relationship to *apuk* itself.

Let's begin with *apuk* for offences or crimes. This is tied the very important matter of pardon by the use of clannish powers, which I refer to as "clan spirit forgiveness". It regards offences against clan members that cause sorrow (such as homicide) and what constitutes true repentance on the part of the wrongdoer.

Over time, the people of powerful spiritual clans who were masters of the fishing spear (or high priest chiefs), acquired a complete understanding of *apuk*. Many anguished over determining its use for offerings such as sacrifices, ritual prayers, mediations, and libations for reconciliation messages of clan spirit forgiveness for offences between different clans, their members etc.

During this chapter, I lean heavily on information provided by Father Nobel, Customary Laws, Chief Justice Wuol Makech, and others.

Before people can clearly understand *apuk*, clan crimes or offences, clan spirit forgiveness, blood wealth for forgiveness, and repentance, they should understand the offence, the wrongdoer, and particularly the effects of the crime on the victim's relatives, loved ones, and their clan.

Simply put, *apuk* is compensation, reconciliation, forgiveness, repentance and the restoration of peace within the clans. Chief

"Apuk" Defined

Justice Wuol Makech, Justice Aleu A. Jok, Robert A. Leitch, Carrie Vandewint, the Dinka Dictionary, and Customary Laws describe *apuk* of clan crime as being about homicides, mistakes or wrongdoing in the clans. When properly explained, we can see how the historical development of *apuk* became the rules of law and customs of the clans. We can then understand spirit forgiveness in the clans, and its link with the wonderful talents of the creator, the Nhialic god.

There are definitions of "Crimes and Mistakes", and "Judgment, the Law of *Apuk* and Forgiveness" found in the *Dinka Dictionary*. Some of this have been described in *Dinka Customary Laws* and other books written by Dr Francis Mading Deng about the Dinka Culture. They are similar to those of the Apuk Clan Culture.

There are many clansmen and clanswomen of powerful clans who believe (or assert that they believe) that through their own efforts they can develop life and the human characteristics that are necessary to bring them into accordance with the life of their creator and spirit. I find the task of convincing them that *apuk* for the crimes of clans is of great benefit to be very difficult.

The Definition of Apuk

A look at the Dinka-English Dictionary definition of *apuk* explains it as punishment or a penalty blood fine for killing, or serious wounds inflicted with the full knowledge and intent of the perpetrators.

There are some principle acts that must be fulfilled before payable *apuk* can be justified. They must be based on true principles of justice that can be documented in a customary law for the specific clans and has the force of law. These are outlined below:

1. Payable *apuk* must have been an immemorial antiquity. Essentially, an old law.
2. Payable *apuk* for crimes or offences is a must, and payment by cultural practices must be on the clan member or clan who asserts the claim payable to the clan victim families.

APUK : A STATE IN WAITING

3   The problem of refuting it lies upon the clan itself against whom the *apuk* of crime doings must be based on clan culture and values.
4   Payable *apuk* of crime done must have been enjoyed as a right in clan custom values.
5   Payable *apuk* of crime done must be obligatory, sure, and specific.
6   Payable *apuk* of crime clans must have been employed continuously, over time.
7   Payable *apuk* of crime type must be reasonable and conform to the courts of clan customs, values and laws.
8   Payable *apuk* is a must and is an obligation of immemorial antiquity for every person or clan member to obey, to adhere to and use to guide their life throughout.
9   Whoever deviates is considered an outcast in a clan, or clan divinity.

Payable *apuk* of crimes or offences is rooted in Dinka culture and clan divinity. It is compensation or reparation. It is a system of fines invoked with a ritual prayer invoking a deity, and using cows or sheep being offered for sacrificial blood. This allows the offender or wrongdoer to achieve communion with ancestral spirits after said contribution is offered to express regret for wrongdoing and to obtain forgiveness in the end.

Payable *apuk* of offence is a blood wealth penalty for reconciliation sought through the payment of damage offences termed Dia,[15] and is donated and paid for by the clan family of the guilty party. Such damage offences in *apuk* prices are paid in a 'currency' and according to a scale laid down under clan culture in their court systems. Dinka Customary Law incorporates the principles of culture in customary courts that settled offences caused by clans against by experienced traditional judges.

My important message to all the readers of this book is to understand the term *apuk*. It was always payable in cattle. The number of cattle is in accordance with the social status of the clan victim and the circum-

---

15   Wuol Makec, John., The Customary Law of the Dinka People of Sudan. Afroworld Publishing Co. 1988.

"Apuk" Defined

stances of the murdered etc. member of the clan. Thirty-one cows, for example, is the standard reparation for homicide.

This reparation helps members of victimized clans, to ease the reconciliation processes with the clans of the guilty party. They can then forgive and restore peace and harmony between them.

Sorrowful Offences and Actions

People are the main investors in sorrowful offences and actions in life. Whether they kill, injure, defame, offend, steal property, or even cause the withdrawal of clan spirits, ancestry spirits and divinities from their immediate surroundings; there must be compensation.

The *apuk* penalty can culturally be achieved through the reparation, reconciliation, and repentance for forgiveness to restore harmony from sorrow regarding crimes of actions in life.

In fact, how the penalty used in our history of customary laws works, is the real message. I must say to readers that individual sorrow for the crime of actions in life is interpreted as the work of evil spirits, witches, sorcerers, the evil eye, broken taboos, perjured oaths, or even the deities, ancestors or ancestral spirits.

The truth is, when good spirits (like the clan spirits, the independent spirits, the deities and divine ancestry's spirits) inflict some physical evil, they do so as a prophetic, corrective, or punitive measure because of the breaking of the true spiritual principles of customary justice of ancestry spirits and clan divinities. They are believed to be for the overall good of the individual and everything needed for life, including both physical things and the obligatory laws of immemorial antiquity.

Every person is created with different aspects that are responsible for the crimes they commit. The divinity has created individual people with physical bodies, body spirit, life, and flesh. These are the principles of life, feeling, thought, and action in people, yet are regarded as a distinct entity separate from the physical body. Life itself is commonly held to be separable in existence from the physical body. The spiritual part of people is distinct from the physical part, and necessary to make our wonderful people what they are.

There is a common belief among the Parum clan that the 'Flesh Heart' is 'sacred blood life' (*ring ee jongdit and ring puou ee jok or jongdit*). Every male and female descendant must honour the flesh deities and the high priests of their clan. The spirit part of an individual clan member is that part which contains what may be called the functions of life and the physical strength and power existing in them.

Clan creatures, divine clans, spirits and priests, are separate and distinct and have characteristics that are distinct in their composition, as well as in the duration of their existence. The body flesh, as clan members know, has an existence which lasts only during the life of the physical body. After that, life ends. The physical body dies and dissolves into its spirit either in the evil creation or in the clan spirit blessings. It can no longer form the same flesh body in the ancestry world of spirits. These sacred flesh and blood spirits are the things of clan traditions, ancestries, divinities and religions.

Apuk Based Laws of Cultural Punishment

There exist native laws of the *apuk* which express the cultures, beliefs and practices that reflect the identity of the people. The origin of *apuk* traces its origin to realistic peace, the use of deity and sacrifice, and persuasion by compensation, reparation, reconciliation and forgiveness.

In applying the real message of culture and its values, *apuk* had its origin to refer to. For that reason, the native laws of the clans and their cultural values became obligatory considerations for the recognized courts when deciding that *apuk* had the force of law[16] and the rule of law regarding cultural history. The law of obligation of *apuk* must be on the person who asserts the application of customary justice.

Whatever the end result, the original goal of *apuk* in general, or of clan crime, is reparation to persuade, reconcile and to forgive by

---

16   Wuol Makec, John., The Customary Law of the Dinka People of Sudan. Afroworld Publishing Co. 1988.

"Apuk" Defined

the use of deities and clan divinities for peace and harmony. Crime, particularly where the circumstances of a specific clan crime were deemed repugnant, or where the killing was likely to threaten order, or would create or increase inter-community conflict, inter-clan conflict, or clan versus clan conflict, became increasingly a matter for the statutory courts rather than cultural. The resulting punishment, which was often the death sentence for the guilty, contributed little to reconciliation and forgiveness among the clan members and was unpopular[17].

Enforceable persuasion to reconcile and forgive helps all. For the people of *apuk*, heaven is that place where everything entering into it is in wonderful harmony with the respective laws of Nhialic and his will regarding the laws of pardon or forgiveness.

Dinka clans believed that there were no independent human practices until man had decided to become separated from religious divinity. However, freedom brought with it toil, suffering, and death, which he had not previously known. It is similar in ways to the Adam and Eve being thrown out of heaven concept in Christianity. When Man on Earth was with God in Heaven, he wanted freedom. When he became independent, he was still dependent in that he had to accept suffering and death.

The separation between heaven and earth, or a divinity from heaven and man on earth, is represented as unplanned. The Apuk people attempt to make efforts to merge together the parts of their world which join when they endure misfortunes like death and sickness.

The ensuing traditional song is a representative of this desire:

The visitors came with doom.
The clannish religion flew away, and the evil spirit succeeded.
Do religions joke and hurt? Sadly, ants of the earth Religion jokes,
Inventor, sadly!

---

[17] Justice Aleu Akechak Jok (LLB), Robert A. Leitch (MBE) and Carrie Vandewint (B.Hu. M, (March 2004), A Study of Customary Law in Contemporary Southern Sudan, pg 11

APUK : A STATE IN WAITING

Our Nhialic brings the rope of the atoch maguen.
That we may meet on one periphery. We, the moon and Creator, clan religion give the rope of the atoch maguen.
That we may meet on one periphery with the moon.
The small bird atoch maguen cut the rope accurately.
The small bird atoch maguen severed the rope, and separated Heaven from earth, and clannish religion from man.

To the people of Apuk, the ethical order is in the end organized according to ethics that usually thwart clansmen. That familiarity and culture measure factually, and that the actions of people cannot change. This is a given, in much the same way as for practical purposes that we regard the physical order to be given. The myths of heavenly separation when *atoch maguen* cut the rope accurately mirrors life according to legend. The Apuk are in a life that is beyond their control. Results often contradict the most reasonable expectations. The spirit who is sometimes a kindly father is also the one that is manifested in the mythological forces of nature and hence has mythological as well as realistic and ethical characteristics.

Our people fear their ancestors, clan spirits, and independent spirits more than they fear the Christian god. Clan chiefs link sacrifices between god and the people, which are usually used to conciliate clans, people with clan spirits, and to promote understanding through the power of prayer.

During ritual dialogues and offering prayers, the master of the fishing spear asks clan divinities, clan spirits, *yath*, and ancestry *atiip* to come nearer to the people for spirit forgiveness. This is done to help them and not to harm them. That is the way the believers have come to dialogue with the divinities and spirits. They believe the creator is close and can listen, see, and order punishment for wrongdoing or disobeying a god. All clans believe in *apuk* of clan offences payable for lost blood values, for blood is life itself and it curses offenders. *Apuk* is composed of inherent components of the antiquities in which the Apuk clans of the have accepted humanity

"Apuk" Defined

and live not considering whether people recognize or enforce them. They further believe that they must incorporate the rules of law and of clan custom spirits into lawful practices prior to clan justice.

Apuk and True Justice Principles

Apuk based on truths represents justice-based principles that have evolved since antiquity through the foundation of culture, belief, tradition, and experience. Each influenced the ancestors during the nascent years of courts and continues to influence the decision-making process of customary justice principles today.

This permits not only the blessing of others but cursing as well. However, this is not to be done in anger, or indiscriminately. Fairly, it is only to be used in such cases whereas it was deliberated, and truthfully and honestly believed by the clans. The clan spirits and ancestor's curses should be adjudicated properly. A curse should be applied in full consciousness in that whosoever curses in the bitterness of their corrupt heart, and not in the light of the truth, will know curse will return upon them[18].

Every legal classification has its procedural rules. Customary law is no exception. To demonstrate how they work in a customary law court it is necessary to understand how rules of procedure differ from rules of substantive law.

This has been described as:[19]

> *"One of the differences between the two systems is that the rules of substantive law define the rights and duties or liabilities of people, while the rules of procedure regulate how the rules of substantive law are to be defended and enforced by a court of law. Rules of procedure mostly answer the question 'how'? For example: how does a litigant open his case or enforce his right against a defendant? While the rules of substantive law*

---

18 http:// encyclopedia.com, Book of the law of the Lord.cite- note -64
19 Ibid

answer the question 'what'? For example: What is the right of an original owner when a thief who stole his property has been convicted?"

Cultural practice refers to local custom court justice originating by usage, or clan practice, and is not applicable to the laws of alien origin. Where murder[20] has been committed against another clan member it is obvious to charge the wrongdoers under the customary court and if found guilty, to award both punishment under said court and according to the victim's customary laws.

The real message is that traditional law allowed the relatives of the victim to decide to seek justice and acts to seek damage offences through the customary rules of *apuk* for the offence of clans that will reconcile to forgive.

Apuk Offences

Apuk offences relating to clan customs and clan culture were the basic sources of penalties for such offences payable to the victim clans prior to the 1820[21] invasion of South Sudan. It became the first invasion in a chain of events that brought irreplaceable influences that altered clan traditional practices.

Any *apuk* determined by culture represents the system of principles believed to have been inspired by their ancestors, clan spirits, or a supreme being. The penalties for *apuk* of clan crimes reflect the rule of law, cultural values and religious beliefs held since ancient times.

The *apuk* of clan killing judicial system requires the perpetrator to pay the injured clan member a reparation of collective responsibility for clan members and that these reparations must have traditional recognition.

---

20 Makec, John., The Customary Law of the Dinka People of Sudan. Afroworld Publishing Co. 1988. At 31. At 26.

21 Lufti, G. A., The Future of English Law in the Sudan. The Sudanese Judgment and Precedents Encyclopedia. Sudan Judiciary, Khartoum. At 26.

"Apuk" Defined

Apuk, Forgiveness, and Peace

I wish to explain the forgiveness and pardon methodology in clans and to enlighten people properly on this subject of which so much is miswritten. Those writings have twisted the real meanings of the customs of the clans and their peaceful coexistence.

In very early times there was no source from which *apuk* could come, either in the spirit or ancestral world. Hence people could not become inspired as to *apuk* based truth and forgiveness.

Payable *apuk* is for forgiveness and repentance that facilitates relief in the people. The penalties for the crimes they have committed are fully paid. This permits them to turn from their cruel, hateful judgments and deeds and to seek forgiveness from the Nhialic creator and to reconcile with the spirits.

If they earnestly seek clan sacrificial prayers for reconciliation, they will find the happiness which is achieved from peace, coexistence and harmony in the clans. Payable *apuk* does not violate any other principal rule of law established to prevent individuals from avoiding the penalties for their violations of the laws controlling their conduct.

The English definition of the law of *apuk* is referred to as compensation particularly where a clansperson becomes penitent in earnest. Via traditional persuasions, the spirit forgives these wrongdoers or sinners of their crimes and makes a new life possible. Thereafter the previous judgment of *apuk* is nullified and swallowed up in the power of the new judgment of forgiveness and reconciliation.

This is forgiveness of guilt, or rather the result of forgiveness. When a someone pays for *apuk*, they are ready to reconcile this forgiveness. The Apuk clans, from experience, believe that this forgiveness is an actual, existing thing. When the victim's clan family receives *apuk* for crimes, they forgive, guilt disappears, and peace exists. This results in harmonious coexistence in its fullness, as justice is done.

Customary Clan Spirit Punishments

The harmony of a clan court of law is based the faith that all punishments from the beginning to the end derive from cultural traditions. Traditional Chiefs' Courts are entrusted with the force of the law to impose punishments according to certain agreed and accepted manners of justice. The overriding punishing power coming from clan spirit creation remains unchanged. However, the ways and means of divinity (*yath* or *jak*) punishment are as numerous and varied and are disastrous if used in an unstable manner. The punishments of clan spirits are threatening, and they teach the accused not to reject the laws of clan ancestors or despise their rules.

There are many who believe that an evil spirit will go after the guilty by enchanting their children, and the following generations of those who disobey clan, ancestry and Nhialic spirits. The threat is inculcated in cruel and unsympathetic members of clans. Specific retaliatory punishments will be imposed by clan and ancestry spirits for mistreating the helpless, stray and innocent.

In the beginning, the punishment of clan spirits and ancestors was independent of, and in addition to, judicial punishment. There were several customary court examples in which a death sentence is settled for a homicide and in addition the threat of clan spirit punishment is multiplied.

Clan Spirit (jok) Retaliation Punishment

The clan spiritual law explicitly states that where the settled punishment is not carried out, the clan spirit will act against that person and his kin by ostracising them. Clan spirit retaliation punishment is certain and is consequently a very effective deterrent. The omniscient spirit will not endure its laws to be disobeyed with impunity.

Clan spirit punishment is expressed in terms of simple death as well as of bearing one's evil or guilt. Sometimes "man shall bear his guilt" is followed by "and he shall die". Sometimes it is combined with the threat "to be cut off". This is sometimes joined with the threat of childlessness, deathlessness, mysteriousness, etc. Where the "bearing of guilt" stands alone, it is meant to impose the duty to bring a sacrifice to a divine spirit, ancestor and creator. This is defined as spiritual wealth or divine wealth by the Apuk. I personally find it appropriate. I have adopted and used it throughout the book.

Spiritual Wealth and the Master of Fishing Spear

Spiritual wealth is a cultural gift to a master of the fishing spear in cattle, goats, sheep and/or money. In return, he invokes the clan spirits *jak*, *yath*, and *atiep* to offer beast sacrifices for rituals on their behalf. The master of the spear is also known as a spiritual priest, spiritual minister or divine priest chief who shall receive spiritual wealth (divine wealth) on behalf of his clan spiritual powers which have been offered gifts in compensation for the spirit and ancestry powers to guide the life of the people.

A priest receives the divine wealth payable to lead ritual prayers in clan traditional ceremonies organized by the guilty clans, or the victim clans, or by a clan party. This is for clan sacrifice prayers to transfer to clan spirits and ancestors for cursed clan families or parties to restore their life in the clan. The clan family uses other spear masters to reconcile clan spirits and the creator of ancestors who chooses to empower the spear master to possess supernatural spirits. This enables healing for spiritual crimes, divine disputes, devil offences, oaths, homicides, bewitching, wrongdoings, and evil eyes that people perceive to have come through the creator.

Divine wealth is the *apuk* payable to the clan spiritual priest and ranges in accordance with the retaliatory penalty for the specific spiritual crime and the circumstances of the victim party or family. Compensation is well defined. The divine wealth to be received by the spear master varies. He is called upon to settle disputes and crimes and shall receive his divine wealth. This is deemed as the spiritual price determined by the level of disputes and crimes that may cause social unrest, victim disability, death, or imprisonment.

Blood wealth is mainly *apuk* that is issued in cattle and may range from one to more than thirty cows for guilt regarding of homicidal acts, causing injuries, offensive behaviour, or damages done with full knowledge and deliberation[22].

Deadly Crime

The Apuk deem deadly crime to be the act by which individual clansmen freely and consciously renounce the clan spirit and the promise of ritual prayer offerings by clan spirits. They prefer instead to turn to something contrary to the desire of clan spirits and clan ancestors. This occurs in a direct form in the retaliation punishments of ritual prayers of those deny their clan ancestors and spirits, as every act of disobedience to the rules of laws of clannish ancestral spirits is a grave matter[23].

Traditional Sacrifices

Here I will describe the one part relevant to the understanding of the Flesh Divinities of spear master clans, including the Flesh Heart divinity.

When there was to be a clan sacrifice in Apuk country, masters of the fishing spear; such as those of the powerful clans of Parum and Pagong, were used to lead ritual prayers over a bull calf tethered on a decorated peg under the shrines. Animal sacrifices have long been the practice in clan tradition for the forgiveness of clan crime acts or offences as part of ritual prayers and traditional celebrations. Clan divinities represent the symbol or emblem of permanent values for the clan. The master of the fishing spear receives clan gifts in return

22   St. Augustine, Catechism of the Catholic Church, 1849.
23   John Paul II, *Reconciliatioetpaenitentia*, December 2, 1984, 17.

"Apuk" Defined

for prayers, ritual sacrifices, mediation and libation for good health or to restore life. He would do so for the clan families that collectively recognize a clan divinity which none of the other clans has. This is *ring* or flesh. The divinity ring of clan Parum is connected to flesh, and therefore the master of the fishing spear invokes and sacrifices a bull calf tethered on a peg in the traditional clan pattern. It is claimed the clan Rum is more strongly inspired by the Flesh Divinity because of the raw meat.

In the myth of the clan Rum, this Flesh Divinity is the same Flesh Heart divinity, *Ring Puou*, that the first deity Rum left behind in the ground for *Ateny Wundior* and other descendants when he disappeared and joined *Deng* and *Nhialic* in the Spirit World.

Ring is the general word for meat in Jieng language. However, flesh is the best *ring* as it is boneless. It is also described as *meat flesh* which comes from a beast sacrificed or slaughtered. One whose death could be observed by Parum clan members where the shivering flesh after a skinned beast is bloody makes it appear to have a life of its own. Moreover, the divinity Flesh Heart and Flesh Divinity are strong indications that the clansmen and pregnant clan women are prohibited from eating the Flesh Heart meat, *ring puou*. Clan members are usually asked to contribute an ox, a sheep, and a quality item according to his or her family status[24] for sacrifices.

Collective ceremonies are performed. In prayers and sacrifices divinity, the general divinities and the clan divinities are commonly asked to come to people to help them with their lives, cure the sick, or guide a war leader or peacemaker in clan traditional practices. This is where the clan members, from the priest to the lowest subject, is to offer a heifer, a lamb, or a chicken to bring to the shrine for ritual sacrifices before the invocations commence so that no clan member is left out.

When the rains are scarce, rainmaking ceremonies are conducted. Beasts are sacrificed, and the rain stone known as *kur* of Deng (*yan-Deng*)

---

24   Book of the Law, pp. 293-94.

is brought out and rubbed with their intestinal fluids. Then water is poured upon it. This stone is sourced from local granite available around the savannah forests. Deng Garang whose spirit is present at the sacred shrine is frequently mentioned in clan Rum mythology as the first son of Deng Garang and Aleek Jiel who exposed Rum into the human world. He is associated with the Apuk cultural hero, Longar, the first son of Jiel.

When a man is asked to say why his marriage is childless for so long, he will simply tell you that his wife is bewitched, or our clan divinity is punishing us for failing to offer Macardit and other general divinities their donation of sacrificial animals.

They believe the divinity invents (*cak*) the child in the woman's belly. When clanswomen are barren it is described by reference to clan divinity. When a clanswoman fails to bear a child despite intercourse with a clansman known to be able to beget children, it is commonly said that Divinity has "refused" her a child. At sacrifices, masters of the fishing spear or prophets commonly ask that Divinity may allow a clanswoman to bear children. Clansmen, however, beget children in relation to the inventive act of Divinity.

Killing the offering is the prerogative of the clan headman[25]. However, witchpersons are specifically barred from participating in this aspect of the celebration of rituals. The divine spirit act permits not only the blessing of others but cursing. This is not to be done in anger or indiscriminately[26]. The curse is only to be repealed upon the deliberate and honest recognition of the creator Nhialic and the ancestry spirits. The chief priest who curses due to the bitterness of his corrupt heart and not according to truths from ancestry spirits will have the curse rebound upon him[27].

Given the practices of the ritual sacrifices for offences in the clan, priests usually require clan offence offerings. He focuses on ritual sacrifice as an element of religious pardon in the forgiveness of clan offences, and religious celebrations. This occurs especially during the commemoration

25   Book of the Law, pg. 199, note 2.
26   Book of the Law, pp. 100-01
27   http://www.strangite.org/Law.html Strangite.org. 2004-01-01. Retrieved 2012-02-09.

"Apuk" Defined

of a clan's own shrine of a deity to ask him in prayers to give life, help clansmen and sometimes to remain away and not to trouble them.

Obligation and Apuk

The Apuk have traditionally agreed that homicide is an offence. The perpetrator and their clan must pay compensation or reparation of collective responsibility to the affected person(s). The payment of reparations, known by the term *apuk dhieeth* or *apuk dhiendu* depends upon the belief and values of that particular clan and may be in livestock and/or currency. Systems exist traditionally to assess clan reparations.

Payment of *apuk* must be made to conform to clan customs they believe were laid down by the clan spirit, or other clan deity who governs according to principles of ancestral worship in ritual sacrifice, truth, and justice. Any enacted crime of *apuk* must be measured by its resonance with the divine ancestral spirit principles of right and wrong. These can be found in the customs, deity doctrines and decrees within the clans, and from their priests.[28]

Local custom is not applicable to laws of foreign origin. Customary Court is commonplace where a case against another clan member can be reviewed. If found guilty, the accused clan member can be awarded punishment according to custom.[29]

The Collective Responsibility

The Apuk share a customary belief that the act of murder is a collective responsibility. The clansperson that committed the act might not have to single-handedly pay the *apuk* for the crime. This person is allowed to appear in court accompanied by the clan family. If found guilty, the

---

28 P.P. Howell, A Manual of Nuer Law, Oxford University Press, 1954, p41
29 Arabs define a penalty fine as 'Dias paid'. It is "apuk" in Dinka for payment of Compensation.

courts determine collective responsibility. The price for *apuk* in the clan is not in any way changed but the overall price is shared proportionally between those deemed by the courts to have blood relations to take upon collective responsibility for the act.

After the verdict or sentence is announced, the Chief is then required to confirm collective responsibility, inform those concerned, and to arrange timely collection. The people of Apuk use patrilineage (tracing descent through the paternal line)[30]. Liability for the act can be taken over by the family or clan members of the guilty party. If the biological father is absent, the maternal uncles take over the liability for the act. The role of collective responsibility in *apuk* for killing is key to understanding that there must be more socially acceptable mechanisms of conciliating victimized parties with the perpetrators.

The Apuk believe that if the person who had killed another person in an inter-clan or inter-tribal dispute, and when they conclude that the person was acting on behalf of others in carrying out the act, then those 'others' have collective responsibility. Therefore, collective responsibility is an expression of the overwhelming solidarity of the entire community. It is the principle of assigning responsibility in a broad sense.

Apuk of Sacrificial Blood in Ritual Prayer

Oborji states that: "Life is viewed as a communion within the created order, universe, spirits, ancestors, one's family, community, and with God."

Apuk is paid to the living spirit of the victim, as well as to the family or party of the body spirit of the victim. It should also include the living blood of cattle and ritual recitation of prayers. Libations are poured on the decorated tethering pegs in surrounding shrines. The cattle should be sacrificially slaughtered by spiritual priests who shall shed blood for the crime committed against physical life, spirit life, spirit body and the evil spirits that falsely cause a person to do wrong.

---

30 The Re-statement of the Bahr el Ghazal Customary Law Act [Dinka Customary Law] 1984, Section 56

"Apuk" Defined

The priest slits the throat of the designated offering to pour its sacrificial blood for purity and to repent in order to restore harmony. When people earnestly pray for penitence, the spirits of the ancestors will forgive their crimes and make a new life possible.

Spear Masters or the High Priests of Deities should not have any blood relationship to the victims benefiting from the award of *apuk* and should not be related to the guilty.

The living animals are the ones to be sacrificed to offer to spirits, ancestors and spirit life because flowing blood is life created by God and must be returned to the spirit in the form of these animals. They will mediate with the spirit of the victim, the victim's ancestors, living spirits, and divinities.

When sacrificial blood is shed, it means culturally that the goal must be a serious one because life is closely associated with blood. It means human or animal life is being given back to the creator and spirits who are in fact the ultimate source of all life, including the living spirit, body spirit and life spirit. In mythology, the life of living spirit has eyes and sees wrongdoers, sinners and bewitchers. Sacrifices may be made by both sides when the lives of many people are in danger. The life of one person is represented in the animal sacrificed in the belief that this will save the lives of many people. Every person wants to reach the spiritual land of one's ancestors and to be venerated by one's descendants as an ancestor. Sacrifice is principally ritual prayer mediation. It allows the person to achieve communion with God through the mediation of the offering.

Blood Wealth

The most unquestionably misunderstood and contentious aspect is that of 'blood wealth'. It is also erroneously called *apuk* or 'the deceased price'. Blood wealth can be described as money or cows brought by a guilty party to the victim's family. The person who is injured or killed brings the blood price, and this price connotes some form of life blood compensation contract.

APUK : A STATE IN WAITING

The form of this blood wealth depends upon a clan's customary justice principles. For the people of the Apuk clans, the *apuk* penalty in blood wealth takes the form of cattle and occasionally, sheep and goats. Contemporary urban people of the Apuk clans have reportedly taken blood wealth in the form of money. At this point in time, currency is increasingly used to pay for blood wealth and the likelihood is that the practice will widely spread across to population with new customary justice values and needs. There are substantial reasons given for the institution of *apuk* penalty in blood wealth. Here are some among the most sacred. They are called *apuk riem*:

1 *Apuk*, known as compensation payable to the relatives of the victim clan, has been considered in some ways to be payment for sacred life and spirit body. The physical body is dead, but the life spirit, living spirit and body spirit live on.
2 The Apuk believe that when a person is killed, defamed or injured, an animal sacrifice is to be used by the spear master or priest to pray for the member of the wronged party. The spear master shall receive "spiritual wealth" for supplication in the form of animals as gifts or donations for the *apuk* of his spiritual and ancestry divinities. Those whose powers have been transmitted to him and because the spear master possesses their powers must be compensated.
3 The payable *apuk* for clan homicide of thirty cows to the family of the clan victim is the reimbursement for blood loss which is life and sacred.
4 The thirty-one cows paid for *apuk* re the deceased person are called "thirty-one cows of blood" or "spirit body", I named them as blood wealth based on explanations I made earlier. Cow of blood is the singular address (*Wong riem*) and plural address as (*hook riem*), cows of blood.
5 Payable *apuk* to the aggrieved clan victim is measurable by the degree of loss. This is usually determined by the chiefs of the traditional courts.
6 Defamation is a crime in the clan and punishable in courts because defamatory remarks can lead to conflict and death. Blood wealth

"Apuk" Defined

and spiritual wealth are payable in cattle for an *apuk* penalty as their spirits will be invited to be used by spear masters who are in possession of the deity spiritually.

7   The payable *apuk* penalty for severe cases can be five to fifteen cows following assessments made by chief's courts, where the aggrieved person may die, lose memory, or limbs due to injuries afflicted in the past.

8   In the Dinka language, we say blood cows (*Wong riem* or *hook riem*) or blood goats (*thok riem* or *thook riem*).

9   If more than two cows are paid as the *apuk* penalty, they are called blood cows, *hook riem* for "lost blood", I have collectively named them as blood wealth as this is how clan members address the *apuk* penalty administered by the master of the fishing spear.

10 If the victim killed was by mistake (manslaughter) and was a member of a clan family, then the decision will lie upon victim's brothers, father, or maternal uncle, who shall receive sixteen cows, in blood wealth for facilitating peaceful reconciliation by the use of spear masters and deities for harmony. The spear master shall receive the traditional spiritual wealth payment.

11 Of the thirty-one cows for *apuk* there is a ritual sacrifice to cut one cow into two equal parts where the homicide causing clan family takes away the back parts and the victimized clan family takes away front parts. This is a sign of acknowledgement that blood, life spirit, body spirit and the living spirit of the clan victim has been reimbursed and is reconciled with ancestry spirits. The other thirty cows blood wealth collected by the victimized clan family members are quickly distributed proportionally among said family members. Spouses of their sisters must take a share of one blood cow, *toong wong yuom* or *wong yuom*.

12 The institution of blood wealth involves an element of prestige for the children, family and relatives. It also may be a disgrace for a family in some instances. A deceased person will be seen as a hero if he or she died in defence of the family, clan, community or for the nation-state's dignity and integrity.

In the event of a failure of payable *apuk* of clan price through lack of resources or refusal, the clan chiefs will order force to be used collect the cows for *apuk* from the clan members.

Apuk of clan payment reduces looming tension and prevents disruptive violence, which frequently leads to damaging disputes and conflict. The clan and the sub-clan of the victim always think of revenge if payment of *apuk* for clan crime is not quickly done.

Any action, which threatens family cohesion in the clan, is viewed with great disdain and is dealt with harshly under clan customary laws and through clan divinity penalties with severe curses for wrongdoers and sinners.

There are exceptions and variations. The people, in the free exercise of their thinking, have gone beyond the limitations of the thirty-cow penalty, which the law of forgiveness and harmony has placed upon them. Hence, they have added one cow to pay as blood wealth for the use of the divine spiritual master.

On many occasions, they have increased the cattle numbers to more than fifty-one cows to be paid to the victim family or member by the guilty family or member.

Although spiritual wealth and blood wealth from their own sorrowful acts of homicide have held them in bondage and unhappiness ever since the original crime, the *apuk* penalty of blood wealth payable to the victim family by the responsible party that has believed in it and submitted to their interventions, has a healing effect. This has been so from the time of the Rum Deity to this very day.

God works no miracles, nor gives special dispensation. No. People must pay the *apuk* spiritual punishment for their evil deeds until the law is fulfilled via true and sincere ritual prayers.

Deng Mabuoch.
Spiritual Priest or an Impostor?

Mabuoch seemed to be in possession of spirit powers at adolescence. He led an expedition from the Ahech-Loch territory of the Wunriir villages in the Machuet section to Bur Apuuk Village before his first appointment as high priest. He was selected as a spiritual priest chief to establish the holy shrine in Maluil Apuk village close to fishing, hunting, and grazing areas. As well, he was recommended by both lower masters of the fishing spear, commoner clans and various diviners for his superior spirituality (or *aciek*) that he had shown in many ritual celebrations.

The divinity Mabuoch or more accurately, the divinity under the name of Deng Kur, descended into the body of the prophet Deng Kur and he claimed he must be addressed as such. He is also known as Deng Mayual, Deng Piol, Deng Dit or Deng. The first son of Mabuoch is called Deng. He proclaimed the prophecy which first appeared in his father and became known as the priest chief Mabuoch Mabior Majur.

Mabior Majur, father of Mabuoch and grandfather of Deng Mabuoch was a blacksmith. He was an artist known for moulding iron into traditional weapons such as spears, axes (*pur jang*, or *puorjang*), and local knives for women to cut thatching grasses and for domestic uses. It was a skill he had acquired at Jurchol-Luo to the west at Ahechloch. He was among the best of his time.

Dengdit is said to be the first son of Mabuoch Mabior Majur. Mabuoch named his son as Deng, who members of the Parum clan believed to be descended from the divinity of Dengdit, with the spiritual powers of Deng Mabuoch Mabior Majur.

Deng Mabuoch decided to announce that he had been chosen prophet by Deng Kur in the heavens to do services on its behalf on earth. Maybe he did so because he was named Deng. However, he was cautious not to come into contact with the Government, and let it be known that he preferred to personally receive anyone who might possibly seek *aciek* in connection with human fertility, evil spirits, bewitching, *yath*, *jok*, *atiip*, curses and bad luck.

Deng Kur means falling ice (hail), or a stone, and is always regarded as a direct manifestation of divinity. Deng Mabuoch announced at Wun-ngap village that he was the representative of divinity under the name of Deng Kur. He demonstrated that this was so by the truth of his assertions and the power of his curse.

The trouble began in communities of the Nyang, Abiem and Apuk North clans where Deng failed to cure women that voluntarily moved to his home for cures by Deng spirits. He claimed that he had been chosen as a prophet with Deng Kur powers for enabling women to bear children. In the process of treatments, the women declared themselves to be his wives. He was reported to have many such wives. They numbered up to forty plus the children. As well, there were many donations of cows that were taken to him in supplication for favours.

He travelled far north to the Abuok and Abiem clans, then up to the Northern Rek clans in Warthou. There he resided with many wives in Gamdhang village and spent time performing prophesy *aciek* for various forms of human sicknesses.

As stated previously, in the case of a clansmen who failed in begetting children despite intercourse with a woman known to be capable, it is generally concluded that divinity had "refused" them a child. Deng Mabuoch stated that he could cure this by communicating directly with the Divinity Deng Kur that he possessed.

If a woman is barren her barrenness is described in reference to divinity. If a woman fails to beget a child, with a man known to able to beget children, it is assumed that divinity has rejected her a child.

Deng Mauoch

The *aciek*, Deng Mabuoch, would ask his divinity for intervention via sacrificing beasts so that such women could bear children. The hymn quoted below may explain the background of the divinity Deng and powers to cure as follows:

> *Deng my father, Deng of all the greatness.*
> *My father Deng, a great person centuries by centuries.*
> *Great Deng denies to hear. Great Deng denies to help.*
> *If not honoured, he is offended, indifferent,*
> *My father Deng do not forsake me,*
> *My father Deng do not abandon me to the powers of sickness.*

Usually, the first rains in the Apuk come violently with a lot of thunderstorms. The divinity Deng is associated with the thunder and lightning which usually destroys, as well as with the life-giving rain. *Thiec of deng* or *thiec deng*, the club of the rain, or *thiec Deng*, the club of Deng, is a name for the lightning which strikes down everything in its way. This is believed to be the direct intervention of divinity in the affairs of people. In thunderstorms, it is traditional to sit quietly and respectfully, for people are in the immediate presence of divinity. Those who died from lightning are not mourned as it was the divinity Deng's work. Houses that have been set on fire by lightning cannot be saved, because this will be seen as an interference with the expression of the will of divinity Deng. The Apuk do not construct a shrine to this divinity, but, poles are put down around the lightning strikes and gifts of cows or sheep are sacrificed to Dengdit. They are boiled in the same place, and the hides cut into long strips and hung on the poles. This shows a sign of sharing and thanks to divinity Deng. It is asked during the sacrifice prayers for forgiveness to continue giving life, to guide life, and to protect the people from evil, evil spirits and sickness.

The number of donations had doubled in the form of girls taken to Deng Mabuoch, in supplication for favours. Barren young women seeking to be cured deserted families or legitimate husbands to go to his house for healing. It was later reported that sick women looking for a cure declared themselves wives to *aciek* Deng, who keeps and cures them.

Aciek Deng claimed that he provided life, remembered the supplications of the donors and young women, and directed his attention to their satisfaction. Relatives of the girls believed that their daughters would be cured and saved from evils and bewitching. However, the men whose wives were sick or barren and surrendered themselves to him, felt that the *aciek* used their wives falsely. Those people became angry and went as far as accusing him of crimes to the government and the British Commissioner of Gogrial District.

The Commissioner then dispatched a government patrol that arrested him in Warthou village with his two daughters, Adut Deng Mabuoch and Abuok Deng Mabuoc as well as their mother, Apuot. He was charged with wrongdoing. However, when his first son, Mabuoch Deng learned of their arrest and impending transport to Khartoum, he travelled on foot to Lietnhom hoping to rescue them and bring them back. Unfortunately, he too was arrested. Later, his father was set free due to his advanced age.

On his part, Dengdit refused to leave Lietnhom and complained that unless his family, was released, he preferred to be returned to jail. The government would not release them. Dengdit did leave Lietnhom to go to a place where the boat that would transport them was docked. He waited until it departed carrying them all towards Northern Sudan via the Machar Rek River.

He watched them being chained and shipped off to Khartoum as slaves. Whatever Deng Mabouch may or may not have been as a person, we can only imagine the anguish he endured.

The Apuk responded to this news and declared war against the government. Paramount Chief Agei opposed all the attempts to establish the Colonial administration on Apuk soil in reference to slain Paramount Chief Malek, his Deputy Ayuel Baak and the agony endured by Deng Mabuoch Mabior and his family.

To lose compassion is to lose what defines what human beings are all about. The greatest crimes of humanity occur when the moral compass, which enables understanding, is made silent due to selfish

Deng Mauoch

justifications. Mature contemporary people can engage in diversity and retain what makes them unique without resorting to draconian actions.

Deng Mabuoch followed the riverboat on foot up to Machar Rek River Port, leaving more than thirty wives behind in Warthou village. I have said before that Deng had forty wives, and it was not so clear whether they included his wives who were living in Apuk. That is where the clan divinity spear was kept by the first wife; mother of his first son. According to the tradition of this powerful spiritual clan, the spear is the power of the nation and cannot be taken out of the house assigned to the clan divinity high priest or deity. It is usually inherited by the first son of the first wife if the family is polygamist.

It was believed that the Clan Divinity was punishing Deng because he broke the laws of his clan and practiced differently from what he was allowed to do by the spirits of *jak, yath*, the ancestors and clan divinity spirits of the Parum clan that guide and give spiritual powers to a spiritual high priest chief through prayers and ritual sacrifices, which cannot be associated with witchcraft, or *aciek* corrupted practices.

Deng remained waiting there but was not allowed to see them until the riverboat got underway away en route to Khartoum. They were never seen again. Deng Mabuoch Mabior died and was buried at the Port of Machar.

I mentioned earlier about how the powers are themselves distinct and how they are recognized in the behaviour of men. The high reputation of Deng Mabuoch's powers crumbled to where they were beneath that of diviner or minor prophet because he abandoned the clan divinity powers and chose life creation, *acang cak koc*, or *acang koc cak*. With the powers of divinity, Deng Kur associated instead with the minor free divinities of Machardit, Garang, Abuk and Deng. *Aciek* is a prophet of this category and is only recognized by minor diviners or lower prophets who may be hoodwinkers and fakes.

Customary Law in the Modern Era

Customary law exists in its unadulterated form in the rural mono-ethnic regions of the south. Questions of harmful cultural practices, draconian martial law, lack of professionalism and jurisdictional uncertainty plague the administration of justice. Customary law in South Sudan largely embraced reconciliation and community harmony which restores balance in the family unit and the community. Traditional values and the community structure that reinforce them are under siege in post-conflict Sudan. (Mennen, 2008:3)

Traditional authority and customary law have attracted increasing attention in Southern Sudan since the 2005 Comprehensive Peace Agreement and the establishment of a semi-autonomous Government of Southern Sudan (GoSS). The largest component of GoSS and the signatory of the CPA, the Sudan People's Liberation Movement/Army (SPLM/A), had already taken conciliatory steps to improve its relations with the chiefs who had complained of abuses by SPLA soldiers during the long war beginning in 1983[31]. At the same time, the international organisations working with GoSS to develop new governance structures became interested in the potential of traditional, indigenous forms of government.

---

31 For accounts of the war and the SPLM/A's relations with chiefs, see e.g. Johnson (2003), Rolandsen (2005), Branch & Mampilly (2005), Leonardi (2007a & b). On SPLM justice, see Kuol (1997 & 2000).

Customary Law in the Modern Era

The Wanhalel Dinka Customary Law adopted in 1927, was a traditional and basic law, whose stated purpose was: "To entrench within basic law the values of the clan customs of Southern Sudan as a traditional society". When the British colonial administration established the Tonj District in 1903, a Mr Wilson was appointed Commissioner. He then appointed Malek Agei Aguelet Agei, a priest chief/master of the fishing spear to determine the *apuk* price for a killing offence. Wilson adjudicated to him trial supervision skills for clan offences regarding judicial disputes resolution and compensation in cattle.

Members of the Traditional High Court of Appeal of the Tonj District and the Government consulted with their colleagues representing the High Court, Chief Magistrates, Local Governments, Rural Councils, and traditional chiefs' courts in the Bahr El Ghazal region in Wanhalel. They deliberated on the prevailing crime rates in the region. The meeting was carried out under the chairmanship of Mr Wilson and attended by traditional chiefs representing customary courts. Court presidents represented the Rural Councils and Town Courts. Heads of Local Government and Provincial Judges represented the Anglo- Egyptian Sudan Government. Before the Dinka Apuk homeland was invaded by the Anglo-Egyptian-Sudan forces, the customary and traditional trial skills of the tribal groups were the primary source of law to the peoples of South Sudan[32]. The invasion was the first in a chain of events, which brought colonial influence to bear over the traditional customary practices and law systems.

The heads of institutions of the government of Anglo-Egyptian Sudan:

1   Took note of the traditional trial skill systems and communications adopted by all the participants that attended the conferences conducted between 1927 and 1931 in Wanhalel.
2   Took note of the reports and recommendations made by the parties.

---

[32]   Lufti, G. A., The Future of English Law in the Sudan. The Sudanese Judgment and Precedents Encyclopedia. Sudan Judiciary, Khartoum. At 2.

3 Took note of the briefings, and recommendations made by the representatives regarding Dinka Traditional Basic Laws regarding the customary law systems, judiciary systems and the investigation and prosecution of offences under both Dinka (Jieng) Traditional Customary Laws and statutory law to strengthen the collaborative arrangements envisaged in the creation of the Traditional Customary Law systems.

4 Acknowledged the proposals made by the representatives in the conference of the traditional systems of communications, especially traditional chiefs of custom courts and steps in the legal court direction that adopted the Wanhalel Dinka Traditional Customary Laws in 1927 in Apuk and urged for their immediate and unconditional implementation.

5 Pledged full support for the recommendations of the conference for the traditional systems of communications to re-enforce the customary law and legal court judges in Southern Sudan.

6 Called upon the Government to recognize customary court systems, customs and the chiefs' courts as institutions through which a many people have interacted quite well with the state.

7 Supported chiefs as having the legal authority regarding judicial trial skills & customary trial sentencing to exercise jurisdiction in their traditional tribal areas.

8 Supported recommendations by the delegations to adopt the customary trial skills that would replace the Mohammedan Law Courts Ordinance 1902 operating Sharia Courts in South Sudan. As well, regarding family relationships concluded in accordance with Mohammedan law or the parties are Mohammedans, that an interdicted or lost person is a Mohammedan, whether being Mohammedans or not, make a formal demand signed by them asking the Court to entertain the question stating that they agree to be bound by the sentencing decided according to Mohammedan law or no.

9 Appeal to the Anglo-Egyptian Sudanese Government to come to the rescue of affected populations in South Sudan by strengthening their presence and mobilizing requisite resources. In this connection,

demand that the Local Government guarantee effective and efficient customary judges for access to customary court sentencing. This is because the primary aim of customary trial sentencing is conciliation and judicial dispute resolution in civil law, and in criminal trial sentencing regarding the reconciliation between the wronged and wrongdoer.

10 Appealed to the Colonial Governor for his approval, to make regulations governing the decisions, procedure, traditional legal systems and jurisdiction of the criminal trials and civil law for trials and court sentences, to ensure a sense of justice and resolution of judicial disputes amongst the disputing clans, and through this means to restore and maintain social stability.

11 Further called upon the parties to honour their commitment that they have entered into when signing the approval on the resolutions of clannish conflicts in the south of Sudan and urged them to fully implement the customary judicial systems as the only framework for durable peace, forgiveness, reconciliation and national cohesion.

The common understanding of the term 'customary judicial trial sentencing skill' is embodied in the traditions which are social conventions and traditional judicial trial skills practised through long usage and widespread acceptance directly governing traditional African society including South Sudanese society[33]. Therefore, the customary "judicial system" is as much a social convention as it is a judicial trial procedure.

Efforts were carried out to define customs together with customary law throughout the years. However, a wide-ranging definition may be found in Osborn's Concise Law Dictionary, by John Burke, on page 108:

---

33 Kur, Dengtiel. A., Access to Traditional Justice Systems & the Rights of Women and Children in South Sudan. Workshop on the Legal Protection of Children. Organized by the South Sudan Law Society. 2000. Rumbek, New Sudan (Definition made by Kur, not published).

"Custom is a rule of conduct obligatory to those within its scope, established by long usage. A valid custom has the force of law. Custom to the society is what law is to the State. A valid custom must be of immemorial antiquity, certain, reasonable, obligatory and not repugnant to statute law, though it may derogate from the common law."

It was through these conferences that the first customary laws operating in South Sudan were officially adopted and documented by the colonial powers. Dinka-Jieng customary judicial systems were enshrined in the passage of the Civil Justice Ordinance of 1929. The customary trial skills of the traditional courts of the Chiefs Ordinance of 1931 was the second important development because it recognized the legal authority of customary trial skills and court penalties by Chiefs to exercise customary judicial jurisdiction in their traditional tribal areas.

"The Chiefs' Court shall administer the Native law and Customs prevailing in the area over which said Court exercises its jurisdiction provided that such Native law and Custom is not contrary to justice, morality or order."

Malek Agei Aguelet Agei

Malek Agei Aguelet was the first spiritual master appointed to the Traditional High Court of Appeal in Tonj District to represent the chiefdom of Apuk by Mr. Wilson. His primary responsibility in the Appeal Court was to oversee trial homicides caused by wrongdoing according to custom and to bring about reconciliations, repenting, forgiveness and harmony between the victim clans and the guilty clans. He was tasked to investigate clan homicides, tried them, and guilty clansmen were given the sentences ranging from fines in cattle, money, kind, and imprisonment for weeks, months, and years. However, death sentences were concluded only by the Chief Magistrate at the district levels in Tonj District.

Malek is from the Rum Deity dynasty and the Parum clan. He is the priest chief that united two principles into his sentences and decisions. He was inspired by his clan divinity and as the inherited master of the fishing spear. Malek had a high reputation as a ritual priest chief that provided sacrificial prayers (*ee ran Nhialic*) as the clansman of divinity representing religious leadership.

The Apuk clans of the southern Dinka Rek in Tonj State, particularly the outstanding Pagong and Pabuor priest chiefs, respected him. The special power of the Parum clan divinity in him was believed to be one of the pillars of his effectiveness. By special inspiration, Malek was able to show necessary powers which could not be possessed by the lower diviners. His courts also made liberal use of the power given to him to authorize summonses, arrest and imprisonment warrants, receipts, decided minor judicial disputes, and other official duties.

Malek, was nicknamed after an ox as Malek Lungbany, Malek Banybeek, or Malek Makuei Aluk as he was popularly addressed. Soon, the belief in his customary trial skills won over the victim clans and finally made the corrupt and wicked clansman become pure and good. The laws of *apuk* showed their immense value in his court.

Malek Speaks About Rules of Law and Justice

Editor's note: All direct quotes from Malek are only edited to match the form of the English language used in the book (UK English) and for punctuation. LE, NE

When Malek was asked about the procedures and trials of customary justice rendered in his Court of Appeal, he answered thusly:

> "Well, you heard what the Government led by Mr Wilson wrote. I can only add that I never sang the songs, which declare that I preached that the rules of laws of English, Arab and Egypt save from crime, or that customary rules of laws were a propitiation for the crime of people in the clans I am representing in this High Court of Appeal tasked to oversee crimes in accordance to clan traditions or beliefs. As I have told you before, many things contained in Government's

rule of laws were written by people outside our clan traditions to carry out certain plans and ideas of the aliens. I never said that alien (Anglo-Egyptian Sudan) rule was a saviour, or that he is equal with the saviour or that outsiders or aliens saved the chiefdom from clan crime acts by reason of any personal characters which he may have had. So, let your mind eliminate these false doctrines and receive the truths, which I the Spear Master shall explain with a completely unbiased mind, free from all preconceived ideas."

"In the context of the laws of damages, in a number of cases of clan crime acts in which the strict foreign letter of the law does not allow the court to impose payment on the guilty damager, the clan offender incurs spiritual punishment. Malek Agei, enumerates four such types of damages, regarding which "according to the strict alien rules of the law, there is no obligation to pay, yet clan spirits or jok, jak, body spirit or ancestry god will not forgive the guilty damager until the clan offender pays apuk penalty". Following are the cases, and brought down by law:" (1) "If a clan man or member or a sub-clan knows testimony that can help his fellow yet does not provide it, either testimony in which one witness suffices, or in which two are required to be Witness; (2) if a clan member hires false witnesses to testify in favour of one's friend; (3) if a clan member hunts near a village in forests closer to neighbour's sorghum farm in the direction of a wind fire in such a way that a strong wind will make the dry grass nearer to the garden catch fire, or if he sees fires nearing his neighbour's farm and he covers the forest in such a manner that the clan man who lit the fire will be exempt from paying damages, and he thereby prevents the victim from receiving payment; (4) if a clan man breaches an unstable cattle keeping thereby enabling cattle of his neighbour to leave, and cows go out and do damage; or (5) if a family member breaches a thong tethering hostile bull thereby enabling violent bull of his family to leave, and bull goes out and does damage."

"Malek Lungdit, clan chief in the High Court of Appeal for criminal trial sentencing acts for the offence by clan member enumerates other sentences for cases in which the guilty damager in clan family is "exempt by human act but liable by spiritual ruling (divine ruling)":

(1) "If a clan member does work with witchcrafts for use of the ritual priest chief invoking white heifer bull with libation water in purifying people who had physical contact with the devil; such work disqualifies the libation water as a purifying agent; (2) if a clan member sets poison before livestock or members of his community; (3) if a clan member allows a burning catalyst in the charge of a deaf person, imbecile or minor; (4) if a clan member frightens member of his community, without physical contact, and thereby causes him to become sick; (5) if a clan member brings a nine-year-old boy from home of his sister to come and help her with her domestic animals and child of six months old, and thereby is attacked and killed by monkeys while protecting the farm; (6) if a clan member has his pitcher breaks in a public thoroughfare and he abandons the water and the broken shards, and another clan man comes along and is injured by them where other cases are brought."

"The legal responsibility of traditional medicine clansmen and clanswomen is a special case. A clansman or clanswoman who, with the knowledge of traditional medicine treated a patient and committed an error, is exempt by human law but is subject to spiritual penalizing decisions. A medicine person who carelessly commits injury will be liable for spiritual penalizing decisions only where he finds out that he has erred and knows what his error was. If, however, he never becomes aware of his error, he is not liable for spiritual sentencing decisions. Malek Agei, spiritual priest chief, distinguishes between a carelessly errors during an operation, in which sentencing case he will be liable by spiritual sentencing decisions, and an error in supplying medication, where not even liability by spiritual sentencing decision is incurred."

"Because of the significance of this incurrence within spiritual sentencing decision, the clan priest determined that a priest chief justice has to inform the guilty clansman that, while the court cannot, in fact, sentence him to pay apuk penalty, he still incurs an obligation regarding spiritual law. Some held that he is disqualified from bearing witness until he pays apuk penalty because he is holding stolen money in his possession. In the clan lineage family, the Appeal Court reversed a lower court's award of compensation for damages in a claim submitted by the relatives of a clansman murdered by a member of the clan family. The clan family member killed the other family member of a clan with a spear given him by the clan family member for clan purposes. The respondents argued that, due to the problematic mental state of the family member, the family should have foreseen that his possession of a spear was fraught with danger. Hence, they argued, the spear owner in cattle camp should be required to compensate the victim family clan. The appeal was rejected because the causal connection between the appellant's (i.e., the cattle camp's) negligence and the killing of the deceased was too weak. Priest chief Malek Lung Dit suggested in his ruling that the court should recommend to the spear owner in cattle camp to go beyond the foreign letter of the law. In making this suggestion, Judge and priest Chief Malek Lung Dit relied on the principle of a spiritual punishment being incurred where, due to the lack of the causal connection required for a wrongdoer's conviction, there is no possibility of sentencing by an act of the human court. In the opinion of many Parum clan families or any other clan families, under certain circumstances an act of human court can even force payment, going beyond the alien letter of the law, upon the defendant. Even so, clan tradition courts, in accordance with Sudan law, lack the authority to do this. Hence Judge and Priest chief Malek Lung Dit suggested to the defendants to follow this practice:"

1   "People must rouse to the fact that they are greater than their apuk penalty in cattle numbering thirty-one cows, because forgiveness can only be possible when the persons found guilty must pay apuk penalty to the victim clan person and that their

cattle numbers are subject to their choice and desire, acceptable to both the victim and offender spirits to reconcile to forgive and pardon."

2   "Whenever I am called upon to lead ritual ceremonies organized to offer an animal, in ritualized sacrifice prayers for a clan spirit, jak, jok, atiip, agoloong, yath and ancestors to forgive the victim and guilty families, I choose a cow of spiritual wealth or divine wealth, because I am a priest chief or spiritual priest that has all the clannish spiritual powers of the clan Divinity that transfers ritual prayers appealing directly to the creator, the clan spirits and the ancestors to reconcile and forgive the acts of crimes to kill in dispute, and the spear bears the power which channels all."

3   "I usually use spiritual prayers appealing to God (Nhialic) through the Rum Wenkook and the Atany Wundior Deities that choose to empower me as Spear Master in the Parum Clan. They always listen to me, they protect me, support me, and they intervene and execute my calls and appeals as the spiritual priest chief in the High Court of Appeal on behalf of Apuk clans."

4   "Whenever, victim and homicide families bring dispute and unhappiness, and cause their desire to be exercised in opposition to the desire of the blood wealth in cattle sanctioned by the High Court of Appeal payable to the victim families by the families of homicide found guilty, then they must be destroyed by clan spirits or indefinite curses."

5   "I am always prepared to issue strong warnings on behalf of the prestigious High Court of Appeal, as Priest Chief or Spear Master, and Judge of customary justice in my Fatherland, to never permit to non-payment of apuk since God works no such miracle, nor gives special dispensation. No. This cannot happen and people with cruel behaviours and committing criminal acts must pay the

penalty of apuk spiritual punishment for their evil deeds until the rule customary justice system rule of law that authorizes the apuk penalty is fulfilled and obeyed."

6 "I have the responsibility to assign victimization and guilt so both parties become the masters of their blood wealth apuk of thirty-one cows, and also to the force clan victim family to receive the apuk penalty in clan crime acts to harm or kill for collective responsibility and be obedient to the great inspiration of their creation."

7 "I always make sure the victim and guilt clan families realize that homicide, wrongdoing, and unhappiness shall disappear."

8 "Their life will come into harmony with the laws of their blood wealth, sanctioned by custom justice systems."

9 "I say to my people that they only have to think, and when thinking, believe that all homicide is wrong and the resulting unhappiness and sorrow crimes of life, are children of the victim and wrongdoers. They are not crimes of the children of God, the creator of heaven and earth. In the conditions of living, God leaves the control, management, and even the life of children, to the will of their parent. They will then understand why evil exists, and why violence, hatred and misery continue to blight the lives and happiness of people. Why, as some say, does the clan spirit permit all these things to exist, flourish, and apparently contradict the truth when he is good, and the source of all goodness?"

"The current blood wealth payable in cattle numbering thirty-one cows can be traced back to the first dynasty, given the example of cattle numbering thirty cows reported as divine wealth received by Bol Mel for the damage crime acts on behalf of fishermen victimized. It demonstrated the past practices continued for the abused crime fine and

Customary Law in the Modern Era

collective fine measurement in accordance with the clan crime acts for apuk payable to reconcile the abused parties and sentence guilty parties."

"The only people who were capable of conveying the Truth, and worthy of belief, were those who would acknowledge that forgiveness is the rule of custom. Not simply because I am Chief of the Traditional Appeal Court and the divine spear minister. Only those clans and sub-clans who acknowledge forgiveness as the customary rule and have received the New Clan Customary Court ruling for reparation, and know anything about the chiefdom, or the spirit devotion of the spiritual master, and the way to obtain it, as in these messages, should be acknowledged. All other people who have not this knowledge, and consequently cannot acknowledge forgiveness as the rule of clans, who should have the sense of hearing crime charging, and is not to be trusted as being True Clan Chief Court of Appeal." Malek Lungdit lamented.

"This is nothing contrary to the laws governing the conduct or beliefs of the Apuk nationalities of clans and people. If a person or spirit either, knows nothing about a certain rule of clans, they certainly cannot teach others its characters or merits. Hence, I was applying an ordinary rule of the law of justice in the way in which clan spirits should be tried in the traditional basic laws and values of the customary justice system as a traditional society."

"In accordance with these laws, a prominent role is accorded to traditional law within the values of the Jieng clans of South Sudan as a clan of the Apuk state. Today, with all of this having occurred, the position of clan traditional law should be given priority. It would be appropriate for the courts to adopt this approach of making such recommendations to complainants or plaintiffs, and under suitable conditions even when compelling them to go beyond the alien letter of the law."

Malek in the Traditional Appeal Court

Malek Agei was asked to give his comments about truth, good spirit and the rule of law in customary justice since clients will be there, waiting to listen to him, because he was the only first Spiritual Priest Chief appointed to prestigious Traditional High Court of Appeal for the clan court hearings and for ritual devotion to the spirits for forgiveness in the Chiefdom.

Malek responded and gave comments as follows[34]:

"The Turkish regime, Anglo-Egyptian Governments and post-historic recorders depicted Parum to be the clan leading the chiefdom with dual control and war management. Rum, Wol, Malek, Ngoth, Rum Agei, Malek Agei, Agei Malek Malek and the descendant line belonged to the clan Parum, and the line continued after Rum Ateny unchained the Pabuor, Padiangbaar and Patiir clans from predatory Lwalla adversaries thousands of years ago, and thereafter the heroic death of prominent broadminded liberators high priest chiefs Rum, Wol, Malek, and Agei who were assassinated for the chieftaincy of the chiefdom in the Southern Apuk in Tonj State."

"The chiefdom accepts that I am the Divine Minister and chief of the High Court of Appeal, descended from the Parum line, based on the promise in the dynasty to the successor sons of the Supreme Deity of an everlasting throne for his descendants so that they guide people, provide life. and pray for goodness of the chiefdom."

"Indeed, many of the chiefdom leaders, as well as deities or high priest chiefs of the powerful Dinka Apuk nation-state, claimed membership in the current Juwiir territory of the spiritual Parum clan. For example, the literary Rum, Atany, Wol, Akuien, Lueth,

---

34 Malek Agei Aguelet Agei had face to face discussions with Madhel Malek Agei from March 1979 to May in 1979 at his court center at Chueibet Malek Village, Jak.

Customary Law in the Modern Era

Deng Dit, Malek, Agei, Akok, Jok, Kom and reigns of the multiple Agei's and Malek's, all came from the powerful Parum descents."

"As history usually repeats itself in, my grandfather Aguelet Agei Malek Rum was dislodged mainly for offences he committed in defence of clan members and territorial ambitions. The causes of Apuk for offences committed by Aguelet Agei angered clan members and they refused to pay, but instead decided to murder Aguelet Agei as the best solution for them. However, Aguelet survived. The children of his sisters Amel and Awien came to his rescue and took him away from among the family and kept him under their protection. Athulueth Deng Thou, his mother, became angry at her brothers in Aliai section who did not intervene to rescue her son and cursed their offspring not to marry again from Aliai section. This curse of Athulueth Deng Thou is still holding to this day. Descendants of Aguelet Agei do not marry girls whose parents are from Aliai today, due to the curse due to the attempt on Aguelet's life by paternal uncles to avoid Apuk."

"My priesthood era in the Traditional High Court of Appeal was a result of past dynasties associated with spiritual priest chief truths, clan spirits, and forgiveness and redemption. In the era of my experience as a priest chief and judge of customary justice, each misdeed verdict received a tenfold penalty with rewards also proportional. I always make it very clear that everyone faced human judgments and spiritual judgments. I became the mouthpiece of divinity on behalf of the sufferers, adding my own spiritual prayers to the divinity and the clan divinities of their clans, to those of the diviners and the people. I also pray to the divinity and the clan divinities of those ancestors most concerned in the clan offences in apuk penalty, and to such minor divinities or powers as are indicated by the offence court. Like other priests, I fully demonstrated that this was possible by the truth of my statements and the power of my curse or cure in clan crimes through on sworn oath taken and the use of spear housing spirit powers that pass on prayers appealing to the Divinities. Some animal gifts could be donated in supplication for favours. I remember the supplications of their donors and direct attention, or intention, to their satisfaction. Therefore, through simply thinking of a clansman, I was able to help victim clans, clansmen or clanswomen on oath swearing, because of the powers of the spear, divinity, and spirits that have superabundant ability on my side."

"My era is derived from divinity on one hand and in dual control of clan crime and justice penalties on the another. This occurs both in the body of the Divine religious priest, which offers the hope of saviour through confession, clan crime penalty after judgment and forgiveness, as well as clan ritual purity. The spear has strength charging through powers invoked in the spear to curse or cure, the Divinity wishes. The clannish inscrutability of clan victims in the homicides of sorrowful life was influenced by the traditional religions of the ancestors. They symbolized the divinity judgments of the individual clansman or clanswoman to tilt the scale of truth."

"Commoner (or kiic) initiates were punished with living heifers or calves that provided orders for navigating the threats of the felonious and addressing justice. The individual clan person who speaks correctly was given spirit forgiveness from the pool of divinity wisdom before joining the heroes who have gone before through clan divinity rulings in the clan crime justice penalty."
"Justice and righteousness are such vital attributes of our Nhialic-God as to have led to the conviction upon every believer that every evil deed and will meet with its due punishment. Catastrophes like thunder, lightning, homicide acts of evildoers, the earthquake that swallowed up the earth and its habitats, and the evil that came upon other adversaries in Apuk homesteads are described by the ancestry spirits as divinity judgments."

"The death of the legendary Malek Rum Wol Rum, Agei Malek, Rum, Malek Agei, Ayuel Bak and other commoners, therefore, was conceived to be the execution of the clan divinities and the general divinities or jak, yath, or agoloong judgment upon all the nationalities of the clans in the Apuk state. This divinity judgment is to take place, according to the ancestry view, on earth and is intended to be particularly a vindication of apuk of clan crime penalty."

"I tell people, and it is a truth and was a truth at the time I was appointed clan master, just as it is now, and always will remain a truth, that every spirit who acknowledges that forgiveness is the rule of law of justice in our customary principles, is a redeeming spirit spiritually receiving a portion of the ritual devotion and is progressing in chiefdom of the clans where forgiveness is now forming. When I gave these instructions to clients in my court, I intended that their communications should be only with those clan spirits, and people, who had received the new reparation punishments now known as apuk in the clans for penalty crime justice."

"I am the divine spiritual master from the Parum clan, and I know that all the clan spirits who have received their ritual devotion in sufficient abundance are good spirits. I am the Spear Minister and the clan Chief of the High Court of Appeal that prays to free good spirits from crime, wrong, or the inclination to influence people not to do anything wrong, which is contrary to the desires of the ancestors and the rules of the laws of justice as set out in our customary principles. While all the other spirits may, or may not, I cannot exorcise the influence of evil in the fatherland."

"We, who are believers in the divine Parum religion, are divine spiritual priests or masters who have the supreme gift of communicating with the clan spirits of the dead through our appeals in ritual prayers, invoking sacrificial beasts. We (the masters of the fishing spear) did communicate so with the body spirit and the life spirit of the dead person. Such communications are made known to the rest of the clan spirits and ancestry spirits, and we believed in them. Henceforward, injunction spear ministers who were not in communion with those evil spirits were not believers of rules of laws in customary justice systems or principles. By this, I mean that evil spirits would try to communicate with individuals and attempt to communicate false rules, as to historical antiquity and its mission."

"Malek Lung Dit said that people must not think that sorrow crime of life is the only stage in which spirits communicate with spirit bodies. I usually say to people that in my spiritualistic time it was much more common. When I am adjudicating clan crime charges for the accused wrongdoers summoned in the customary court of the rules of laws, and when I am invoking beasts offered for ritual sacrifices in clan ritual ceremonies, often in private, I usually make these communications to the people of Apuk state with the help of the clan divinity and spirit as spiritual minister and spiritual priest chief of the Traditional High Court of Appeal. This was an important part of my adjudication services which I was rendering to the people in the customary justice courts. It was the one that kept people and me in constant harmony with the life, spirit and the spirit body of those who live in the spirit form, and from whom I received my spiritual powers of calming and of adjudicating well in many other ways while conducting my spiritual legal justice."

"In those days, calming the clan victims of sorrow crime life, and judging the guilty clan family members, were very important parts of my work of dual control of the clan customs, as Court Chief Judge and as spear master or priest chief. I believed in what Rum Wenkook and Atany Wundior had told the Parum spiritualists. I increased my faithfulness and performed many court works, which the people who did not believe as I did, thought were miracles. To me, the calming of the accusing party and the judging of these crimes was just as natural as eating and sleeping. I said to people that my faith was a certainty. I possess the Core Spiritual Judgment that the Parum clan Divinity and Ancestry Spirit speak of. I sit in judgment of clan crimes and adjudicate vendettas, just as I breathe, and am able to judge material beneficial to brothers and the chieftaincy in the chiefdom."

Malek Speaking in 1979 at Chueibet[35]

Chief Malek Agei spoke to his son, who quotes his father below, about the custom court established in 1948 to replace the English and Mohammedan Laws in Apuk. It is important to note that the British Administration took Malek to the Rual Mei School established at Thiet for training children of chiefs, divine deities and influential diviners of clans and sub-clans selected from all over the Tonj District.

Malek is quoted as follows:

"I am the First Master of the fishing spear appointed to represent the Apuk in the High Court of Appeal with the capacity of clan chief. I want you to know that no alien judiciary legal system existed before the invasion of the Apuk by Government. The divine priests, custom rules and other traditional beliefs were the primary sources of law to those peoples[36] of nationalities of clans or sub-clans of the Apuk. The earliest foreign instruments[37] were the Mohammedan Law Courts Ordinance (1902) which sought to empower Sharia Courts. Customary laws were addressed through the Civil Justice Ordinance (1929) and the Chiefs' Courts Ordinance (1931). Again, I want you to know that disagreement existed between the judiciary of the Government era, which advocated a restrictive definition, and the Sudanese courts, which favoured a wider definition to include the canon law or personal laws of other communities. The judges were allowed to decide whether a custom is 'reasonable'. They in turn, must make judgments about the concepts or values of a society in the light of their own rules, values and customs."

"I established the clan tradition court the same time in 1948, and was ready, just after the moment of the newly created Traditional

---

35 Malek Agei Aguelet Agei discussed how he was first taken to School and later assigned to court with defined roles and function in 1979 with Madhel Malek Agei.
36 Lufti, G. A., *The Future of English Law in the Sudan*. The Sudanese Judgment and Precedents Encyclopedia. Sudan Judiciary, Khartoum. At 2.
37 Ibid. At 6.

High Court of Appeal for customary legal principles, to live the lives of the dynasty of Apuk chiefdom. I know it has been said that the first homicide people have had their court tried death sentence not according to the customary court system of our culture. The homicide court found the party guilty and sentenced to the reparation rule of the customary court and is not applicable to the imported rule of law of alien origin. I disclosed this message earlier that the death verdict for the guilt contributed less to the rules of forgiveness and reconciliation of the communities and was not popular. The imported rule of law of foreign origins developed from the Anglo-Egyptian judiciary of the different order, and as the process of evolution proceeded, this rule of law was stopped. Crime charges were being screened. To the end, a person found guilty received a sentence of English legal code systems, with all the rules of law of their justice and orders. I am saying that the English legal sentence was not acceptable in our customary justice systems."

Malek as a Teenager

"Young men acquire their nicknames after an event or an ox. However, our culture demands a nickname for any young man which may derive from what a beautiful ox possesses or an event that earns you a nickname in honour of situation that had occurred. I was nicknamed as Banybeek, Makuei-Alukwath. This was combined as Malek Banybeek, Malek Makueialuk or Malek Makuei-Alukwath after my ox of beautiful natural black and white colours of the first category. This ox was marial with a red nose, white head. Black colours on its eyes, ears, neck, back part, and tail covering portion to the legs behind it. It was such a beautiful ox that it made me popular and earned me those nicknames that made me the proud son of Agei Marialdit in the dynastic chiefdom of Apuk."

"When I was appointed, I was a wonderful young man in my physical fitness as any man ever became, from that time into the present chief of customary Appeal Court. In fact, I believe, that at the time of my generation we were more wonderful than people are now, because we, in the generation had no physical ailments, no sickness, and no deformity of any kind."

"Before I was appointed to represent the Apuk Juwiir as Chief Court of Appeal, I was a young leader of a generation called Madoot of the Chiefdom. The Apuk Chiefdom was asked to bring a calf of a buffalo captured alive for the British commissioner, Mr Wilson. This was during the reign of fourth Chief Agei Malek Agei Malek Rum, son of third Chief Malek Agei Malek Rum, who was slain with Ayuel Baak with many captives by British Royal Army in Chuei Ajai. He was the son of the second Chief Agei Malek Rum, also slain in the battle where also his venerate elder son Aguelet Agei sustained multiple gunshot wounds inflicted by the adversaries, who was also the son of first Chief Malek Rum Wol Rum who was slain around 1908 as well. Chief Agei dispatched the Sub-chief Ajang Ajang Akol Arop, who brought the message to the Lietnhom cattle camp. I organized strong young men and went hunting in the grassing green forests for buffalo around Toch looking for a young buffalo calf. We captured one alive, tied it with ropes, drugged and took it to Mr Wilson. When Chief Agei joined our caravan, he became a happy and proud chief of Apuk chiefdom. After the Apuk Chiefdom handed the calf to Mr Wilson, I was put in the record and my appointment to the High Court of Appeal was seen as a result of the gift."

"We certainly were healthier in face and form than people now are or have been for many long centuries. Besides, our bodies lasted longer than do the bodies of people at this time. I do not know why."

"Before the alien arrival, we were very happy in our Chiefdom. We knew not troubles or worries of any kind, and never had anything to make us afraid, or draw us apart from each other, or from the creator, the spirits or the ancestors. When the great temptation years came and were gone, and then because of our overblown ideas of our greatness, influence, and want of dependence on alien Governments and its creation, we fell. Never again were we to be restored to our position of comeliness and happiness that were ours at the beginning of our lives in great Chiefdom of nationalities of clans."

"Of course, I must say to you there were parts played by the peoples who were the inventors of their sorrowfulness and wrongdoing to kill, to injure, to defame wrongly, to offend, to disobey or deny divine spirit, to steal, to destroy a property and of the disobedient of the rules of laws in history and the devil from the Chiefdom of Apuk clans. Sorrowfulness is understood to mean the work of evil spirits, witches, sorcerers, evil eye, broken taboos, perjured oaths, and even the prophet."

High Court of Appeal[38]

"My duties grew together with the custom courts and Chiefs by adjudicating social obligations, liabilities for homicide and for injury caused by defamatory damages, clan crime acts to kill, to injure and another injury or death caused by animals. The custom court of Chiefs administered the Native Laws prevailing in the clans or sub-clans or tribes where the court exercises its jurisdiction provided that such Native Laws are not contrary to justice, rules, laws or orders. The newly created customary justice systems of the Appeal Court is comprised of tribes or sub-tribal units (nationalities of clans), where chiefs, sub-chiefs and committees, normally of kinship networks, exercise core social and legal powers the chiefdom enjoys in the clans Apuk chieftaincy."

"I used to adjudicate the justice of making the great effort between the

---

38 Direct interview with Chief Malek Agei in face to face discussions from March 1979 to November 1981. Madhel Malek Agei conducted this interview and he was from time to time writing order letters for Malek Agei which was issued to his police called Bill Akot also referred to as bazinger or police for the chief. The letter was written to the accused with charges to appear before the court to answer charges against him or her. Observations during the court time by Madhel Malek.

High Court of Appeal and the Courts of Chiefs and acted as court chief in trying to obtain the justice for the great chiefdom of Apuk. As far as I am concerned, for I did not tempt, or seduce, the Arab judge working with me to do great wrong. Neither did he seduce me to enter into the effort of their justice decisions to the contrary."

"But all this is in the past now. Many years have gone since the chieftaincy fell. My chiefdom has suffered much because of invented sorrow crime life. I have explained before that many years passed since the time that I forfeited the Alien Laws (English Law and Mohammedan Law) until they were replaced with our rules of laws in custom principles and made known to the people under my Appeal Court chieftaincy."

Forgiveness, Faithfulness, and Apuk

The rules of payable *apuk* of forgiveness are the greatest rules of law. Every other customary law is subordinate to rule of forgiveness and must operate in unanimity with rule of law in the Apuk chieftaincy. How the Apuk entered into rules of laws of justice in custom systems is via the allegiance of faithfulness. When given to people, and they possess it, this *apuk* fulfils the rules of forgiveness. This allegiance of faithfulness frees people from all rules except the rules of clan spirit retaliation itself. The Apuk chieftaincy is a slave to no rule and is free indeed because it possesses the allegiance of faithfulness to the payable *apuk* of crimes in clans for forgiveness.[39]

The rules of payable *apuk* and all rules of laws not in harmony with the rules of laws of forgiveness and allegiance of faithfulness have nothing enchanting with which to operate in the life of the people.

---

39 Recorded court discussions with Chief Malek Agei conducted by Madhel Malek Agei in May 1980 and consultation with Bill Akot.

Summarized Malek Quotes

"The most important message I can pass on is that individual clansman must understand is that families of clans are greater than their thirty-one cows for apuk of clan victim and that their thirty-one cows are subject to their choice and desire."

"I always make sure I have passed my spirituality message clearly that whenever, by your survival (existence) and functioning, clan victim and homicide families bring revenge dispute and unhappiness, and cause their own clansmen's desires to be exercised in opposition to the desire of the blood wealth spirits of thirty cows for apuk of clan victim and one cow for oath in blood sacrifice by the use of Priest Chief that ritually prays, then you, the victim and homicide clans must be destroyed by body spirits, jak, yath, life spirits and divinity spirits."

"Since I am the Priest Chief of the Appeal Court for clan offence sentencing, I warned those victim and homicide clans to never be permitted to come into a continuation of revenge dispute again."

"Let the victim and guilt clans become the masters of their blood wealth of thirty-one cows for apuk and blood sacrifice ritual be obedient to the great inspiration of their creativity."

"The victim and homicide clan families will realize that homicide, wrong, and unhappiness will disappear, and their normal feeling will come into harmony with the laws of blood wealth that members of guilty clans or families have donated as their supplications."

"If the people will only believe, that all homicide and wrong and the resulting unhappiness and sorrow of crime life in the community are children of their own creation, the clan divinity and even ancestors will leave the control, management, and even the survival of these children, to the spirit of their parent, or their clan."

Customary Law in the Modern Era

"They will then understand why evil exists, and why wars, hatred and misery continue to blight the lives and happiness of clan peoples. Why, as some say, do clan spirit permit all these things to exist, flourish, and apparently contradict the truth Clan Divinity is good, and the fountainhead of all goodness?"

"The use of the deity and spiritual master practices derives from ritual prayers that the laws of apuk penalty must rule according to the customary justice system in all the apparent harshness, suffering, and want of forgiveness. The belief of the customs overshadows the victim and finally makes the corrupted and wicked clansman become one of purity and goodness. The law of apuk penalty terms of compensation is necessary to preserve and bring about the reconciliation, forgiveness and harmony between the guilt and the ancestors and spirits, which is absolutely necessary."

Apuk Cultural Curses

Introduction

In Apuk culture, curses and blessings are a physiological and mental experience. Like any other significant life transitions following the death of a loved one, the bereaved individuals need to adjust and go back to a normal life. Apuk culture has described this misfortune in the family as something to do with a curse. Nothing ever "just happened". Someone or something caused it to happen. This holds true whether it be death from mosquito bites, snake bites, a nail wound that caused death of a family member, or the sickness of a child. It is a conviction that endures to this day in several parts of South Sudan.

It should not be forgotten that sometimes the accused shared the same belief in the power of ill-wishing, suffering, evil eye deaths and cursing. There are examples of deaths caused where people believe they are under a curse and is the mirror image of the excuse effect. This chapter focusses on the practices of curses and blessings in mourning sacrifice rituals among traditional rural and modern urban Apuk communities in South Sudan. A particular focus will be on the challenges and changes observed in the way these curse and blessing sacrifice rituals are practiced in Apuk communities and in other Jieng Dinka communities throughout South Sudan today.

Certain curse sacrifice rituals practiced in the past seem to have diminished in many South Sudan urban environments. Some communities have been forced to forgo some of the cursing and blessing sacrifice rituals and adapted Christian and/or Islamic denominations in their living environments. The people have had to deal with one death after another within a short space of time as a result of war and upheaval. Snake bites, malaria, life threatening diseases, suicides and traumatic road accidents also take their toll. This could have impact on the effectiveness of practices regarding proper traditional curse and blessing sacrifice rituals.

The Apuk state has gone through a period of political, economic, cultural transition during past centuries that continues still. In the past, many clanspeople migrated from traditional environments in the rural villages for mainly economic reasons. Some of them relocated themselves to clannish groups based on ethnicity and security sharing. This became a home for the majority of the Apuk people. As a result, they found themselves in separate environments that were somehow not conducive for them to continue with their traditional rural lifestyles. Among these included practices of various curse and blessing sacrifice rituals.

Curses in Apuk State

The use of curses has been practiced by many cultures. The most universal method of laying on a curse is by an image or model, or sculpture, which is an image or representation of the victim, or the person to be harmed. Curse related sculptures were common in ancient Rek of Apuk Jieng Dinka in South Sudan, India, Eastern Asia, Egypt, Africa and Europe. They may be constructed clay, wood and even stuffed grass such as the reed practices by Apuk culture. In Rek and especially Apuk Lith culture, black goats, sheep, and chickens are used to represent the person who is wished to be harmed. Usually the sculpture is marked or tied with ropes to look like the victim. It is thought that the closer the sculpture resembles the victim, the more that person will suffer when the sculpture is harmed or destroyed.

It is important to use living animals with living blood to represent victims who are to be harmed or destroyed with living blood. The theory behind harming or destroying a sculpture or killing a living blood goat or sheep to do harm to a victim is pure sympathetic magic. As the animal is harmed or killed, so the victim is harmed in similar fashion. By the vowing speeches during cursing sacrifice prayers thereof, the persons that they bear the name for curses, may be continually debilitated by poor health or die away by continual sickness.

The ancient Apuk state cultures often used a wrapped reed image of the intended victim, who was the enemy of the community. The master of the fishing spear or chief priest would pour water, and oil into the mouth of a goat or chicken or smeared ashes (in liquid or dust form) on the animal. It was then wrapped in reeds and thrown into a lake or river. As the animal drowned inside the lake the master of the fishing spear pronounced a prayer saying:

> "Ancestry spirit, creator, life spirit, I call you to this judgment, the enemy cannot come again, you enemy and you devil spirit, you go far away, you good spirit and you good life come closer and whenever I call upon you, Heavenly Father, the goodness, it is because your people are in danger, they need help and you have that help to sit down here, and you clan divinity spirit protect ants, they are your children."

The ashes of the grass pulled out from the hat or house of spirit power, *yath, agoloong* is usually worshiped and served with cow butter and fat from ritual sacrifice animals. These would be mixed with excrement or ashes and thrown into another forest or lake. A black animal is often taken to the forest during the night, in darkness, tied down and left to die alone. Ash dust, oil and libation water in are left under shrines and on tombs. The special spear of animal sacrifices for rituals in the family can then be removed and returned to the house. This is the role of assigned woman doing all ritual functions.

Most of what I have heard about people's experiences with culture curses during or after cursing experiences is actually very similar to ancient culture curses. There is a sense of curse or blessing assurance. There is often a feeling of a bless and a curse beyond a magician

Apuk Cultural Courses

or priest's ability to describe them. Usually there is help offered afterwards that seems to come out of nowhere. I am talking about the "core experience" here. Not the curse and or blessing when a priest has time to think it all through and then make up assertive beliefs about what he experienced.

Curses and blessings can be more effective and successful if said properly. This is true whether they are said by a high priest Deity, or by a person on their deathbed, or witchcraft, or any other methods. There is no real Deity implicated. Curses and blessings are customarily succeeded by a spirit. This means that you may place trust when you admit that you were a physical and emotional wreck when it occurred. Curses and blessings feel like you had a brain seizure. That explains all the bright lights and visions.

If you go and say to a believer that they are cursed, they will, by the sheer force of fear, believe that they are cursed and fear they will perish. To attain such a level of effectiveness, the curser must initially be known to have such a power. Pagong, Pabuor and Parum spiritual masters or priests would be a good example. It is a perfect exemplary of the priest spirit power of causativeness. A real high priest Deity knows that this power, once set into motion, will be demonstrated. They believe that what you put out in culture and into the life, comes back to you in due course like Karma. It is not in the interest of a spiritual high priest to curse. They warn that any person who desires to curse another must be ever prepared to suffer the same curse as their victims. It is like throwing a spear straight up in the air and predicting where it will land.

Like blessings, curses have universally been bought and sold throughout the Apuk centuries. Witches and sorcerers were reported to have been hired and have practiced both blessings and curses as a service to others. This is because high priests and magicians call upon supernatural powers to effect a change. They have rendered these services to buyers for barter, or in carrying out customary judicial court sentences. Plato mentioned in his Republic: "If anyone wishes to injure an enemy; for a small fee, sorcerers will bring harm on good or bad alike, binding the gods to serve their purposes by spells and curses."

Wrapped reeds, black chickens, goats and sheep were popularly used by numerous spiritual priests from the dynasty era of the Pabuor, Padiangbaar, Patiir, Parum clans right through the colonial development period in Apuk state.

The Definition of a Curse

A curse is an offensive word that people use when they are angry. It is the spiritual use of the words that are said to cause trouble or bad luck for some. It involves the use of words of sworn as an oath, calling for harm as soon as they are uttered. A curse is a cause of trouble or bad luck inflicted by a supernatural power. It can come in the form of a prayer, an imprecation, an execration, a god, a natural force or a spirit. A curse is an expressed wish that some form of adversity will befall or assign itself to some other thing, like a person or people, a place, or an object. It is a series of words or an expression used in swearing calling for harm to come to village or place or to someone. A curse is an evil or misfortune that comes as if in answer to someone's request, or to utter an oath to call upon a divinity or god to inflict harm or destruction.

In Apuk culture, the Deity, the elderly, the disabled or a person on their deathbed is believed to have the power to bless and curse. The culture also accepts as true the evil eye, which may be the consequence of envy, except it is believed to be the consequence of a deliberate curse. These accursed creatures stand in the vanguard of the Evil One. They are liars and sons and daughters of liars, and spirit power curses them to the ground as Moses cursed the Egyptians. As Jesus cursed the money changers.

Clan divinity spirit power curses dark influences and casts them out in the name of clan divinity spirits and ancestry spirits. For the devil is accursed from the tongue of the creator God and the Heavenly Spirits. That which comes from the tongue of dark evils are only curses and twisted truths. The curse and its accompanying rituals are belief systems that have some causative force in the end.

In the history of curse, like the angry mother who cursed her fatherland, 'curse' means a wish or pronouncement made effective by a spiritual power in Apuk culture, such as the Creator Nhialic, or gods, a spirit, or a natural force, or else as a kind of spell by magic or witchcraft[40]. The Jieng Dinka language describes 'curse' using the word *theeth, cieen, kueeng, wiew, lam, wak* or *wieel*. Cursing through *wieel* is a result of an evil eye effect and *wiew* is an act of food denied to a person in need, or an offering of sacrificial meat neglected to waste without proper use on intent rituals in the society.

According to texts, the term "curse" signifies not only to curse, but to speak contemptuously, disrespectfully, or to make light of a person so that all speeches which have a tendency to lessen our parents in the eyes of others, or to render their judgment, piety, etc., suspect or contemptible, such as is she or he included; though the act of cursing, or of treating the parent with injurious or opprobrious language, is what is particularly intended.

Traditional Cursing and Blessing

Anywhere there is a clansman, there is traditional religion. And where a clansman is, there is his chief priest to maintain his own tradition. As Moses said:

> *"Honour your father and your mother,"* and: *"Whoever curses his father or mother must be put to death. But if a man says to his father or mother, whatever you would have received from me is a gift committed to God." As God prophesied of people who are hypocrites, as it is written in the Bible: "These people honour me with their lips, but their heart is far from me."*

Wherever there is an Apuk clansman, he worships and prays to the divinity spirit in everything he does. Wherever he sleeps or eats, he prays to a divinity spirit. Wherever he hunts or fishes, he prays to a

---

40   Chauran, Alexandra (2013): Have You Been Hexed? Recognizing and Breaking Curses. Llewellyn Worldwide

traditional divinity spirit. Wherever he harvests his farm, or if he is a cattle keeper, he prays to a divinity spirit for blessing. If he has diseased animals, he prays to a divinity spirit to curse and strike evil eye spirits and black devil spirits to suffer the worst fate. He prays to a divinity spirit to bless him where he fights enemy in battle or where he faces danger. He prays to divinity spirit where he buries a corpse.

Apuk clansmen pray for divinity spirits using animal sacrifice. These prayers are used when calling for damage to come to a village or place, or someone to be destroyed or to die. Apuk clansmen also worship divinity spirits with prayers for blessing. They use divinity spirit power to curse children, fathers, mothers, the fatherland and descendant children that stand in the vanguard of the Evil One. The power of a divinity spirit curses liars, sons and daughters of liars, by cursing them all to the ground. As Athulueth cursed the place that forced descendants not to marry girls from Aliai-Buong in the Apuk clans. Jesus curses dark evil spirit influences and casts evil spirits out through sacrificial prayer. Everything which comes from the lips of dark evil spirits are only curses and a sick twisting of the truth.

Even though all effects of transformation, technological advancement, and the challenges of secularisation; curses, blessings, rituals and sacrifices are still cultural practices and are as relevant today as they were in the past in the Apuk state of South Sudan. Whether Muslim, Christian or the traditional Jieng-Dinka clannish ethnic religion, the people of Apuk in their overwhelming majority are deeply religious. Religion in the form of clan Divinity is the most important and integral part not only of their private, but also of their social, political and military actions.

Not accepting this fact, may be based on experience with Christianity, Islam, Buddhism or merely based on the individual's limited understanding of religion. To try to justify actions or political developments or even to contribute to Apuk judicial resolutions, one repeatedly will reject and leave out important values, motives, actors and opinion makers. They will only ever have a limited understanding. However, a social encounter with members of the Apuk clans of nationalities could certainly become difficult or lead to embarrassed circumstances if you have no knowledge of their historic beliefs.

You will cause offence if you are not prepared to follow the free offer to start a ceremony or ritual sacrificial lamb with a prayer speech, to bless the good people, to greet ancestry spirits or *yath* or *jak* or *agoloong* of guiding principle of dual control, to respect the emblem of Divinity spirit, the creator or divinity festivities, to give offer on holy shrines and tombs in form of tobacco, to pour milk on decorated pegs in a shrine or tomb site, to stand on right hand side on a holy shrine or tomb in a sacred ceremony, or at least to remain behind the crowd to learn by seeing. Never simply regard the singing rhythm in Sacred Shrines or the tomb of a spear master as cheerful attractions or, is not able to just abstain from any comments after realizing astonishing emblems or rituals in community parts.

Apuk Blessings and Curses

Apuk communities bless and curse other communities. This is acceptable between different cultures, communities and religious beliefs around the world. It is not even a crime to bless and curse among Christian community. As I have said earlier, many members of the community curse evil people within their and other communities. The community has the duty to know the people who cursed were good, decent, and morally upstanding and to know they were descended from spirit powers of a divinity spirit of the clans. That they were considerate people who were innocent of having done anything to evil persons to provoke a curse.

A curse is a saying that causes deaths, injuries, destructions, or bad luck inflicted by power of clan divinity spirits or prayers. We know the people of divinity spirit have supernatural powers to curse. We know why the elderly person cursed them and we know the ones the elderly person on their deathbed blessed and cursed. And we find no references anywhere in any culture, religious faith or spiritual path that does not allow curses for cursing and blesses for blessing to be uttered from the same lips, whether you are old, on your deathbed, or a clan divinity priest with supernatural spiritual powers. In my experience with traditional curses, the community has wrongfully cursed other innocent communities, condemning them as evil, like those who curse the Jews as a group.

Still, the high priests of clan divinities with spiritual powers from the same Apuk clan community will bless different communities and various religious beliefs out of the same lips. Here, in this Apuk state, we have one among us who has blessed and cursed out of the same lips. He has lied, used witchcraft, condemned community members who were innocent, and have done many other things all of us might talk about, but did not do. The entire history of curses made to the fatherland by angry mothers is in fact a blessing and a curse coming from the same place!

Still, none of this is just cause for punishment. Apuk culture remains faithful to blessing and cursing. The culture is aware what an act might entail. One is not punished for blessing or cursing from the same lips.

Eve is known to have sinned first. But Adam is seen as the original sinner because Adam is the first man and the natural hereditary was passed down from Adam to his descendants. According to Genesis 3:17 (English Standard Version):

> *And to Adam God said, "Because you have listened to the voice of your wife and have eaten of the tree of which I commanded you: "You shall not eat of it!" Cursed is the ground because of you! In pain you shall eat of it all the days of your life!"*

Jesus blessed people and cursed people as well, all out of the same lips. Chief priests with power of clan divinity spirits do more like Jesus himself, who cursed and blessed people and still had "the Love of God," which Jesus shared with his Christian followers. However, he often withheld from those he felt were undeserving. Without this then the evil would never know verbal retribution or castigation.

Apuk Cultural Courses

Background

Malek the son of Rum was the leader of clan divinity spirit with war control, in the Apuk chiefdom. He was the descendant from Rum Wenkook deity, Jiel deity, Atany deity, the Pagong clan, the Parum clan and ancestors with supernatural spiritual powers.

Deng the son of Thou was the descendant of Bek Amuuk, the Padiangbaar clan and ancestors, and each of them had his own ancestors. They include ancestors from the Pakuieth, Paluet, Patiir, Pabol, Pathieu, Pabuor, and Pagong clans among others in Apuk Lith of the Rek Jieng Dinka clans of nationalities.

Agei and Athulueth Unite Two Families

Athulueth had her own clan and land as did Agei. Their language was the same widely spoken by Rek Jieng or Muonyjang together with the Apuk Lith clans of nationalities. Deng Thou agreed to give his daughter Athulueth to Agei, first son of Malek Rum, in the marriage uniting the Padiangbaar clan and the Parum clan as well as the two families. Agei was a mighty warrior like Rum who came and defeated predators. The Agei and Athulueth marriage begat a mighty warrior son whom Agei later named 'Aguelet' for winning wars fiercely by the Apuk people in very precarious series of battles fought from the 1870s through the 1890s.

Agei said, "I will name him 'Aguelet' because I survived wounds of battle that when I decapitated a man of that name who was leading enemy regiments."

Aguelet is a name referring to heroism, acquired in the horrific battles Apuk people had fought. The most common disputes that affected cohesive resolution were caused by sharing of water points in the swampy wetland of Toch for animal drinking and grazing. This caused the spread of bitter and persistent interclan and intercommunity fighting for many centuries.

Various battles fought against this warrior called "Aguelet"

APUK : A STATE IN WAITING

became noticeable due to the large numbers of men he and his forces killed. The Apuk clans were in psychological terror and fear for years.

Thus, when Agei adopted the name of Aguelet, whom he decapitated, he also named his first son "Aguelet"[41]. He was born in the generation that fought many battles of conquest and slavery with weapons and tools manufactured out of iron, bronze and wood. Clubs, such as *bolong, bolong-nueer, bolong-many, cuoor, bolong-cuoor, coruop, atuel, kueer,* and *makuith* were manufactured from wood.

This was one of the best duels between Apuk combatants and adversaries ever fought after the Bur Apuuk camp wars. Agei as the dual war commander of Apuk combatant warriors and Aguelet Matiat as the commanding leader of adversary warriors tried to outmanoeuvre each other in a battle of nerves, instinct and intelligence. The multi-talented Agei directed his regiments deep into enemy territory and killed Aguelet. This remains one of the most memorable hand-to-hand fights in our history. A total estimate of one to two thousand corpses were reported counted over two months of fighting. This was the second of its kind along with the war fought in Bur Apuuk. That fight nearly wiped out an ethnic group which compelled the two rivals to make semi-permanent peace. This was led by high priests from the two sides that made the vow and submerged a spear of oath into the ground on the borders

---

41 The name Aguelet is not a family name. The name was first heard from enemies during the war in Toch, swamp wetland, where cattle grass and drink in the dry season. The enemy called the name Aguelet whenever he hit the target and he killed several people in the name of Aguelet. People did not know what was meant by Aguelet, even today. It was also known as Aguelet Matiat. But it was reported that Agei succeeded when he penetrated inside enemy zones. He charged inside with his spear and killed the person who kept calling the name of Aguelet. That immediately caused enemies to run and nobody on the enemy side mentioned the name of Aguelet again. Many enemies lost their lives on the run. They were defeated and defeated until the war ended. The death of their war hero called Aguelet Matiat scaled down the number of wars for many years. This earned Agei a reputation for heroism. When Agei married Athulueth to be his first wife, he named his first son Aguelet in memory. However, Aguelet Matiat turned out to be brave son and fought many wars, defeated many enemies, saved many lives in danger and made relatives to pay for apuk penalties that ranged from small injuries, severe injuries to death of enemy victims.

Apuk Cultural Courses

with oaths to prevent further war between the two neighbouring communities[42].

In the war of words between the Apuk Lith and its adversary, the war song of the Apuk Lith threatens them and promises them that: "Apuk will give their flesh to the birds (*coor tit*) of the air and the beasts of the battlefield when we clash in Toch Apuk, and everywhere we battle. Great Apuk Lith is a force which strikes an adversary down and destroys its country. The corpses of the dead of war shall be as cow dung on the surface of the ground. They shall perish by the spear, and as spear dying people, their corpses shall be food for all the birds of the air and all the wild beasts of the Toch and border Apuk Lith. Great Apuk is always ready to destroy its adversary anywhere, any time. Wherever an Apuk warrior clashes with his adversary, there is nobody left to frighten away the birds of the air and the beasts of the earth, in Toch Apuk Lith, in border Apuk Lith and everywhere fighting occurs."

From the ancient sources, death in war resulted from the sin of disobeying the Divinity and not obeying Divinity Laws. Another curse associated with war was leaving corpses unburied for hunting beasts to prey upon. In Apuk culture, denial of burial and exposure of the body to predators was considered as a severe curse. This mirrors the beliefs in antiquity that not to be buried was worse than death, because the life spirit, blood spirit and body spirit of the dead could not rest and would never reach the spirit world.

If you buried the person punished to die on the battlefield you will also be punished for similar sins to die on the battlefield. For this reason, death in war is amongst the curses and threats against the Apuk which also included the curse of non-burial.

Agei and his wife Athulueth lived in Akuwei homestead in Machuet section of the Apuk nation.

In all he had five wives. Agei was the traditional chief, spiritual chief priest and war leader. After his first wife, he married Ajok, Adut, Athieng and Ayak. Although Ajok, Adut, Athieng and Ayak had more sons, Athulueth had the one named Aguelet.

---

42 Elders of Apuk and Nyang knew this story. Apuk and Nyang communities vowed not fight with each other because previous wars destroyed people many years ago.

APUK : A STATE IN WAITING

Agei and Athulueth also had two daughters. They were named Amel and Awien. Agei arose to the chieftaincy throne of chiefdom in Apuk after his father Malek Rum had sustained severe injuries as the second Paramount Chief when the British colonial administration was established between 1899 and 1900s in the Jur River District of Tonj.

The Traditional Chief was given the responsibility of local administration, tax collection, and customary judicial trials for the resolution of social and political issues, intertribal and intercommunity conflicts.

Worshiping

Agei travelled from his home village to Jak temple site, where he worshiped the spirit divinity, and offered sacrifices. His father Malek was high priest of spiritual Parum clan there and his elder son Aguelet served with him as successor priest. Whenever, Agei offered a sacrifice he gave some to his wife Athulueth and his elder son Aguelet to divide the meat with Ajok, Adut, Athieng, Ayak etc. Athulueth was given more because she was the first wife, as was Aguelet given more as the first son and successor to the high priest and the dynasty.

One day, when sacrifices had been offered, Athulueth got up and requested a high priest performing the rituals to pray for her and her son Aguelet. She was broken-hearted and was crying as she prayed to all powerful god spirits and ancestry spirits together with priest, saying

> "I am your poor woman, but I am so miserable! Please protect my son Aguelet from his enemies. I will support him in his services to spirits, and he will always care for security of his people who will also service the clan divinities and spirits as long as he lives. His success will never be stopped."

Apuk Cultural Courses

The Angry Mammy Oath for Cursing

Cursing by vow or oath is not easy. It not only demands time but an environment that will allow the high priest to readjust at his own pace. What a clan person is depends upon is the character of that individual person. What a clansperson does, and what people think of what that clansperson does, depends upon the environment where he or she lives.

In fact, if a clansperson makes an oath to the Ancestry Spirit or takes an oath to bind himself with an obligation, he shall not violate his word. He shall do so according to all that comes from his lips. Furthermore, if a girl makes a vow to the Ancestry Spirit, and binds herself by an obligation in her father's house in her virgin age, and her father hears her oath and her obligation by which she has obligated or bound herself, and her father says nothing to her, then all her oaths shall stand and every obligation by which she has obligated herself shall stand.

Still, if she is married and she swore in her husband's house, or obligated herself by an obligation with an oath, and her husband heard it, but said nothing to her and did not forbid her, then all her oaths shall stand and every obligation by which she obliged herself shall stand. If she vows a binding oath to humble herself, her husband may confirm it or her husband may void it. But if her husband indeed says nothing to her, then he confirms all her vows or all her obligations which are on her. He has confirmed them, because he said nothing to her on the day he heard them. But if he indeed annuls them after he has heard them, then he shall bear her guilt.

The Plot to Kill Aguelet Agei

Aguelet was a man who received his name because of wounds and risky fights his father survived during wars of the Apuk Lith. He was the most respected son in the family of mighty warriors, spiritual priests and chieftaincy.

APUK : A STATE IN WAITING

As the forebearers of Aguelet Agei included Rum Atany who served in the predator's jail and in the wars that defeated them during nomadic Bantustan era that established modern Apuk state, those who went to war for him did so out of a sense of patriotism. These people truly were the greatest generations and saved the Apuk society from the tyranny of both nomadic Bantus, slave hunters and colonizers.

Without their sacrifices we very likely would be living very different lives. Thank you to all who risked everything to secure our freedom. The stories in this book give a glimpse into the hell our combatants endured to secure those freedoms.

Parum clan priests are cursers, ritual sacrifice prayer givers and libation bearers. The plot to kill Aguelet at served to inflame his angry mammy to hate aggressors and to curse the relatives from the Aliai Buong Section who did not help her son. They thereby encouraged enmity, fuelled by penalty *apuk* blood in collective responsibility charges of 201 cows of blood fines payable to clan victims felled or wounded in the battlefields.

The resulting assault left Aguelet Agei with knee injuries after he was forced to jump out over the fence, in a planned raid on the Mangar Agaach village, apparently carried out by nine aggressors. Ironically, the aggressors came from paternal family members. They disobeyed customary judicial trial sentence charges of the blood wealth penalty of *apuk* in collective responsibility. They objected to pay their share determined by blood relation charges payable to clan victims wounded or killed by Aguelet during battles. They believed that they must kill him so no warrior could kill, injure or bring fear into our family again. As soon as the relatives who hated Aguelet said this, an argument ensued, and the relatives started taking sides. Some did not believe in disobedience or that the death of Aguelet would stop wars or bring back life to the dead on both sides. But those who hated Aguelet believed otherwise, and therefore there were secret plans made to assassinate him at night in his home.

Aguelet crushed the besiegers in their attempt to gain possession of oval mud wall-blockhouse fence. It was solidly constructed

Apuk Cultural Courses

around his fortress home at Mangar Agaach, south of the Manyiel cattle camp. Even the third attempt after Aguelet sustained multiple injuries on both knees utterly failed. These hostile acts angered his mother (or mammy) and the Apuk community. It brought families, children and native communities to the brink of war.

Some hours later, news reached the children of Amel Agei and Awien Agei saying that their uncle Aguelet was assaulted with murderous intent at night because of the blood wealth fines.

Another interesting incident took place.

Aguelet's mammy Athulueth was present at the time of the attack. When the assassins were after Aguelet, mammy Athulueth became hostile. She dashed out the front door and into the clash to rescue her besieged son.

As well, his brother in law, Matik Ngor Bak, heard Aguelet being attacked, and stormed out to rescue him. They repulsed the assassins, and Aguelet asked Matik Ngor Bak to tend to his knees. He did and so told Aguelet to remain calm and sit with mammy Athulueth.

Aguelet felt the pain slowly ease while in his mother's arms. The grief she was going through after her son was attacked by his own family members was plain to see.

Due to his courage he was given the nickname of Matiat. Now he was a true hero. He was trying not to defend his own life, but to rescue the people he dearly loved. He truly he earned his heroism by all accounts.

After the attack, Matik Ngor Bak Matik accompanied his sister Adut Ngor Bak Matik and Aguelet to pick up by children of his sisters Awien and Amel. Both his knees were stiff and he couldn't walk well.

Even if Aguelet survived, both knees were now crippled. Now, few would commit to rally to his side. One young man, out of sympathy for the suffering and bravery of this warrior, did volunteer and held his arms. Another young man brought him a supporting stick and held him until they got to the house of Awien and put him on the little hut to the rear. His brothers in law were anxious for him and they thought he might die before they got him their destination.

The trigger was when people of same blood tried to kill their own mighty warrior to save the expense of a few cows. Aguelet had always protected and cared for them. He always made them proud at battles. This betrayal caused angry outbursts.

His mammy, of all the Parum and Padiangbaar families, stirred strongest against clan relatives. She stood up for her proud Apuk battle-hardened son against all enemies. The oaths she swore regarding the plot to kill her heroic warrior son is key to understanding where penalty *apuk* blood wealth has the power to trigger or activate hatred of blood relations. This creates a psychology of enmity. There must be more socially acceptable mechanisms of conciliating victim parties with guilty parties than penalty blood wealth numbering 31 cows. In an individual case, the payable amount to clan victims by those found guilty regarding collective responsibility to kill might be reasonable. However, the sheer number of cows Aguelet's relatives were forced to pay due to his successes on the battlefield simply overstrained the system. A system that worked regarding a single homicide was fatally flawed in times of war.

In this case, traditional chief's courts had determined the blood relation penalty objected to by Aguelet's relatives. They refused to contribute their share of the blood wealth proportionally payable between the Padiangbaar and Parum clans. This was in the context of collective responsibility for acts of the clan homicide crime guilty blood fine. It numbered 201 cows of blood wealth reparation payable to those clan victims killed or wounded in many battles fought in water points, grassing land and social functions. The first blood fine of 155 cows of blood wealth was to be paid for *apuk* of five clan victims dead. The second blood fine for severe wounds was 4 cows of blood wealth per victim. A total of 32 cows of blood wealth was needed to be paid for *apuk* of eight persons severely wounded. The third blood fine was that one minor wound was 2 cows of blood wealth. Thusly, a total of 14 cows of blood wealth was needed to be paid for *apuk* of the seven persons wounded.

It was deemed the clan battles were acts of the Padiangbaar, Parum and the entire communities fighting for their security and were considered as the collective responsibility that Aguelet had carried out in their name. Acts of injury and killing were not at any point the single-handed acts of one heroic warrior.

When Aguelet was not supported by relatives of his mammy from Padiangbaar in the Aliai Buong homeland, Athulueth became angry and she concluded that people from her fatherland wanted to destroy her family. It was not just that negative perspective. "They wanted to destroy me, and my siblings, and family members" she said. She reiterated that they engaged in supporting aggressors. "They were intent on destroying my son Aguelet and our family."

As Aguelet's mother she expressed her oaths with curses as a married woman to understand where collective responsibility has power to trigger hatred, which creates a psychology of enmity amongst clans linked by family blood relations. As an angry mammy she also expressed oaths with curses to promote understanding where collective responsibility must change to be a more socially acceptable mechanism of conciliating the war victim parties with the war guilty parties regarding blood wealth payments.

> "Why" she said, "do I, Athulueth, daughter of Deng from the Padiangbaar clan in Aliai Buong, wife of the spiritual leader of the Apuk clans of nationalities, call to the unheeding, to the deaf ears, twanging the futile noise of my lips? Which way can we turn, you Parum ancestors? You Padiangbaar Ancestors?"

Athulueth said:

> "I am ashamed that attempted assassination happened to my son Aguelet and I take full responsibility for what relatives of my father have done. By remaining quiet and letting the blood of my son run on the ground on this land shows they do not care about his death. His blood becomes a curse and root cause of curses on descendants for them. I now put a curse on your very spirit and blaspheme you in the spirit of family house. The Aliai Buong shall be the only fatherland to suffer this curse for you[43]."

---

43 Elders and surviving great grandchildren of Athulueth interviewed. Great grandchildren of Athulueth still will not marry any girl from Aliai Buong homeland until the curse is traditionally wash away.

What an interpretation on the cursing words of Athulueth regarding the guilty charge of courageous battle consequences in collective responsibility payment!
a) What power to trigger tacit approval and thereby encouraged psychological hatred of enmity indoors has angry mammy Aguelet used?
b) What favourite swearwords and blasphemies has angry mammy Aguelet used?
c) What are the curses of spells has angry mammy Aguelet provoked?
d) What misery has angry mammy Aguelet engendered?
e) How bitterly have clans, as well as individuals, within limited boundaries of angry mammy Aguelet, understood experience by suffering?
f) How many cursing and vowing lessons has experience taught families and clans of Bek Amuuk, Rum and Apuk nationalities?
g) How much pain has wickedness brought in its experience?

In my own experience, the great Apuk state cannot long remain quiet. If it ceases to have adversaries abroad, it will find them at home as powerful federations challenge all external attacks but are wasted away by their own internal lack of strength. The desire for tranquillity. The interests of property. The horror at cruelty. The lessons of experience. The force of clan Divinity (religion), and the bitterness of suffering re-induce the desire for order, and to restore the influence of the Apuk state in Rum period.

For the Rum and Bek Amuuk descendants and in all historical accounting, this memorable attack will ever stand onward. The attack was the subject of undying interest from succeeding Rum, Bek Amuuk and all Apuk generations. It is a lasting beacon to our descendants amidst the folly and senselessness of future spells.

Communities even direct prayers to sovereign powers. They direct prayers to the clan deity to observe potent curses of the slain to see the remnants of the line in their helpless plight. They direct prayers to cast out evil spirits from house and home in dishonour. They also turn clan divinity prophecies to fairer issue, even to a war hero that cares for the throne, community protection, and preserving the ancient inheritance of the clans of nationalities.

Athulueth was exceedingly angry with assailants, and fraternal nephews. In her affliction she made supplication to the clans of Aliai Curses, poor wretch. She hurled a bitter curse at the Padiangbaar for showing a negative attitude in face of the enemy and attempting to destroy Athulueth's family by assassinating her son because Aguelet is a child of a daughter of the Padiangbaar clan.

This was where she talked about the ways in which collective responsibility security and protection of lives and clans have the power to trigger or activate an assault to hate family members amongst other people, creating a psychology of enmity.

Both clans had lost many cows on payment of blood wealth punishment for the past fights. In every violent conflict between clans, Aguelet had inflicted injuries or deaths. The Parum clan said they struggled to pay the blood wealth obligation.

In separate violent clan fights, the community cited numerous battles involving clan members assaulting cattle herders at water sources. These incidents and disputes caused injuries and deaths on both sides some years back. Members of Agei clan were battling accusations regarding *apuk* payment of penalties that drained up blood wealth and the use of collections of cows from paternal and maternal uncles paid for guilty punishment *apuk*. Those paid to victim clan members following devastating violent fights in the Akuwei, Paduer and Manyiel cattle camps and went to chieftaincy courts in Apuk homesteads. Athulueth protested to the assailers of Aguelet and to her nephews.

This kind of collective responsibility for security and life of family allowed tacit blood wealth approval of the penalties and thereby encouraged the psychological hatred of enmity.

Every clansman or clanswoman is a potential cheat or rogue and also a potential good clan member. What a clansperson is depends upon their character. What a clansperson does, and what we think of what a clansperson does, depends upon his and our environment and upbringing.

APUK : A STATE IN WAITING

As the angry mammy said to her relatives:

"Why have you done such a terrible thing? You fear for your life when life of your own sister was under attack with intent to kill. The same life blood flowing in you is same life blood flowing on ground from the heroic warrior son of your sister. You have seen him bleeding. Because of the wounds inflicted on Aguelet, the son of your sister, you are guilty of disregarding the vow of blood relations to commit blood relation care for a blood relation act of crimes. I now put curse on the Aliai homeland for you. Our descendants will always remain apart. Our descendants will never again love one another, and no happy marriage will take place again between them."

Perhaps her responses were questionable and antagonistic. But she has free will too, and if people plot to kill her only son, people should expect anger. Aguelet and the sons of his sisters Amel and Awien fought to repel the aggressors. He never claimed he was walking a perfect dual spiritual and warrior path. No heroic warrior can claim that on this earth. This still does not imply the spirit may not speak to whom and through whom it pleases.

Athulueth was exceedingly angry with her father, uncles, cousins, nephews, aunts, nieces and all relatives of clan descent. In every instance of her affliction she makes supplication to the cultural curses on that poor wretch the cursed Deng Thou for standing outside the attack doing nothing when his grandson Aguelet Athulueth Deng Thou was battling the attackers alone and preventing them from killing everyone. All this even though Deng had maternal obligations to keep protecting the children of his sisters.

It is believed that the authority of the angry mammy who lays the curse on, increases its strength and potency and causes it to be more formidable. In Apuk clan culture, the women, the poor, the destitute and the dying have no other recourse for justice other than spirit power. They call for prayer for offered sacrifice rituals attended by a variation of priests possessing spirit power such as those of the Pabuor, Pagong, Pathieu, Patek and Parum clans, and persons possessing magical skill like sorcerers and magicians. Deathbed curses are the most potent, since all the curser's vital energy goes into the curse.

By morning, news reached the children of Amel Agei and Awien Agei that their uncle Aguelet was assaulted at night due to the blood wealth fines.

They took Aguelet to their sanctuary at a village in Kuach while shouting their battle-cry against the Aliai clans and the descendants of the Malek Rum lineage. Then they sacked the properties of all the perpetuators. They laid fire to the fields of Manyiel village at Mangar Agaach within the Kongdeer section in Machuet of Apuk.

Aguelet and his mammy Athulueth lived few years in Pachien in the home of Amel Agei. Athulueth died few years after arriving to her daughter's home. Aguelet died ten years after. They were survived by Agei Aguelet senior, Agei Aguelet junior, Atany Aguelet, and Angou Aguelet. Aguelet was buried in Pachien in the house of Amel Agei who was married to the Baak Anei family in Kuach of Rek Dinka. The body of Aguelet was later returned to house of Agei and reburied in Chueibet Malek village at Jak in Apuk State.

Athulueth Curses the Aliai Buong

Swearing an oath or a curse is the 'unfiltered, genuine expression of emotional truths. It is not until the fourth or the fifth generation that the cursing punishment for transgression drops. It is felt in its full bitterness for that length of time. The extension of war experience, the diffusion of cursing, the oath revealing the conflicting attitudes of the community towards cursing, the frequency of cursing harm ranging from annoyance and psychological stress to physical illness and suffering, to childlessness and even death to the heirs, to the family lineage died out, to the lingering break of peace and the blessing of life. In effect, the consequences of killing and wounding have fast-tracked the march of events. That which was slowly smouldering in former eras by the numerous successive generations, by the continuing change of home desires, has now been brought to maturity by the burning spirit, commonly disseminated, and the vehement desires which are everywhere released into action.

Athulueth said to them:

"Because of what you have done. Because you remained quiet. You will be the only clan to suffer this curse for so long as it holds. Our descendants will always live apart because you failed to protect life of the child of your own daughter in fulfilment for the love obligation of maternity and parentage. Why have you done such a terrible thing?"

"Because of your foolish actions, you will never be able to marry off your daughters to my descendants again. If you try, it won't produce anything for you. From now on, you will be apart from us, and our descendants will be apart from you." (Note: These descendants of the angry mother became famous dual control heroes, warriors and high priests or masters of the fishing spear.)

Historic Example of a Curse

My interpretation of Exodus 21:28-32: A bull that kills someone with its horns must be killed and its meat destroyed, but the owner of the bull is not responsible for the death. Suppose you own a bull that has been in the habit of attacking people, but you have refused to keep it fenced in, if that bull kills someone, both you and the bull must be put to death by stoning. However, you may save your own life by paying whatever fine is demanded. This same law applies if the bull gores someone's son or daughter. If the bull kills a slave, you must the pay the slave's owner 30 pieces of silver for the loss of the slave, and the bull must be killed by stoning[44].

---

44   Exodus 21:28-32 (Murder and Other Violent Crime),

chapter title

Outcomes

In the final outcome, the Curses raised their piercing cry.

Athulueth directed her prayers to sovereign powers of the Parum clan deity to observe potent curses of the slain. To see the remnants of the line of Rum in their helpless plight, cast out from home.

Thusly, she cursed the Aliai clans.

Athulueth said:

> "As the daughter of Deng Thou from Aliai, I am ashamed that this happened and take full responsibility because my fatherland and the Padiangbaar clan failed to act to protect life of son of their daughter".[45]

The relatives of Athulueth Deng Thou did not bring support to Aguelet like the relatives of Angou Anei Akol Kuot and Adut Ngor De Malek did. Matik Ngor De Malek and his three brothers joined their sister Adut Ngor De Malek, when she was married by Aguelet Agei, and Wol Anei Akol Kuot joined his sister Angou Anei Akol Kuot when she was married by Malek Rum. They both remained loyal allies to family members of Malek Rum and supported them whenever they were in trouble, in battles and facing security threats.

The Curse from Chief Priest

There is a belief that if the victim knows that he has been cursed and believes that he is doomed, that the curse is more potent as the victim helps to cause his own demise. However, many high priest chiefs and magicians claim that curses can be just as effective without the victim's knowledge of them. They further say that they would never let the victim know the curse had been laid on him because then he might go to another spear master of priest chief seeking to get it broken and cleansed.

---

45   Elders report from the family, Aguelet Agei, descendant, Awien Agei descendant.

This has happened. Persons feeling that they have been cursed will go to a spear master or magician (sorcerer). Sometimes they are in ignorance of person who put the curse on them. If the spear master or magician has laid the curse on the person, then he makes an additional barter for taking it off. When two opposing high priest chiefs or magicians are involved, a divine spirit war might erupt to see who has the stronger spiritual powers.

In the diverse traditions of clans with supernatural powers, witchcraft is against the ethics and laws of the divinity spirit craft as a method for the laying of curses. Most high priest deities abide by this, thinking that the curse will return to the curser in the same form as given. However, some believe that cursing one's adversaries is justified. High priest chiefs from ethnic cultures such as the Parum, Pagong, Patek, Payii and Pabuor clans, and the Pakuin, Padior and Dedior branches of the Parum Rum Wenkook clan, also believe that cursing is justified.

Cleansing and Reversing Curses

A curse is believed to be reversed or eliminated through ritual removal or disconnecting processes. These usually require elaborate rituals or prayers supervised by high priests invited or hired from clans holding spiritual powers.

The descendants of Athulueth can never fully take back what she said and what their children and descendants have done. What has been done stays forever in our past. We cannot go back in time to undo our mistakes or take back dirty things we have said or done. Every second that we use in our lives, never comes back.

Athulueth cursed the Aliai homeland because she was sincere to them. People who curse a lot tend to be more honest, upfront, and loyal with their family.

To break and disconnect this curse requires a process of ritual prayers and payment to the body spirit and life spirit of Deng Thou, the Padiangbaar clan, and the Aliai homeland itself. Such ritual and sacrificial prayers must be initiated by the descendants of Athulueth and Aguelet Agei Malek Rum on behalf of their grandparents.

As many methods exist for cleansing away and reversing curses as there are for making them. If a chief priest or witch or magician cursed object has been hidden in in the dwelling of a cursed person, it could be discovered by divinization and ceremonially destroyed. Usually, expelling rituals or protective workings are used to overpower the curse. Protective strings, such as pieces of skin hides of beasts sacrificed in rituals can be worn around the wrists or legs. Ashes of dung and the blood of animals that can be smeared or rubbed on the face and body can also be used to attempt to cleanse a curse. This can wash curse and neutralize it. A general side-effect in cleansing and disconnecting a curse is that its energy can recoil on the person who hired the spear master to make said curse. If such person has not taken adequate precautions, the person may end up receiving the entire effect intended for the victim.

How to View the Apuk Cultural Curses

I have attempted to provide a few answers to future generations regardless of what clan or colour they are. Firstly, there is no good reason for the Apuk people in South Sudan not to learn their history. Secondly it important that learn history about people, cultures and use of curses practiced by our ancestors as they now form parts of our culture.

Look at what is taking place here in the Apuk clans and in our own country of South Sudan. We are losing a fight against a bunch of money-grubbers because we do not understand our situation or the history of our natural resource wealth. Our country is sliding closer to an apocalypse because no one remembers what took place here. When our resource wealth vanishes, we will quickly rush to write off revolutionaries and hate groups as a minority of extremists, forgetting that often in history those same groups are the ones that take power due to the laziness and ignorance of the masses.

Furthermore "Those who cannot remember their history are doomed to repeat it." So, we can choose to ignore the history of curses practiced by other cultures and the history of an angry mother that cursed her fatherland in Apuk Lith state in South Sudan. In the future when our descendants are ruled over by zealots and sceptics, they will regret not learning our history of curses. Our predecessors will curse 'us' for our ignorance. Hence, this writer of history may have a distinctive bias when predicting a possibly sad future for the South Sudanese people.

The reason why people seem less fortunate in Apuk state is purely because they are cursed, nothing more and nothing less. This writer implores them in the words of Isaiah 18 and 19,

> "They will be food for vultures during the summer and for wild animals during the winter. They are those tall and smooth skinned people who are feared all over the world, because they are strong and brutal. I will punish them with civil war. Neighbours, cities, kingdoms and chiefdoms will fight each other. The Nile River will dry up. Its streams will stink. The tall grass will dry up and the fields along the Nile will be completely barren. Every plant will disappear. The people who fish in the Nile will be discouraged and mourn"[46].

This Apuk state is one of riches. However, the appetite and desire of our own people has wrecked it in particular and South Sudan in general. The exploitation of national wealth by phantom companies led to money shifted outside to banks in foreign countries. Now we are struggling recoup everything we lost.

We must ask ourselves important questions:
- Why is dirty money a disease?
- How can we bring our money back from foreign banks?
- How can the prayer of millions of people curse the dirty money of those criminals who stole it?
- What next can our Apuk state do before calling the whole world

---

46 Ethiopia Will be Punished: Isaiaha 18:1-7, & Egypt will be Punished: Isaiah 19:1-10,

to pray for them so that these dirty money spirits are cursed to wither and to die?
• Why is religion a brain seizure? Why does South Sudan have a religious brain seizure?

The case of South Sudan is a classic example of state brain seizure enabled by a small group of political and commercial allies who have used public money to privatize the natural resource wealth of the country. These resources span from gold, to aluminium, to oil, to timber and to livestock. Nearly everything else is misappropriated.

We are worried that our people are confused and do not know what to do next. When our money is brought back home to roost, as inflation spikes, the currency devalues, and hunger increases. We fear that our people do not know how to use public money adequately to reduce economic collapse, the breakdown of the rule of law, or to prevent acute malnutrition, hunger. This includes how to reduce number of children going without education and improve poor health care services. Our people do not have anything to offer to their own people with whom they fought to liberate to enjoy their freedoms and rights.

We in the Apuk state are disgracefully choked. We even wonder how vices wrecked our state and has thrown all South Sudan into acute poverty during our generation. We see dissatisfaction shattering our ability to sacrifice for peace and harmony. We must sacrifice before it is too late, or we will be punished and cursed by future generations.

The Apuk Concept of a Hero

A hero may be described as a person who transforms care, love and personal virtue into heroic action in Apuk culture. In doing so, he puts his best self forward in service to Apuk in particular and to society at large. A hero is an individual or a group of heroes. They take action on behalf of others in need, in defence of integrity or a moral cause. Heroic action includes:

- Engaging willingly on behalf of others.
- Steering and shepherding in service to one or more people or the community.
- Not connecting a risk to physical comfort, social stature, or quality of life.
- Starting without the expectation of any reward and/or material gain.

There are different interpretations of the word hero and the term heroic action made by Rum when he first arrived. This holds true for Malek, Agei and Aguelet's heroic actions. It is the antagonism Aguelet faced that made him a hero with most salient moral characteristics of courage. To be a hero it takes a strong will and great courage to face wickedness head on.

Aguelet's heroism was indeed a welcome and much needed change. In many ways he broke the mould in that era. He was overwhelmingly seen as a symbol of triumph for overcoming the odds against him and emerging victorious. He organized the community and led and defeated Arab slave merchants and various adversaries until order was restored in his society.

However, the reality of it all is never clear-cut. The burden and scars of the hero can be left with us. This comes as a result of what they have learned and the trials they have undergone. It all may leave them dispirited and calling for even greater amounts of courage to deal with the outcome of the journey. At other times there is no clear triumph as the journey might mean having to live with lifelong pain, as in the case of post-traumatic stress disorder, injuries or brain damage.

Behind every crisis, there is a hero to solve it. Behind every life that shatters, there is the opportunity to put it back together. Heroism is a gift bestowed to all of us, which, if left unrealized, becomes a curse and the root of our problems. Sometimes the cost is simply very high; so why be heroic?

Consider this. Whatever comes our way, and whatever battle we have raging around or inside us, we always have a choice. It is the choices that make us who we are, and we can choose to do what is right. Many have argued that most of the time it is not about good or bad choices, but choices that were simply not good enough. In their conclusions, those choices are the only ones that make the most impact in a world where heroism is absent.

As far as grasping the need for heroic deeds that are not so obvious, but generally apparent, I think that what stalls any actual participation in worthwhile heroic action is the perceived risk to loved ones. If there will be a risk to one's family, that is an honest and rational barrier. However, to see the long-view risk to their loved ones of NOT taking action is an intellectual endeavour not so easily ignored.

A definition of a hero or heroine is very difficult to make. However, one can immediately recognize a heroic act and the actions of a true hero. We see it when a person is running into a river that is about to draw someone under, or charging towards a fight on a battlefield, or rescuing a baby from a well. Heroism ensues in the environment daily in large and small ways. Heroes and heroism inspire future generations to act heroically when the occasion rises.

In the wake of every clan crisis, there is a hero. In the wake of every act that shatters a clan, there is the opportunity to put it all back together. Heroism is a gift bestowed to all clan members. Agei did not face what his son Aguelet faced, due to the changes as a result of colonial laws integrated into Apuk law courts. Today, we need heroes more than ever before!

A Very Fishy Tale

Historically, hunting and fishing were the main sources of livelihood for the people of the Apuk. Priest chiefs, as masters of the fishing spear, were usually consulted to pray to the clan spirits, *jak* and *yath* on behalf of hunters and fishers before they ventured out. They were expected to return with gifts for spiritual prayers.

There was a fisherman many centuries ago, and a master of the fishing spear called Bol Mel from the Pabuor clan. He loved his daily morning fishing trips. That was why he was nicknamed *Bol Chiirial*, meaning "Bol left in the morning". It reflected his early fishing forays into the wetland river called *Toch* or *Toch Bol Chiirial*, as it was fondly known. There was very little recorded history of any rules regarding fishing conduct until the 19th century AD. At this point, the Government intervened, formulated rules and demarcated borders to regulate, control, and to limit conflicts between competing clans over the ownership of the Toch regarding fishing activity rights, cattle grazing on the green wetland islands, fishing camps, and drinking water springs.

Most fishing activity stretches up to the Akarap islands, bordering other clans from the Luachkoth to the extreme east and connecting to the border of the Jieng (Dinka) with the Gok clans and from the Thony clans to the southeast of Toch Bol Chiirial currently known as *Toch Apuk* or *Toch Juwiir* or *Toch Apuk Juwiir*[47].

---

47 Bol Mel's children usually reported to visiting family members and friends that Bol aa cii rial bii la meei ee rec tooc, meaning that, "Bol has gone for fishing at rivers in the swampy areas."

Body Odour and Fish

In the minds of most people, malodorous body odour was not viewed a justifiable defamation damage in the common dispute context of collective responsibility. Rather, for some it was an unjustifiable defamation damage because eating red meat, other foods and even fishing activities increase body odour. For others, it degenerated into that non-payment category that could be presided over by the judgment of a blood feud and common disputes. In this connection, the 'defamatory damage dispute' was waged between the 'people' and 'those with fishy body odour' during festivities. However, the fish, the water, the rivers and the people were all created and loved by God.

Little did the people at the Aguudi fishing camp and Madhol Village know of a rule of a spiritual master based on the act of spirit revelation where divinity punishment originally and ultimately derives from clan divinity, the sacred divinity that creates both people and fish. They were all frightened when Bol Chiirial offered himself as a living sacrifice. Divine ritual cursing prayers called upon the creator of fisheries, fishing, wetlands, water, trees, grass and fish eaters and declared that divine punishment should be enforced on those people found guilty of an unjustifiable defamation damage crime.

Before we get to Bol, lets discuss body odour and fish!

There are many types of fishes and eating them increases body odour in a distinct way just as garlic or any other strong food does. Fresh fish and other water dwellers including crabs, lobsters, shrimp, and shellfish etc. have a light smell when they are first caught and should never smell distinctly fishy. However, as time goes on the smell increases exponentially.

Heredity determines more than a person's eye or hair colour. It also drives their body odour signature. The natural smelly body odour emitted from oil and sweat glands may occur anytime.

Fishing communities eat fresh fish. Fish tissue contains an odourless chemical known to be responsible for body oxides. After the fish is caught and eaten, the body secretes a naturally occurring bacteria on their skin that produces the distinctive scent people identify as body odour.

All people have a distinct combination of multiple numbers of bacteria types living in their sweat glands which therefore causes their own unique smell altering natural body odour.

What people eat can have a major impact on their scent, at least temporarily. While most people understand that consuming onions and drinking cow's milk will affect breath, people might not realize that such foods as meat can significantly raise the volume of body odour. Compounds are absorbed into the body and secreted in sweat. Body odour can change for the worse as early as one hour after consuming these foods.

Mostly this is noticeable when people with different diets interact. Fish eaters don't smell it on each other. Nor do meat eaters. However, for example, when a fish eater and a meat eater are near each other, they both detect an odour.

The amino acids in meats leave a residue in people's intestines during digestion. Intestinal enzymes break down that residue, which then mixes with the bacteria on the skin during perspiration and intensifies body odour. It has an effect that is hard to avoid. Since meat is harder to digest than other foods, the body must work harder to process it. As a result, sweat glands may respond by secreting at a higher rate.

People can emit odour within two hours of eating meat. Depending on the personal body chemistry the change in the scent brought on by meat consumption can be minimal or can linger for as long as two weeks.

There is no argument over the health benefits of eating fish.

Years of research have shown that fatty acids, commonly found in fish oil, are critical for brain function and play a key role in reducing the risk of heart disease. Meals that include fish have become a commonly accepted and beneficial principle. But some eat their catch too soon after being caught in swampy rivers. These may secrete an organic chemical compound that produces an extremely fishy body odour. In a few people, consumption of fish can contribute to "fishy body odour syndrome." This can be treated by dietary change.

chapter title

A Criminal Act?

Eating fishy foods was considered to be a divine criminal act for the reason that the malodorous body odour breathed by others and was brought by fishers into the festive celebrations.

Ancient clan culture dictated that the rules for Apuk regarding that damage is a prime law of the custom court in memorial antiquity. Cultural evidence suggests that the Apuk descendants of the ancient Kushites from southwestern Rek Dinka of South Sudan used the laws of the custom court to ease the burden of the rule of law of defamation damage in collective responsibility in the chieftaincy and increase trial sentences for the damaging crime of those guilty individuals.

Bol Comes to the Rescue

Bol Mel loved eating fish, tortoise and mammals; especially, hyrax, antelopes and impala.

The fish odour purportedly smelt by those attending a community festivity caused mocking attacks and sparked up the crimes of divine disputes. The defence was that fishy body odour from fish food was created by divinity and not by the fish eaters. Fishers argued that they were created equally with the other peoples in the festivity. Bol Chiirial made the point that there was collective responsibility for divine dispute crimes since fishy body odour, fish eaters, fish and people were created by God. Fish eaters accused of fishy body odour were vehemently booed, abused, shamed and rejected, which offended fishers together with their leader and spiritual priest. Bol Chiirial became furious.

Bol resorted to divine curses on those people so they would not catch any fish at spots located in areas controlled by the Pabuor clan due to the fact those people were biased in creating a malodorous body odour law directed against fish eaters at the social dances.

Defamation

The compensation known as "defamation *apuk*" is contained under the protection rules of the laws of custom as obligation laws which require court decisions to deal with damage awards.

Using the name of a person in an unjustifiable defamation statement is regarded as a grave crime in clan culture. The protection of an individual's name is the primary objective of the family, and whosoever spoils that name threatens to reflect said spoilage on the family as a whole.

Family protection rules are therefore important rules of law in the custom courts of chiefs for defamation[48] damage *apuk* and are payable in cattle. The spiritual act and punishment exist in most customary court systems to deal with defamation damage, sacred blood loss, sacred life loss, in the spoken word and importantly, in song. It is argued that the defamatory damage is more serious because it spreads quickly and is enduring. These damages are serious divinity breeches and are often held to be the causes of wider violence. "You look very important or noble when people tend to criticize you, whether rightly or wrongly[49]". But the counter-argument of defamation damage is that no one bothers to criticize a clansman or clanswoman of low status.

Defamation and Body Odour

Bol Chiirial believed that the people who brought forth defamation disputes for unjustifiable malodorous body odour during collective festivity celebrations, were acting on behalf of the community and that the community had collective responsibility. In this interpretation, collective responsibility is an expression of the overwhelming

---

48   Dr Francis Deng, SLJR 1965, p 560
49   Quoted in Wuol Makec, John., *The Customary Law of the Dinka People of Sudan*. Afroworld Publishing Co. 1988.

solidarity of the total community, who shared the same thoughts for regarding body odour.

Unjustifiable fish food body odour acts that condemned fish eaters and fishers, offend Nhialic who created fish eaters to eat fish and henceforth smell like fish. Bol together with community leaders, spiritual priests, and influential leaders determined *apuk* in cattle numbering thirty cows of collective responsibility. The community groups confirmed collective responsibility, informed the concerned parties and collected the collective divine punishment of *apuk* as compensation.

Punishment

The creator and clan divinity spirit may punish an entire people. They call down the guilt of the ancestors or ancestry spirits on the children for generations to come on any who reject the creator of all living things.

Bol Mel said there is no forgiveness until the community succeeds in getting rid of the hatred for fish smell body disorders. This can only be attained by communities realizing the fact that their crime is the result of their having damaged those fishers verbally and in their thoughts. Also, that they were out of harmony with the purpose of the spirit, and the rules of laws governing the creation of people.

There can be no evil on the part of the fish eater, or of the body odour itself. The evil act was in the condemnation of fish eating in a manner antagonistic to the purpose of the spirit that created fish and fish eater alike. They were affected by inharmonious criticisms directed against them, the fishing community, and the impelling directions of purpose that caused some to commit the evil defamation act. An act which was the outsider's demonstration of the inharmonious criticism of the body odour.

The law asserts therefore that the fishermen and fish eaters were falsely attacked, and their names damaged because of their fishing activities and odour disorders.

Spiritual Disputes

The fishing activities the cursed carried out produced no fish whatsoever. The people rightly assumed that Bol had cursed the fish away using divine spirits for revenge for the damaging acts committed against fish eaters for fishy odour. People went directly to their spiritual priest to bring the payable *apuk* price of thirty cows per the collective responsibility penalty. This was the payable *apuk* price of damage crime compensation, reparation and appeasement for the abusive language and unjustifiable defamation statements.

Criminal actions committed against the spiritual priest in spiritual disputes were measured by their resonance with the clan divinity rules of laws of right and wrong. It seems the time away spent crossing rivers, as well as the time spent driving back thirty cows from the sedentary agricultural village to the island of Aguudi did the spiritual minister some good. Several months later Bol allowed the fish rivers to ease fishing sports activities to include the previous offenders.

The *apuk* Bol Chiirial had received became popularly known as "Apuk for Bol Mel" and may have existed all during the dynasty and recurred so as to provide the new *Apuk* of Bol Mel or *Apuk* of Bol Chiirial justification regarding intention in the Muonyjieng language. Many people tend to believe this to be so.

Apuk and a Return to Innocence

There is in clan custom, a principle which makes the clan spirit of one who has not yet been involved, suffer the penalties for the acts of clan crime and evil of which they may have been guilty during their community life. There is no forgiveness of these acts, in the sense that forgiveness is explained by the spiritual masters and people with collective responsibility for their clans, or communities. The only forgiveness is the end of the memory of the damaging acts, so that clan members become as though it had never happened. As the member of the clan returns to innocence and is in harmony with the rules of creation, he begins his life anew. Then, and only then, forgiveness takes place. Clan divinity does not forgive by the mere act of pronouncing forgiveness, or by any judgment and sudden cleansing of clan crimes. It removes the condition, which results in harmony.

Collective Responsibility

The best way of resolving defamation damage caused by fish created malodorous body disorders was through collective responsibility. The *apuk* price in spiritual wealth payable to the spiritual priest"[50] for damages inflicted should be shouldered by all members of the community. The penalty for *apuk* claims that certain conditions must be fulfilled for the collective responsibility to be recognized by the court of law as having the force of law. The recognition of thirty cows of spiritual wealth has the force of law to reconcile all parties to the dispute.

Bol Chiirial believed that those who carried out the defamation acts might not pay the *apuk* price and so he cursed them. This way, the people, themselves had to change their attitude towards the fishermen. Collective guilt must be peacefully resolved by the use of priestly prayer. At whatever time defamatory damages, partialities, and appetites are eliminated, then that clansman returns to normal through forgiveness for harmony.

There was no assurance for forgiveness from Bol, or any other spiritual clan members that can remove that which is the cause of the defamatory damage crime, or the result of the cause. That is why the Apuk entered into the historical justice of the customary court that sanctioned cattle be transferred to clan spirits and ancestral spirits that pardoned people. Thereby, the divine wealth cattle were paid to parties who were victimized. This preserved social cohesion, forgiveness, peace and harmony that allowed people again to return to normalcy and coexistence.

---

50 If a cow is given to spiritual master directly for praying on behalf of victim or guilt, he will call the cow as *wong bith*, which can be translated as cows of spiritual powers.

APUK : A STATE IN WAITING

Without Apuk There Can Be No Peace

In order to protect people and fish bearing rivers, forgiveness was seen as a means to an end. Bol Mel threatened the community and stated that guilt for spirituality disputes would not end if there was no formal acknowledgement specifying that the fishermen offended by foul language offences would be compensated by rituals of *apuk* payable to the creator and to the ancestry spirits concerned.

He further stated that without *apuk* there can be no peace. Instead, the unresolved disputes of offences for divinity spirits can and will spread to infect other peoples, fishable wetlands and villages. In particular, where there are undisciplined people who think they have something to gain from spreading defamatory statements.

These new thoughts regarding spiritual wealth were widely understood and accepted

Apuk for ritual sacrifice prayers is a very divine element in forgiveness. The clan spirit does not, and the spiritual priests and defamatory parties cannot forgive damage crimes in the manner mentioned. However, spiritual wealth for true *apuk* of clan offences and sincere prayers for forgiveness to the clan spirit regarding defamatory damage to the victims will bring its answer.

True *apuk* for clan offences or crimes and sincere prayer, change not the defamation offence but change the damaged life and situation of damaged victim clans. The purpose of defamation offences, partialities, and desires was thereby influenced in such a manner that they received and realized the help offered regarding changing partialities, desires, and in turning their judgment to those issues that would enable members of victimized clans to remove from their memories the offending clan acts and offences.

The Apuk nationalities realized these truths. When they desire the forgiveness of their offences and pray to God for help in turning away from these thoughts, and when they implement their will in accord with the Divinity's will, and not expect forgiveness or removal of their defamation damages, they find themselves well on the way to true forgiveness.

Conclusions

The extensive oral tradition of the Apuk regarding the penalty of damage sentencing and punishment for spirituality disputes is decided by the chief. He chooses the number of cattle for *apuk* to forgive the collective guilt in divine disputes.

The price in domestic animals appears to have been thoroughly determined by reputable spiritual leaders, village leaders, elders, prophets, lower diviners, and chiefs or priest chiefs to deter people from offensive behaviour in the dynastic era. The spiritual wealth price in cattle was a conceived deterrent for other offences that might occur. It was the fee that will forgive people found guilty of deliberate defamation damage offence crimes in sacred blood feuds, divine crimes, and divine disputes.

The divine wealth price of thirty cows applied as *Apuk* Jok or *Apuk* Yath or *Apuk* Atiip is still being applied to this day. The dynasty conceived *apuk* for resolving critical issues which could disintegrate clans and clan alliances.

This is the real reason for the telling of the fishy tale. While fish odour may seem a small thing, it brought about a major change. It influenced the first thoughts conceived regarding payment in cattle for *Apuk* Atiip. The *apuk* of price in cattle distinguished Bol Mel and recognized the fishermen victims that had fishy body odour. It was recognized as natural, and the work of the creator.

People were compelled to see that there should be divine wealth for *apuk*, so true forgiveness could occur, and good relations would be restored. The payable *apuk* price helped the dynasty back then and still helps those of the Apuk today. Help from *apuk* supplication to spear masters and the spiritual clans sought to effectuate the issues. This belief was true and brought the relief prayed for.

An Afterthought

Fishing is one of the most peaceful and rewarding of all outdoor sports. Whether you're spending time with family and friends or fishing on your own, it is a great way to enjoy the outdoors and come head-to-head with a vibrant array of fish. Making the first trip to the sporting goods store with its overwhelming array of colourful lures and fishing rods and reels is fun.

Fishermen plan trips to where the best varieties are. They pick a place where they will enjoy spending several hours outdoors and where they will have a high probability of success. Lakes, rivers, and ponds are usually their best bet.

In Apuk, lek, aguer (diing), walleye, apooth, chot, abiliin are popular, as well as machar Ageer or rech chol.

In Machuet at Lake Ahom, Goor, Cheng-Gak Abekthii, Cheng Gak Abekdit, Kiir, and Ayihoou are popular spots for fishing outside of Toch Bol Chiirial.

In Toch Bol Chiirial, in the War-Apuk, Wathgoy and Baleek Rivers, the following fish are available: chot, lek, chur, atek (rechchol), including bowfins are common in rivers and swampy locations. Flounder and perch are also commonly fished.

Lake Baleek swamp in Toch Bol Chiirial is a great sport for garfish.

War-Apuk Spiritual Master and Tayau are fishing destinations for all sorts of varieties.

In Wunreel Apuk River and Wanhalel River, rainbow trout, chur, chot and other varieties are well stocked and common. They are distinctive for their reddish and pinkish stripe from the gill to the tail. Crappie, walleye, and atek are also common in the rivers of Toch Bol Chiirial.

Women, boys and girls are adept catching catfish in the rivers and lakes throughout the area. However, in this species the chemicals break down into derivatives of ammonia and therefore smell very bad. Waterway catfish, blue catfish, and flathead catfish are all commonly caught.

When fishing for catfish, anglers usually look for deep water at the mouth of large creeks and rivers and keep an eye out for sudden cut banks or drops. Catfish love these spots but will head for deeper water when it warms. Toch Bol Chiirial is a popular spot. Fishermen establish camps there regularly.

The Dinka Apuk People

The Jieng history begins with cultural heroes of the clanspeople such as the spear masters, or prophets & spiritualists. The Biblical Book of Jacob (which refers to Israel) describes God's or *Yiath's* repudiation of a spiritualistic line arising from the tribe due to its sinfulness. The Bible traces the Israelites to the prophetic and spiritualistic Jacob, who was renamed Israel after a mysterious incident in which Jacob wrestles all night with God (or an angel of God). The tribes of Jieng trace their roots, connecting culture, worship and beliefs in a similar way. Rum was captured and kept in captivity by predators with whom he wrestled all day and night. Today, the Apuk and the Jieng, both recognize themselves as communities with an authentic Israelite origin.

The power of clan spirit is one of the pillars of traditional Apuk culture. This is otherwise known as the 'High Priest Deity', or 'The Powerful Clan Spirit People'. It is a religious dogma remarkably difficult to pin down and define. The powers of clan spirit solicit the help of the water spirits via ritual sacrifices, invocations and dramatic representations by high priest chiefs. Powerful clan spirits are important symbols of identification and a significant factor regarding historical identification, social cohesion and managing clan security and control.

The Apuk can trace their initial development stages through early Dinka Jieng symbols and drawings that were primarily of livestock. Similar drawings had appeared in ancient Egypt that linked them

The Dinka Apuk People

with the introduction of domesticated cattle herds. In the mythological development era, herders[51], who also fished and cultivated, put down roots in the largest swamp in South Sudan. The floodplain there is fed primarily by the Wanhalel, Jur, and Machar rivers.

The subclans of the Dinka Rek of Apuk are branches that gradually developed from the original ancient settlers in the southwest in Tonj State. They spread out over the area perhaps between 600 and 1600 AD[52]. These subclans defended their domain against the Ottoman Turks in the mid-1800s and repulsed all attempts of slave merchants to convert them to Islam. Otherwise, they have lived in isolation.

The Apuk have many subclans that originated from the unique economic, political, and social interest/insecurity challenges caused by inter-clan and inter-subclan fighting during the migration era. These subclans were controlled using the spiritual powers of the high priest chief (master of the fishing spear) and traditional justice systems. Subsequently, as many Apuk clans became settled they changed their Rek clan views, values, rituals and traditions.

Oral traditional literature asserted that the process of historical expansion together with the consequent migration forced a larger proportion of the population to seek fresh settlements in the hunting, agricultural and cattle grazing areas of Apuk. This resulted in people creating new settlements known as Malony, Aliai, Tarweng, Manging and Angol.

Their lands in Jaang state are referred to as Jaang Rek country. It comprises vast sections along the Wanhalel River from Toch (Toch of Bol Chiirial) in Tonj south.

A distinction should be made here regarding the Dinka-Jieng Ngok, Twic, Luanyjang, Ciec, Atuot and Aliap subclans. They are different and, not part of the Apuk clans of the Jieng Rek people in Tonj South. However, the Dinka nations living in the Upper Nile region covering the Eastern White Nile River called themselves *Raan de Jieng* subclans, or sub-tribes.

---

51 Lienhardt, R.G. Divinity and Experience: The Religion of the Dinka, Oxford: Clarendon Press, 1961.
52 Lienhardt, R.G. Tradition and Modernization, New Haven: Yale University Press, 1971

APUK : A STATE IN WAITING

The Apuk Identity

The primary purpose of identity is security in common and to have greater group interest whereas members will be more likely to look out for each other because of that shared relationship. Identity may exist along religious, ideological, geographical, ethnic, or national lines. In every case the bond between people sharing identity has a security factor. "I know you because we have this common thing. I can trust you more because of these shared features."

The Apuk clans have their symbol of identity within the Rek nationalities. They are Rek branches of the river, wetland and lake Nilotic peoples. The clansmen who were named 'Dinkas' by travellers were native clans and among the first ancient Sudanese people. They were the original sources from which the Apuk branched out.

The first function of defining Dinka-Jieng identity is an exercise that must identify all the indigenous ethnicities where there is a branch of the Apuk clan. Today, ignoring the Apuk is clearly a comfort for those who have already ascended to become the dominant upper class.

Any foreign explorer who travelled to the south of Sudan, upon reaching a village, asked the clansmen what the name of their clan was. Instead of saying Jaang or Muonyjieng, the name which they supposed everybody already knew, the clansman gave the name of his chief. He or she would say: "We are the people of Ding Kak", a very common name among them. The explorer simply wrote down *Ding* and *Ka*. Thusly, the word *Dinka* circulated widely around the world as the name of a nation of people living around the lakes and rivers in the region.

That was how Jaang or Jieng was marginalized. However, the neighbouring tribes still used the name *Rek* regarding those tribesmen who were known to them as people of the Jaang. This was the name given to those tribesmen of the Malual, Aguok, Awan, Kuach, Lou, Abuook, Nyang, Looch, Akook, Leer, Luackoth, Apuk, Thony, Muok, Yar, Abiem, Jalwau, and Thiik clans among others. They were

172

The Dinka Apuk People

collectively known as people of the "Jaang Nation" or *Muonyjang*[53] (a more correct cultural identity name).

Language

The language of the Dinka Apuk clans is one of the oldest Nilotic languages (Nilo-Saharan Languages) dating to the 9th century AD.

The Apuk people speak a variation of closely related languages categorized into five broad families. Each subgroup calls its own speech by that group name and more than thirty (30) related sub-languages have been identified among the five language groups as follows:

1. The North-Eastern Jieng spoken languages of Padang, Abaliang, Dongjol, Dok, Ageer, Rut, Luac, Thoi, and Ngok groups.
2. The North-Western Jieng spoken languages of Ruweng, Pan Aru, Alor and Ngok (Ngok of Abyei in Kordofan) groups.
3. The South-Eastern Jieng spoken languages of Bor, Nyarweng, Hol, Athoc, and Tuic or Twic (eastern Nile Tuic).
4. The South-Central Jaang (Jieng) spoken languages of Gok, Agaar, Ciec (Chiech), Atuot, and Aliap groups.
5. The South-Western Jaang spoken languages of Malual (Malual-Rek), Rek, Tuic or Twic, Luac or Luac-jang groups.

They encompass all the known languages of Jieng speech.

Ongoing research and analysis entail a continual revision of the formal classification of Jieng speech forms. A standard reference for these languages and all languages of the world is being developed to be the official language standard reference guide.

The Jieng language of the Dinka Rek, consists of dialects (related sub-languages) categorized by the English/Dinka Dictionary. A chart of the dialect codes being used by various nationalities is based on the initial survey results.

---

53   Nebel, Arthur, The Dinka Dictionary, Published by Veronica Fathers, Wau, 1954

APUK : A STATE IN WAITING

The Apuk state language of identity is here among the spoken Jaang/Jieng languages of Rek as below:

Rek Language	Location	Nationality	Identity	Rek identity Name
Jaang or Muonyjang or Muonyjieng (Jieng) Rek	South-Western Jieng Rek (Dinka)	Aguok, kuac, Lou, Kong-goor, Abiem, Abuok, Awan, Kuei, etc.	Eagle (Fishing Eagle)	Kuei
Rek Jieng	South-Western Jieng Rek	Apuk	Eagle (African Eagle, or Martial Eagle, Crowned Hawk Eagle	Apuk-Lith
Rek Jieng	South-Western Jieng–Dinka	Apuk	Eagle	Apuk-Lith
Rek Jieng	South-Western Jieng-Dinka	Apuk	Eagle	Apuk-Lith
Rek Jieng	South-Western Jaang/Jieng Rek	Malual	Gier-Nyaang	Malual Giernyaang
Rek Jieng	South-Western Jaang/Jieng Rek	Tuic or Twic		Twic Mayardit
Agar	South-Central Jieng	Agar		Agar-Marol
Gok	South-Cenral Jieng/Jaang	Gok		Gok-Ayiel
Aliap, Ciec, Atuot	South-Central Jieng/Jaang	Ciec		Ciec
		Aliap		Aliap
		Atuot		Atuot

The Dinka Apuk People

The Nilotic people in Tonj South

The oral literature regarding our origins is extensive and has largely been recorded. It describes a people overwhelmed by Bantustan terrors. Subsequent wars of expansion by nomads and predators drove people out of their villages to seek sanctuary and survival along the many banks of lakes and rivers in southern Tonj State.

Eventually, anthropologists came and renamed the fish-eaters and the meat-eaters. These peoples and others were then referred to as *Nilotic groups*. This relates to a Nilo-Saharan group of languages that is also spoken by the Apuk clan groups of Dinka Rek peoples in regions of the White Nile valley.

The Nilotic peoples who settled at the river and lake banks still live near their warm and moist homeland. Wetlands and lakes are synonymous with the Apuk clan. They have retained the Nilotic tradition of life as pastoralist people. Like other Dinka-Jieng of Rek clans, cultivation is done by both men and women. It is still the men who clear forests from November to March. There are others who specialize in fishing. They make their trips to the wetlands and rivers from December and remain there until May. They deal with the annual cycle of one long dry season and one long rainy season.

Both girls and boys tend goats, sheep, and cows while they are under the age of 13. This role will change for the girl at 14 years old or when she has shown maturity through attaining her monthly cycle.

The clansmen are responsible for herding and are proud of their cattle management. These animals are dominant regarding Apuk prestige, dignity and culture. A woman will give a special name to a particular ox and compose love songs and dances about it and the clan. A man identifies with one special ox in accordance with Rek Apuk culture. He feels proud about the ox and calls himself by its name. This is an honour to him at his adulthood. The ox will be referred to by many reference names as variations to its direct name, which reflects its colour.

The Apuk clans are unique regarding compound names for a cow with multiple colours. A cow having black and white colours can be called: *rial, marial, gak, makur, majok, ajok, magak, akur,* or *akeer*. A bull with black and white colours is *marial, majok, magak, mangar, makur, marialgak, maker, makuei,* and so on. Only the Dinka culture has this system of combined colours in Africa. Males of the species can be referred to as cows on occasion.

English word	Jieng/Jaang Rek language word
Cow, cows	Weng, hok or weeng
Ox, oxen	Muor (mor), mioor
Bull	Thon, thoon (two or more)
White cow, white cows	Yar (female)
White bull, white bulls	Mabior, mubioor (two or more)
White head with black body colour for female cow	Kuei, Kueeth, Makuei, Mukueeth,
White head with black body colour for male cow (s)	Makuei, mukueeth
White head with red body colour	Mayom, muyoom
White and black colours on one cow (male cows)	Majok, Mujook. Marial, Murieet, Magak, Mugeek, Mangar, Mureer, Makur, Makuur or Mukuur, Maker, Mukeer
White and black colours on one cow (female cows)	Ajok, Ajook, Rial, Rieet, Gak, Geek, Akur, Akuur, Ngar, Ngeer, Akeer etc.

The Dinka Apuk People

Like other Jieng Rek people, Southern Apuk have a diverse vocabulary used to describe their world. Apuk itself has an estimated number of up to 400 colours to refer to cattle alone as well as their movements, diseases, and their variety of forms.

Showing generosity to others is crucial to achieving status in Apuk society. They base their life on the values of honour, dignity, and supremacy. They discuss and solve problems in public forums and are more republican in open debate by nature. They also value unity of purpose, sovereignty, interest, and security of their property and lives. The southern Apuk exhibited quality leadership back to Rum dynasty era with only minor internal conflicts.

The Battle with the Bantustans

There are many ancient references to the battles fought between the Bantustans and the Apuk spanning many years. Some Apuk clans were led by a master of the fishing spear as both the war and priest leader.

The duty of the priest "the master of the fishing spear" was similar to that of the divine priest chief, or monarch. In war, the priest guided the people and mediated the peace in the end. During that period, the main duty of the divine priest chief was to provide life. He was considered to be the holder of life. The priest believed that his life was tied to the life of his people.

However, when the divine priest with dual authority, Bol Mel, participated in the battle between the subclans and the Bantustans, he exhibited no willingness to appease the clan spirits for fear of a conflict of interest. That created clan Divinity weaknesses who then did not guide the military in the battle against the predators, who then conquered the clans.

That marked the end of Bol Mel's mastery over the subclans causing severed links with clan members, and resulted in the destruction of the garrisons, homesteads, cattle camps and byres along the great rivers and lakes. Soon, Bol died at his homestead in Maluach. The social, political, and military organizations diminished, creating divisions in the subclans and ending Nilotic clan dual control in north-western Machuet.

To fill the vacuum, the culturally distinct Rum, master of the fishing spear, emerged as the war leader. He freed by battle the devastated Pabuor, Patiir, Padiangbaar and Parum clans that had fled to escape the massacring, abducting, looting and torturing. Following the battle, the master of the fishing spear operated under his new military and spiritual powers. Rum performed spiritual prayers at the holy tomb shrine sanctuaries built for the ancestral spirits, before launching counter-offensives in retaliation against the Lwalla.

It was recorded that Rum, had experienced a dramatic event in this ancient battle between the Lwalla and the Rek Jaang. According to sources, Rum (identified as Rum Atany) looked up to the sun before the battle and saw the light of a bright star appearing above it, and with it saw the words of Nhialic:

"You will conquer the Lwalla, destroy their armies and build an independent country comprising the subclans with undifferentiated divinities."

Rum relayed this message to his forces. Rum's invocations and mediations achieved their goals and the Lwalla armies retreated. Rum wrested back control of areas as far away as the southern rivers and swamplands. He ejected the predatory Bantustans for good. The symbol of clan divinity that unites subclans after a victorious battle still bears the image of Rum.

He commanded his troops to adorn their shields with a spiritual symbol of the supreme creator god, Nhialic, whose spirits can cause adversaries to be cursed, suppressed and defeated. Thusly his troops would emerge victorious. Rum Ateny guided and commanded them in battle and was again victorious. The Lwalla were weakened and driven southwards. Rum had a small army but again drove out the enemy at Wunriir. His successor also defeated his enemies, taking the south in the process, and then sent a powerful army further southward yet.

The Dinka Apuk People

With the retreat of the Lwalla, there ceased to be any written record or information about them or about the Nilotic clan activities in the region over the next three hundred years. The alliance of the Nilotic clans emerged as an independent homeland which slowly expanded its authority and influence into other chiefdoms which were controlled from Wunriir. Successors went further relentlessly, launching full-scale attacks, and weakening adversaries who were never again to invade or terrorize the Pabuor, Patiir and Padiangbaar clans. The predators were defeated to such an extent they never truly recovered.

Earliest Apuk Settlements

The earliest clans settled first in Machuet from the west to the north of the Apuk subclans, at habitable places. They made many cattle byres, mud-walled homesteads, and villages that embraced the legendary Machuet of imagination from the early centuries. The first peoples were settled in a sedentary way of life in well-protected villages. They supplemented wild meat and fish with grain and herds of cattle[54] which were kept at the byres and camps around their homesteads.

Machuet is described as "the mother centre of the Nilotic clans that constituted Rek"[55]. This is where the Dinka Apuk clans branched out to settle in western Rek and became clans of the current Apuk[56]. Their habitats were all along the banks of many lakes and river tributaries. These were of great importance due to the annual flooding of the savannah. The swampy lowlands are connected to many major tributaries like Bur Apuk (*Bur Apuuk*) along the Pagol river, Ahoom Lake, Ayihoou Lake, Goor Lake, Jak Lake and others on the western side of Machuet and Malony Apuk. There are also those flowing into the Wanhalel, Wanh Goi, Madol Apuk, and Nyin Akum Rivers.

---

54 Simson Najovits, Egypt, trunk of the tree, Volume 2, (Algora Publishing: 2004), p.258
55 Herodotus, 1. Translated by J. Enoch Powell, Oxford: Clarendon Press. 1949, 121- 2.
56 David N. Edwards (1998), "Meore and the Sudanic Kingdoms", The Journal of African History 39 (2): 175- 193. JSTOR 183595

This aided with the production of fish, pottery, iron ore and water availability to the homesteads and allowed for the rise in power of its people[57].

When the priest chieftain emerged, he revived authority and incorporated the military/priest leadership that salvaged clans from the governance of the conquerors. The outgrowth and administration of the Rum dynasty extended down to the southern and eastern waterfalls and towards the clans of Malony from the southwestern frontiers to the clans of Machuet in the west to the northern Akon Agiu and northeastern Adhoth-Nhim borders. Clan sources recorded lakes and river tributary waters reaching far to the Apuk clans in the extreme north bordering the Pagol River and upstream to the confluence of the Bur Apuk and the Majok Apuk Rivers bordering Jurchol-Luo in the northwest. The clan divinity priest chiefs[58] ensured the loyalty of clan traditional chiefs by conscripting their clansmen to serve as messengers and defence guards at the cattle byres and homesteads around the country. They also expected tribute gifts in the form of goats, sheep, ivory and gold to offer in ritual prayers as sacrifices.

Lwalla Persecution

The first recorded persecution of the clans by the Lwalla predators was in the first century AD, when, as reported by historians and anthropologists, chief priests and commanding officers attempted to blame outcasts for the great sins punishable by god in what is now called Dinka Apuk[59]. According to Pabuor clan tradition, it was

---

57 L. P. Kirwan, "Rom beyond the Southern Egyptian Frontier", Geographical Journal, 123 (1957), pp. 16f

58 "Early History", Helen Chapin Metze, ed. Sudan A Country Study. Washington: GPO for the Library of Congress, 1991.

59 Dinka or Jieng definition of clan or sub clan, or tribe is autonomy, state or nation or country. According to Dinka, country refers to wut, gol, and all are semi-autonomous or independent from each other and can unite for individual interests, political issues, security reasons, wars and natural disasters.

The Dinka Apuk People

during the reign of Bol Mel that Rum the stranger was martyred. However, many modern historians debate whether his administration distinguished between the divine Pabuor clan and the divine Parum clan prior to the divine heir of the divine deity Rum's modification of the divinity tradition of divine divinity controlled by the use of spiritualized priests in the 10th century AD. From that point practising lay persons paid spiritual incentive gifts to spiritual Pabuor clan priests and spiritualized clans did not have to pay any incentives. All somewhat confusing. History often has uncertainties.

The Padiangbaar, Patiir, Pabuor clans and their subjects, suffered from sporadic and localized persecutions over a period of three and a half centuries. Their refusal to participate in the imperial cult was considered an act of treason and was therefore punishable by execution. Most widespread official persecution was carried out by the Lwalla. During this era, the spiritual master ordered the villages of three clans to be deserted and their sacred gifts collected and sacrificed under the supervision of the Pabuor clan priest chief. Native clans were arrested, tortured, mutilated, burned, starved, and condemned to gladiatorial contests to amuse spectators. These persecutions officially ended when an offspring descended from Rum, the senior commander, issued a proclamation of toleration which granted the Padiangbaar clan, Patiir clan and other subjects the right to practice their religion, though they would have to seek spiritual help from a reputable priest with a powerful clan divinity to restore evil spirit protection to them. The divine Pabuor clan, the Padiangbaar clan and the Patiir clan were involved in this proclamation of toleration. It has been speculated that Rum's successor's reversal of his predecessors standing policy of layperson clan persecution has been attributable to one or both of these co-spiritual, supernatural powers.

Rum was persuaded to marry a woman from the Padiangbaar clan. This marriage indigenized nativity permanently into the southwestern Dinka Rek Jaang of the Apuk homeland in current Juwiir. It is possible but not certain that Rum's successor's wife exposed him to laity (non-ordained priests etc. such as in Catholicism). In any case, he was over 35 when he finally married, and the Padiangbaar clan integrated him into their clan culture. Speaking of laities, Rum made clear that he believed that he owed his successes to the protection of the High God alone, with the help from the Divine Deity of Parum descent.

The population that resulted from the mix of cultural and racial lines developed rules, laws and social cohesion/order over time and progressed into the Dinka Apuk state as we know it. The Parum, Pabuor, Patiir and Padiangbaar clans were originally hunters and fish eaters. The Nilotic people were essentially almost identical, and thus the concurrent advancement of divine spirituality leadership, militarism and political principles in successor rulers[60] advanced smoothly.

The subclans of the Nilotic ethnic groups progressed, spanning the occupation period so many centuries ago. Excavations in the Jak holy sanctuaries at the Chueibet, Piokkoi, Adeejook, Ahoom, Manyiel, Maluach, Aguurpiny Arop Kon, Akon Agiu and Aheechloch lakes, revealed evidence of an important high-ranking culture and burial temples near settlements. These were concluded to be our first ancestral burial sanctuaries in Machuet Apuk. It is important to note that the Pakuieth are a sizeable Nilotic clan who came and settled widely in the clan enclave of the Machuet subclans. The Pakuieth clansmen, Arop Kon, emerged as military commanders. The wealthiest, such as Akol, or Arop Akon of the Pakuieth clan of Agurpiny, dominated social settings in the period of Rum, Wol, and Malek and Agei.

Wunriir Machuet Apuk

Although Maluach and Jak remained religious centres, the western and northern clans of Apuk eventually fell into disorder. They had come under pressure from the Luwala invading the territory

---

60 S.O.Y. Keita (1993). "Studies and Comments on Ancient Egyptian Biological Relationships". History in Africa (JSTOR) 20: 129–154. Retrieved 2015-04-11.

The Dinka Apuk People

through the southwestern frontiers by crossing the Dinka Muok and Dinka Yar borders and the River Wanhalel. Additionally, the Apuk maintained contact with Bantus and Jurchol traders along the upper western plateau borders and incorporated Nilotic cultural influences into daily life. Inconclusive evidence suggests that the technology of manufacturing weapons including spears (*bith*) with the use of iron smelters, may have been transmitted northwest and eastwards across the savannah belt to the Maluil near the Wanhalel and Swamp Rivers in the east, Malony in the west, Machuet ranging from centre to extreme north, and to Aliai in the east.

Relations between the Apuk, Thony, Yar and the Luanykoth were not always peaceful. As a response to incursions of the Apuk into western Luanykoth, northern Thony and Yar, a Luanykoth army moved west to the swampy river valley and the Thony army moved northwest to the swampy river at the border with Apuk for military confrontation. The commander of one force quickly abandoned the area, however, deeming it necessary to resolve a confrontation with a neighbouring community peacefully. That compelled the Thony military brigades to pull back and resulted in a negotiated solution to the conflict caused by water points and grazing land bordering the three Nilotic clans.

The Parum Clan and the Rum Dynasty Era

The legendary Rum Deities were high priest chiefs, believed they were descended from the divinity of the powerful clan Parum, which ruled Apuk from unknown centuries past. Rum Wenkook controlled as a Deity and high priest chief. His offspring and heirs succeeded him in priesthood, military leadership, and in establishing the tradition that descendants intermarry with those of conquered clans to assimilate different cultures and to unite the nation they lead. For centuries, this offspring led the nation of subclans, beginning from the unknown to the known to the present century. They controlled the chiefdom through the dual authority of high priest chief and war leadership.

Rum founded the Parum clan of divine spirituality. Their belief was that the clan prophet would be of the Nhialic god line, based on the Creator's promise to Nhialic of an everlasting throne for his offspring descended through the divinity powers of the Highest Holy Spirits, and others from god like Dengdit, Deng Kur (or Deng Mayual), Garang, and Abuk Apiny). Strangely, there is rarely any mention of Apiny Ayak.

Many of the Jaang leaders and prophets of the Parum-Pagong clans claimed membership in the tribe of Jacob. For example, the prophets Rum, Deng Mayual, Jiel, Garang, Abuk, and Apiny, all belonged to the tribe.

Not all the struggles of the people of the Apuk clans were caused by the arrival of the Arab slave merchants. At the beginning of the nineteenth century, a major scrambling to carve up Africa by the colonial powers led to an explosion of violence that lasted for generations. It was called the 'Era of Fears'. In fact, the primary reason for the Apuk raids into the Condominium Colony was to get away from the fears coming up behind them.

At the centre of the storm was the Apuk. To protect themselves and their cattle, they united under a single chiefdom led by Malek of the Parum clan. Malek rose to the top because he was a skilled and innovative leader, war strategist and master of the spear. He organized his warriors into *riec* or regiments and gave each *riec* a distinctive arm tie and headpiece commonly called an *ajom*. It was made from ostrich feathers covering a protective helmet.

A few of his officers were even more skilled. Akok, Aguelet, Wol, and Kur, were descendants of Rum the spiritual master. Bol Chiirial of the Pabuor clan, Aguet-Lokbaithok of Patiir clan, and Bek Amuuk of the Padiangbaar clan had acquired ancient military skills before the son of Rum arrived at the Apuk of Bol Mel.

Malek Rum grew up bitter and lonely amongst the people who despised his forbearer (the Rum who was kidnapped), the guest and fatherless son of the Parum spiritual clan. When he got the chance, he became a herder for the clans, and later joined its defence. Here he found an outlet for his aggression and fought

The Dinka Apuk People

so well that he rose rapidly to a leadership role. The spiritual masters descended from Bol Mel liked Malek descended from Rum Ateny who escaped in Lwalla detention camps and led Apuk clans into victory in the prehistoric period, and ordered the transfer of leadership of the clans to him. Then Malek sent messengers to call the Apuk clans to war by beating a big drum throughout the country of Apuk chiefdom. Malek became the Pabuor clan's spiritually chosen heir and was made the chief commanding the defence of the Apuk clans. The first thing Malek did as chief of the Apuk Chiefdom was to get revenge on the Lwalla and ordered the massacre of them all.

Many years later, a deputy was killed by a tribe that refused to submit to his authority. In the civil war that followed, Malek seized control of the Toch Bol Mel and the savannah territories to the south of the Ju base near the swampy rivers. He then eliminated the leaders and the defending forces of most of the other enemy clans. Thusly, he added their people, resources and territories to the Apuk controlled by him, and the tables were completely turned. The weak clans migrated to Apuk for protection, and the predatory nomads became part of the Apuk clan. They remain so to this day.

Military innovations were the key to the success of Malek. He imposed far more discipline on his troops then predecessors had. He forced warriors to traverse harsh terrain and forbade them to marry until they had distinguished themselves in battle, or their term of service was coming to an end. His regiments, to use the English term, were divided into four groups. Each was named after the colour or appearance of a bull. The main body of troops was called the *rieny madot*, or *madol*. There were two wings called the left and the right that ran ahead to outflank the enemy. The fourth were frontier troops called the *aneem*. They were scouts are sent ahead to check the direction, size and formations of the enemy. There was also a reserve force called the Bridges. They were under orders to hold back until the others were engaged in combat.

Up to this point, Apuk warfare was mainly a matter of getting close enough to an enemy to throw spears. Casualties tended to be light, with most of those on the losing side living to fight another day. Malek thought this way of fighting was ridiculous and replaced the short spear with a long-bladed version created by the blacksmiths. It was a spear of medium size with curved hooks which could not be easily removed. It was also wide-bladed and couldn't be thrown, forcing the warriors to charge and stab an enemy in hand-to-hand combat. Clans called the new weapons: *tong alool*, *binh yuai* and *binh nyueth* after their shapes. He added a larger shield, which the warriors could use to knock an opponent off balance. Other new weapons included: the *tong abanban, tong yar* or *tong hier, tong col, binh laak*. The names were determined according to design, colour and need.

Putting all this together turned the army of the Apuk clans into an unbeatable, efficient killing machine. Soon, enemies were fleeing the bordering territories, trying to put as much distance between them and the Apuk clansmen as possible. Many simply crossed sides or ran for safety to the Apuk and were assimilated. Apuk boundaries generally existed as fiat boundaries created by communities themselves reflecting natural boundaries such as common borders between the Kuach Akeen, Nyang Akoch Majok, Luach-koth Bol Malek Jok and the Yar Ayiei.

It is important to note that Malek Jok was the descendant of Rum Wenkook with the identity symbol of clan divinity of the Parum with the dual control of war leadership and high priest chief of Apuk clans. This has always served as an advantage for peaceful coexistence between the Luach-koth Malek Jok and the Apuk Malek, Apuk Rum, Apuk Malek Agei, Apuk Agei, Apuk Malek Mathok and their descendants.

Territories and Cattle Camps

The valley of the Apuk Lith clan, within the territorial boundary the Apuk clans, is occupied by nine major clans. These are the Kongdeer Machuet, Agurping Machuet, Maluach Machuet, Malony Maluil, Aremrap Aliai, Buong Aliai, Angol Maluil, Manging Maluil and Tarweng Maluil. Machuet is the oldest homeland, and

The Dinka Apuk People

it is where the Apuk Lith began and widely expanded to the other territories.

According to legend, at its height, the Pabour, Padiangbaar and Patiir Clans were the primary clans of the Chiefdom. They were followed by the Parum of the Rum deity of Apuk Lith. They occupied most of the territory of the kingdom, except for a small area in the east occupied by the Luac-koth, and an enclave towards the northwest which was occupied by the Jurchol and Nyang clans.

These were initially the main territorial boundaries of the Apuk clans of the Rek Dinka clans in the Bhar El Ghazal region. The main cattle camps within the territory of the clans include Git Cattle Camp in the Manging section, Pankiir Cattle Camp in the Malony Section, Akuwei Cattle Camp, Paduer Cattle Camp, Malou Cattle Camp with holy tombs and shrines, Jak Cattle Camp on the most Holy Tombs and Shrines of the High Spritual Priest Chiefs from Rum to Ateny descendants, Manyiel Cattle Camp in the Kongdeer section of the Machuet Division, Pan-nhial Cattle Camp and Angui Cattle Camp in the Aliai section.

The clans of Maluil Apuk were separated administratively in the secession of 1976. However, the clans of Aliai and Machuet remained under the Chieftaincy of Malek Mathok Malek and were loyal to his management. It existed from 1976 onward until the Apuk Juwiir was re-divided again politically and administratively by the liberation movement in 2000. The population was distributed according to proportional sections as follows:

1 **Malek Mathok Malek of Parum clan:** Continued as Paramount Chief for the Kongdeer section of the Machuet region. Machuet was subdivided into the Kongdeer, Maluach and Agurpiny sections. The main clans of Kongdeer clan division are the Parum, Pakot, Pakuieth, Pagun, Pagoor, Panyier, Pabuor, Patiir, Patiop, Pagong, Payuom, Padiangbaar, Pangok, Patiir clans.
2 **Arop Akol Arop of the Pakuieth clan:** Selected Chief for the Agurping region. The main clans are the Pakuieth, Pagun, Pagoor, Payuom, Padiangbaar, and Patiir clans.

3 **Malek Akuien Lueth of the Parum Clan:** Selected Chief for the Aliai subtribes which were carved out from the Machuet region and from the Chiefdom of Chief Malek Mathok. Aliai is subdivided into Aliai-Aremrap and Aliai-Buong. The main clans of Aliai area are the Parum, Padiangbaar, Pabuor, Pagoor, Pakuieth and Padolmuot.
4 **Akot Makuac of the Pabuor Clan:** Remains Chief for the Manging region. However, the Malony, Tarweng, Angol subtribes were carved out. The main clans of the Manging are the Pabuor, Padiangbaar, Pachool, Pakoot and Patiop.
5 **Manut Baak Athian of the Pagong clan:** Selected Chief for the Malong region that had been carved out from Chief Akot Makuac. The main clans of these subtribes are the Pagong, Padiangbaar, Pakoot, Pakuieth, Payat, Paweet and Palueet.
6 **Chol Yuot of the Pakot clan:** Selected Chief for the Tarweng region that was carved out from Chief Akot Makuac. The main clans in the Tarweeng are the Pakot, Padiangbaar and Parum.
7 **Deng Aruop Mabuoc of the Parum clan:** Selected Chief for the Angol region that was carved out from Chief Akot Makuac. The main clans of the Angol subtribes are the Parum, Paweet, Pakoot, Pangok, Pakuieth and Panguet clans.

Background

The Apuk of Bol Mel consisted of clans and subclans of the main Rek clans of Jieng. They worshipped what they considered to be the one true God, or *Yiath*. This figures prominently in Jieng traditional history through their spear masters and is found in books on African traditional religion. Most religious scholars agree on this, although the written form was subject to distortion and post-distortion alterations undertaken during the era of the Christian reformers in the 12th to 13th century AD. The Apuk Lith has been traced back to branches of Rek clans when the Pabuor, Padiangbaar and Patiir clans separated during a large migration period and first settled in this territory.

The Dinka Apuk People

The original three were migrant clans that later became the those of the Apuk Bol Ciirial around the 16th century. Spear masters allocated the land among the major tribes. Priest leaders ordained portions of the land which is described by many as encompassing most of Parum, Pagong and Pabuor clan shrines within locations in the three major divisions such as the oldest Apuk Lith of Machuet, Maluil and Aliai Apuk.

The three main clan divisions are subdivided into sections (or Wuts) of the Apuk Bol Ciirial (or the Apuk Juwiir).

The following nine clan Sections of the Apuk Lith are known as:

1 The Kongdeer Machuet Section
2 The Agurping Machuet Section
3 The Maluach Machuet Section
4 The Aremrap Aliai Section
5 The Buong Aliai Section
6 The Malony Maluil Section
7 The Tarweng Maluil Section
8 The Manging Maluil Section
9 The Angol Maluil Section

South Sudan: The Language, People, and Cultural Identity

The Apuk clan language is of Dinka-Jieng ethnic origin and is one of the oldest of the Nilotic ethnic languages in South Sudan. It has predominately oral core values. Nilo-Saharan languages date to the 9th century AD. The ethnic Dinka-Jieng still uses its native script every day and everywhere, with several million speakers in the country. Also, about a million Rek speakers inhabit the Western Nile.

The Jieng appear to be among the largest speakers of the Nilotic language. It is divided into northeastern spoken language, northwestern spoken language, southeastern spoken language, southcentral spoken language, and southwestern spoken language versions.

There are about a million speakers of it along the eastern and western White Nile River in South Sudan. There are likewise different divisions of Nilotic languages within the speakers of Nuer regarding the Shilluk Luo, Jurchol Luo, Acholi and Anyuak clan languages. The most linguistically diverse region in the country is in the Equatoria region inhabited by Nilo-Hamitic, Bari, and Azande speakers. There are also border regions with a second native script used by the Nilo-Hamitic clans.

A script is more than contemporary technology for recording in vernacular or the modern-day ability to write the spoken word. It is a vital form of communication, a core value and a cultural symbol of a people and their identity. The mere sign of Chinese script carries the power of the Chinese people as Arab script carries the power of Islam and Islamic people. Every time we understand written English and Arabic we understand the might of their cultures. Writing is a powerful political tool used all over the world to show national identity.

South Sudanese Identity

The history of the Apuk originated in the history of Jieng-Dinka ethnic group of South Sudan. The Arabs called Dinka-Jieng the people with "dark skin colour" or "black skin colour" and described 'Dinkaland' as the land of "Black People" or "Soudan" or "Bilad as-Soudan" (the lands of the blacks). Black peoples occupy South Sudan, Sudan and most of the continent of Africa.

Fixing clan nationality identity to South Sudan makes sense; but fixing clan nationality identity to any hypothetical dark colour or black colour does not. Dark colour and Sudanese or South Sudanese are not interchangeable in any course or even ideologically synonymous. Dark colour segregates skin colour for clan nationality only, and not the land of origin, or the land of birth-rights, which are the fundamental factors and the most critical bearings of the clans of nationalities of South Sudan.

Hence in this scenario, where do 'dark people' or 'black people' come from? Or "Bilad as-Sudan", "Soudan" or "the lands of blacks"! There is no way of escaping this squabble. Therefore, 'dark' is superfluous and South Sudan is relevant. There are no 'Dark South Sudan people' because there are no 'dark clans', no 'dark cultures', and no 'dark customs' in any clan family. Even in the South Sudan family, there is disagreement regarding 'black Africans' from the 'the dark continent of Africa'. For instance, many Ethiopians have light skin colour. Others, such as the Amharas, do not all have dark skin colour. South Sudanese clans such as the Azande and Pojulu have light skin colour. Even though Ethiopia is a Greek word for dark skin colour, the Amhara people pledged allegiance to be Ethiopians.

Dark colours are often associated with anything bad or evil. The Bible describes devils and evils as being dark. There is an Arab League and Arab Council, and there are the Islamic League and Islamic Council for the preservation of the identity of those Arab Nations of northern African countries from Mauritania to Sudan. Their maps have been politically attached to "the Arab World" and their geopolitical maps curved out and annexed to the "Islamic and Arab World Maps".

Why an Arab identity? Why are some African countries attaching their identity to the Arab identity? Or the Islamic identity? Or the Arab World Map identity? These questions have no single answer. But one thing is clear, the Arabs are sharing a geographical location in this 'dark' African continent. They are members of the African Union and they are members of Arab Leagues and Arab Councils. They are members of Islamic Leagues and the Islamic Councils of the Arab and Islamic World.

Clan Identity

Why is a clan council considered to be a 'tribal council'? Or Tribalism Club or Tribalism League? Blanket arguments such as "a clan league is bad" or "a clan council is bad" or "a clan council is tribalism and it is bad" or "a league of clans is not a good thing". These are not academically constructive critiques.

APUK : A STATE IN WAITING

Why is a clan council needed? Because the voice of the marginalized clan communities cannot be heard over the deafening thunder of politicking. To counter this bizarre inequity, the focus of this council deals with a clan-centric national view. It centralizes the issues, core values, cohesion, opinions and concerns of clanspeople.

Whether it be the Bari clan in Jubek State, the Moro clan in Amadi State, or the Padang clan of the ethnic Jieng in Ruweng State and the Apuk Lith clan of the ethnic Jieng Rek in Tonj State, they all have tools and progressions for accomplishing cohesion, people rights, controls, checks and balances, non-discriminatory rules of law and embracing traditional core values.

Clan cohesion is a progression and a result of inculcating and empowering all members of the clan community to have a sense, as well as a feeling, that they are members of the same nation. That they are members of the same kingdom, clan, state, fatherland and society. These clan members engage in a common enterprise and face shared challenges.

Clan cohesion should be used to deal with senior citizenry supervision and the reconciliation of differences, pardons, spirit forgiveness, fear of clan divinities for their collective punishment of wrongdoings and evil crimes, competing interests and the demands faced in our society.

Clan cohesion is based on the knowledge that individuals can only attain their full potential when living and working together. A clan goes beyond peacekeeping and violent conflict supervision.

The basic tools and progressions for attaining clan cohesion include good authority, influence, ability, the introduction of non-discriminatory practices, diminishing disparities, differences, embracing and implementing a clan's traditional values and principles of governance.

Clan core values are beliefs of a community guiding the actions and behaviour of clan members. Its principles of governance are patriotism, community unity, sharing, and the decentralization of power on clan checks and balances, the rule of law, democracy

The Dinka Apuk People

and participation of the people. Clan values also include collective dignity, equity, social impartiality, customary judiciary, comprehensiveness, equality, people's rights, non-discrimination, and protection for the weak and the poorest of the poor. We need good governance, integrity, transparency, accountability and sustainable progress.

The clan values and principles of governance should bind all clan state agencies, clan functions, community or society functions, all clansmen, clanswomen, clan youths; boys and girls whenever every one of them applies or interprets the constituents, and enacts, applies or interprets any clan judiciary, community judicial disputes resolution or makes or implements community policy decisions.

Clan core values define the clan state and authority systems and in extension the constituents. The basic means of legitimate understanding of the clans are; patriotism of the people, representative democracy, principle of majority, principles of power checks and balances, and protection of minorities, principle of separation of power, principle of inviolability of basic rights and freedoms. Each should be a resourceful clan governed by rules of law and principles of supra-inhabitant rule.

A society which is pluralistic, open, and in the process of formation of political willpower, fulfilment and the application of political decisions, permits easy political development in a socially acceptable atmosphere.

Politicking poisons the life conditions of people in the various clans of South Sudan. It makes people hate the clan council before they even know it. The government defined the term 'council' in a way that a person from England, Turkey, Ghana or Egypt perceived a council to be. They never saw it or interacted with council members. So, what they have done is poisoned how people of different clans relate to each other.

Inequity robs the hope of people by marginalizing the potential contributions from a major sector of the population. The cure for endemic diseases, cancer, or a new mission to the moon, are stuck in a village and rotting because of the 'Tribalism Council Community'. They are stuck in a political favours marketplace network system. Stuck by the sticky fingers of the money-grubbing official. Stuck by the policies of misinformed agencies, and corrupt leadership.

The biggest untapped resource is not in the ground of South Sudan, it is in the people. However, this is in jeopardy because of the prejudices residing in the country. The identity and pride debates still rage on unabated.

The identity of South Sudan is that of a diverse society with multiple cultures. Today, the native natural environment and the primary function of defining the identity of South Sudan is first and foremost an exercise in political self-interest by state leaders and institutions. The power of definition must remain with the majority and today South Sudan is simply an umbrella term for all the high societal native ethnicities and their contemporary descendants for the stockpiling of ill-gotten gains. Avoiding clan identity is clearly a comfort for those who have already ascended to become the dominant classes. For South Sudan in particular, clan friction and violence are a consequence of that domination.

Understanding our South Sudanese Identity

It is difficult to understand the history of South Sudan from the context of a clan member standing on his or her cultural land. This is doubly so when looking at it from the perspective of the conquered community victims whose idea of what a country should be is not the same as that of the powerful criminals who abuse the idea of a 'South Sudan'. The first step in any examination must deal with these distractions and limitations so that the South Sudanese people alone can begin an authentic discourse into the history of South Sudan.

South Sudan's people must accept that identities and terminologies change as circumstances change. If there's not any such thing

The Dinka Apuk People

as a historical South Sudan identity[61], then the groundwork must be laid for the people to grow into a mutual identity. Within that framework, there can also be an Apuk clan identity, a Dinka-Jieng identity and a Bari or Kuku identity. This is then melded to the South Sudanese identity.

The most important facet of identity is security. If the clans of South Sudan share a greater interest in the federation, they will be far more likely to look out for each other because of that shared linkage. In all areas, not just that of the clans, identities exist. These run along religious, ideological, social, economic, political and interest of security lines. They can also thrive within a federal framework.

People are now overly critical regarding historical and diverse clan identities and of the South Sudanese identity. Some people have expressed the desire for archaeological exploration to find the 'real' South Sudan. What does all this imply? Does it mean the clans of antiquity? Do they think they will find a place where the clan identity was fully authentic before the Arabs came and gave us the name of our country? One where everyone was beating drums and pouring libations onto decorated pegs, shrines, deity tombs, tree gods, clan spirits and ancestors? Is it possible to find perfection in this regard?

In the entire history of humanity, no such perfection exists anywhere. Every developed state that has ever come into existence has done so with the influences of dissemination, diffusion, and sharing with other groups. They all evolved from a melting pot of ideas, cultures and races.

---

[61] The goal of identity is clan security, political security and social security. Something in common is people and clan interest to look for each other and shared association identity may exist along religious lines, ideology, inter-marriage, personal interest, political interest.

Our Identity Today

This sphere where South Sudan exists has been in place since the time of the great population migrations of the past. What do people mean when they refer to 'pure people'? What core value should this have in any historical assessment? A clan, as real as it is today, can only be defined by what it is today. People cannot transfer contemporary clan formations into ancient societal historical identities and say: "These people were or are the real clans of South Sudan." Those ancient people are defined by how they saw themselves, not by how people choose to see or define them today. None of those clans ever identified with any land area larger than their own clan territory. Our country in a sense has been 'manufactured' by the necessity to survive against the north. Its diverse elements should be celebrated, not scorned.

Some fools believe that if we go back in time we will find a real ethnic clan of cultural antiquity in South Sudan. One where the culture and its people, was 100% authentic, 100% perfect, 100% self-identifying and 100% black! One that proves that there is one true South Sudanese identity and that falls precisely within the borders of the country of today.[62] Ridiculous!

The goal of identity is social and political security. The logic being that people that have something in common are more likely to grow other interests together.

In ancient history the terminology: the lands of the blacks or the lands of the dark skin colour as an identity would have had no meaning. This was an identification from the outside by people who knew very little about what was inside the area we now call South Sudan. The ancients defined themselves as members of clan chiefdoms, clan kingdoms, high priest chiefs, or high priest deities of religious beliefs etc. They identified themselves by using clan divinity symbols or emblems. These identities are still a part of the people in

---

62 There is argument of going back to old cultures to find an originally Indigenous South Sudan!

The Dinka Apuk People

the region people call the Nilotic clans of Jieng, Nuer, or Acholi, the Bantustan clans of Bongo, Azande or Moro, or the Semitic, Sudanic and Hamitic clans of Ndogo, Lokoya, Lulubo, Kuku, Pojulu, Mundari and the Baka region. Anthropologists have categorized the Bantustan clans as members of the Sudanic and Nilo-Hamitic Clans of South Sudan.

With greater interaction between all the various clans, this dream of a centralized generalized people's identity may take root via ethno-genesis[63]. The name 'Sudan' is a term imposed on us at the time of the conquest by Turk and Arab oppressors, never by indigenous ethnic clans themselves. The clan names, however, connected the people to their lands of origin, therefore became their birth right and geographic claim. They argue that the name South Sudan or even Sudan disconnected them from their land of origin, birth and even culture.

How are We All Connected?

The people of a united South Sudan are surely more than just a name. They are connected by nativity rights, clan nationality identity and the issues of sovereignty. Dark skin colour is not a verification of being Sudanese per say. It is a definition that fails within the identity of many South Sudanese people at every level of history, culture and in political contexts. Similarly, dark skin colour is a definition that fails the identity test of many African people at all levels on the continent. For example, think of the people of the Apuk clans or the Jieng, the people of the Bari or the Moro clans, the Shilluk, Nuer or Morley, the people of the Twic Dinka clans and the Latuko

[63] People were neither Pabuor, Padiangbaar, Payuom, Parum, Patiir, Pakuieth, Pakot or Panyier or any other clan. Ethnogenesis (from the Greek ethnos "group of people" or "nation", and genesis, "origin, birth"; plural ethnogeneses refers to the process of formation or emergence of ethnic groups. Using this term in "quotes" because it usually specifically refers to an ethnicity rather than a race. So, the Ethnogenesis of the Bari, Apuk, Ngok or Padang people commences with the emergence of a distinctive Bari people, Apuk people and their cultures.

clans and the people of the Azande. They are all native clans. Their diverse hair textures, skin colours, heights, and builds are all specific adaptations to living in the diverse geography of South Sudan. For this reason alone, dark skin colour is certainly not a symbol for the entire South Sudanese identity. Many native clans, depending on geography have light skin colour like Azande clan of Gbudue State and Tombura State, the Bongo clan of Tonj State and Pojulu clan of Yei River State to mention just a few. These adaptations and cultures are originally clan based. Historically the clans, whether fixed or nomadic, were essentially 100% of the population within the borders of what is South Sudan today. While that is changing rapidly in urban zones, the rest of the country remains clan based.

The most common feature of this South Sudanese identity, beyond comparative cultural similarities, is its history, without exception. Historically, the lack of consideration for the clans by the government is the overriding factor defining the boundaries of dark skin colour in this country. This is regardless whether the dark skin colour is clan colouring in the region of the Nilo-Hamitic people, inter-marriages in cities or the "Falata droplet rule" of Wau city of the Bahr El Ghazal Region. In every demand, the 'dark skin colour' hypotheses have been fashioned to serve the interests of foreign people.

It turns out to be life-threatening in contemporary pluralistic South Sudan. This is broadly extended to other African countries and the wider world in which the question of identity is left to the people wearing those identities. No matter how else South Sudanese people define themselves, whether as Muslim, Christian, Sudanese, Jieng, Bari, Nuer, Azande, Falata, Fartit, Lulubo, Pojulu, American, Ethiopian, South African, Acholi, Madi, Apuk, Ugandan, Kenyan, Aguok, Awan, Ivorian, Twic, Luanyjang, Luanykoth, Thiik, Akok, Gok, Agar, Bor, Atuot, Padang, Jie, Jurbel, British, Australian, Norwegian or whatever, they should also be South Sudanese.

It is that identity that impacts their link with the broader culture and with the social order of all citizens. It is not the only consideration in their lives, but surely a very central one.

The Dinka Apuk People

Diverse peoples live within the South Sudanese family. South Sudan is, therefore, a way of saying all of the native ethnic clans and their dispersions have a South Sudanese identity and are part of our family. Today, when some say the South Sudanese identity is skin colour and an intentional legitimacy by regulation, they are wrong. Being South Sudanese is different from being Arab. Because Arabs are connected by a combination of language, politics, and both historical and cultural identities. State, culture and nationality are three factors embodying identity. The state or nation is the largest community. It should embrace both clan and culture with their tools and processes for attaining core values and cohesion, all of which supersedes nationality.

Nationalities are more than just the colour of passports of individual clansman and clanswoman, or the territories people pledge allegiance to. Subsequently when Uganda became independent, overnight the Sudanese, Rwandan, Congolese and Kenyan people in the new borders became Ugandan. When Eritrea became independent, overnight the Ethiopian and Sudanese people in the new borders became Eritrean. When South Sudan became independent in 2011, overnight the Sudanese Falata people, Ethiopian Nuer and Anyuak people, Congolese Azande clans, Ugandan Madi and Acholi people, became South Sudanese.

The Padang Jieng people inhabiting the border territory of the Dinka Ngok of Abyei were politically and artificially divided where those Padang of Ngok people cut south of the border became part of the south. The Abyiei territory that belongs to Padang Jieng ancestors is nothing more now than a Sudanese political territory. The population from the divided clans bordering today's South Sudan and Sudan still speak same the Padang language, worship the same clan divinity, worship a single divinity symbol and offer prayers to the same ancestry and clan spirits. Some Padang clans pay no taxes at all and others pay their taxes to different governments.

Similarly, the populations from the divided clans of Acholi, Nuer, ethnic Dinka-Jieng, Anyuak, Azande, Falata, Kakwa, Kuku, Madi, and many other clans of bordering countries like Kenya, Sudan, Congo, Central African Republic, Uganda and Ethiopia still speak the same languages. The only difference is their 'nationality'.

The same is true for the Dinka-Jieng Padang of South Sudan and of Sudan, the Falata of South Sudan and of Sudan, the Nuer of South Sudan and of Ethiopia, the Anyuak of South Sudan and of Ethiopia, the Toposa of Kenya and of South Sudan, the Azande of Congo and South Sudan, the Madi of Uganda and of South Sudan, the Acholi of Uganda and South Sudan, the Kuku of Uganda of South Sudan, the Kakwa of Uganda and South Sudan. They have the same ancestry, Nilotic and Nilo-Hamitic languages, etc. There are similarities in various African countries such as the Tigray of Eritrea and of Ethiopia and Zulus of South Africa sharing common borders and having the same ancestry, same language.[64]

Escaping clan identity and its cultural identity, with doublespeak, political correctness, obfuscation and naivety, is clearly a comfort for those who have already ascended to become the dominant upper class. For everyone else, clan engagement is a consequence of that domination. Therefore, South Sudan's identity is found in its diverse cultures and nationalities. The primary function of defining the country's identity is seemingly an exercise in political self-interest by certain players and institutions. Subsequently, either South Sudan's people can self-define and profit from that definition, or be defined, frozen, marginalized, and exploited by special interests[65]. There those who are South Sudanese by blood and those who are South Sudanese by soil. Because they do not meet the narrow definition of a 'true' type, or selectively defining certain traits like Nilo-Hamitic speaking or Nilotic speaking, simply ignores the complexity of genetics.

---

64   Loisel (2004: 4) argues that in 1990 almost 87% of African borders were inherited from colonial era

65   Ethnic definitions are subject to change over time, both within and outside the communities. For example, Post-Islamics, have altered the "Arab" makeup of the word, causally merging non-Arab people into an Arab identity. Another example from 19th-century was how Europeans classified Jews and Arabs as one "ethnic" group; the Semites or Hamites. Later the term Hamites came to be associated with Sub-Saharan Africans instead.

The Dinka Apuk People

Identity should be a foremost consideration, for if it is not then subsequent work would not be grounded. Then people could see how the question of compensation, land ownership, citizenship, free-movement, the unity of political parties, and unity of people, all hinge on a clear definition of identity. History is South Sudan's clarifier and its memory. The dilemma of our culture lies in the non-existence of social justice services and the lack of social equalities. Today our people still must fight for their very basic rights. What we first had in common with each other was a unified reaction to Arab slave merchant and colonial regime oppression. That form of oppression identifies our people by their culture and clan identity. This happened throughout the region. To this day, every generation in South Sudan procrastinates when determining how to self-define before allegiance. And while they fiddle their thumbs people are being defined in a way which enhances their oppression.

Clan identity does not have to equal the politics of hate. Being proud and defining the identity of the Apuk Lith and Apuk Juwiir clans of Rek Dinka-Jieng does not impose upon, threaten, or obscure the identity of the Bari, Kuku, Azande, Fartit, Nuer, Anyuak, Pojulu, Kakwa, Atuot, Agar Jieng, Ciec or Gok clans and cultures. People must evolve enough to where they are no longer threatened by their differences of clan identity, cultural identity, religious symbol identity, food, social traditions, clan divinities and divinity symbols. They do not have to be rejected using rivalry, hateful speeches and subjugation.

People misunderstood the Kokora within the Bari cultural identity. When clarifying the Bari Kokora definition of who is a Bari and a Bari speaking clan they ended up denying non-Bari clan members the right of acquiring resident rights in Bari land and Pojulu land because they are non-Bari and non-Pojulu who do not fall into Kokora definition. South Sudan's citizens failed to understand the cultural identity emerging from Pojulu in Yei River State, Balanda and Fartit in Wau State, Fartit and Falata in Raga of Lol State, Agar in Rumbek in Western Lakes State, and Ngok Lual Yak in Malakal and Shilluk in Pashoda State. We should learn from Israel, regarding their rules when clarifying a definition of who is a Jew and denying the right of return to Israel to those who do not fall into that definition.

False definitions allow those who have traditionally exploited South Sudan to continue to do so. It must be realized that cultural immunity defence systems of the clans and their identities have been the most damaged. For a clan group interested in self-preservation and self-determination, the question of who belongs to the Apuk clans of nationalities or the Bari, Agar, Aguok, Awan, Kuku, Padang, Pojulu, Shilluk Luo or Fartit or any ethnicities, who has interest in those ethnicities will be paramount. This is particularly true with the Apuk identity experiencing oppressive economic development and political marginalization on all fronts.

Symbols and Rituals

The Cow

The cow is a symbol of the clan of the Apuk. It is often represented in Apuk art such as the sculptures made by children outside a wall and on the roofs of grass houses. It is a symbol of pride and is used for honour, marriage, compensation, reconciliation, and pardon for spirit forgiveness.

This chapter presents the discussion of Apuk as defined during analysis. Insights were generated from historical experiences, the meaning attached, specific feelings about the Apuk identity, culture, emergence of the dynasty era, high priest chiefs, ritual sacrifices, ceremonies and practices in the Apuk community environment. The aim is to show the identity of the Apuk and the needs of the people living there.

The Eagle

The African Crowned Eagle Hawk is known for taking flight with one of the heaviest weights proven to be carried by any flying bird.

These eagles may target prey considerably heavier than themselves. Such prey is too heavy to fly away with. It is either eaten at the site of the kill or taken in pieces back to a perch or nest. They tend to lift the larger animals into the air and drop them. This will incapacitate or kill them. The authors of several books about eagles: David Allen Sibley, Pete Dunne, and Clay Sutton have said that African Crowned Hawk Eagles have killed creatures weighing up to 30kg. The Martial Eagle found in South Sudan, Sudan, Kenya and other countries in Africa has been recorded as killing a 37 kg mammal. This is well over its weight.

The Clan's Relationship with the Eagle Symbol

The exact origin of the eagle identity symbol is unknown, but it is believed to derive from the African Crowned Hawk Eagle, which the clan called *lith-toong*. This term explains the dark-coloured, swarthy, black/grey wings used for sweeping attacks from the sky and as a reference to the plumage, *lith* (simply put: 'Eagle that fights'). The ancient clans traditionally used it symbolically in their rituals. Clan priest chiefs offered animal sacrifices to worship the feeding eagle. There are several versions of the Apuk clan symbol in creation myths. The main identity symbols of the various clans are birds, trees, cows, grasses, snakes etc.

Writers such as Lucan claimed the eagle was able to look directly at the sun, and that they forced their babies to do the same. Baby birds that blinked would be cast from the nest. This belief persisted in the Clan Parum lineage from the onset of Rum dynasty until the modern era.

Lith Symbol of Clan Identification

It is reported that the eagle symbol of the clan was introduced by a naturalist and prophet with dual control of war leader and clan divinities in the era of the Rum dynasty. *Lith-toong* became the ancient clan patron animal and divinity emblem. It was believed to have provided the power of the Lith clans (eagle clans). There are numerous artistic depictions of the *lith-toong* symbol with young clansmen bearing the mythology upward. These trace back from the beginning of clan traditions to the present era.

Symbols and Rituals

The Apuk clan tried to reunite parts of their world which were torn apart when they suffered various misfortunes following from the Luella incursions. The following statement from an elder is a representation of this desire:

> "I, Eagle, the Crowned Hawk Eagle, King of Birds in sky and ground, have fought the good fight. I have finished the race for you to be known as Eagle King, and I have kept the faith to defeat the adversary Eagle King"[66].

A lot of what the Apuk say about their symbols of clans and clan divinities is connected to the notion of the eagle symbols. It matches very closely with their experiences in life, of the relations between kin, and of the values of clan kinship. The clan symbols together with clan divinity are a type of ancestor. The emblems are a type of clan association or federation.

Clans are in fact differentiated from each other by incoming generations, *reec/riech*, by personality, or by family and lineage. The symbols of the clans of the Apuk, perhaps by virtue of their being birds or animals, can be thought to form a single undifferentiated association. Each eagle, for example, is seen by people as the equivalent of a clan or people. It is not fully realized, for they are persons, members of extended families and lineages, and are noticeably differentiated from each other in these ways. The clan is an association, union or federation unity. But in relation to the clan, its symbol and clan divinity, the Apuk transcend the divisions between themselves.

So, *lith-toong*, which became a symbol of identity dedicated to the

---

66 My discussion with one senior Apuk man, made me to believe that they identified themselves with eagle as it behaved in a way they admired. Apuk people see themselves as fighters like the Crowned Hawk Eagle.

identification of the Apuk clan, to provide the practical consciousness of the Apuk clan, by the Apuk clan, for the Apuk clan. It refers to an eagle that can fight flying in mid-air, attack prey from the sky, can fly for hours and attack prey on the ground and in the forests.

The identification of eagle and clan was split based upon the noticeable distinctions in morphology and anatomy. Genetics obviously indicate that the species of eagles and humans are totally separate and distinct animals. However, the clansman may wear a feather headdress and use the attack tactics of the Crowned Hawk Eagle, thusly winning an eagle clan name.

The clansman carries a club called *atuel* used to strike the skull and kill instantly. Meanwhile, any monkey caught by the eagle will be seized by the skull and killed instantly.

An eagle is a common form in Anglican symbolism for spreading the Gospel all over the world. Additional symbolic meanings for the eagle include the pronouncements to the Israelites in Exodus 19:4; Psalms 103:5 and Isaiah 40:31. Eagles are an exceptionally common symbol (USA etc.) and are considered the 'King of Birds'. Another is the lion, the 'King of Beasts'.

They were popular in the Holy Roman Empire. Its eagle was pictured as being two-headed, supposedly representing the east and west divisions of the old Roman Empire. The *Lith* or eagle of clans is a common symbol representing the divisions of clan associations or federations, South, east and north of the states of Jieng Rek and going to Jieng within Rek and Jieng across the eastern White Nile River the symbol of identity may be a fishing eagle or a Crowned Hawk Eagle. There is a *lith-toong* clan known as the Apuk Lith and there is Kuei clan as well. It represents the Apuk clan tradition of symbolic expansion.

The birds are usually given names due to their colour, behaviour and appearance as translated in the language of clans. *Lith*, the eagle of prey, is referred to as *dit yap* or *dit-toong* according to its behaviour. It may have different colours, for example *lith, lith-toong, kuei, acu* and *acuil*. A few eagles are described below along with eagle symbol or emblem of its Apuk clan.

Lith-Toong

The African Crowned Eagle (aka the crowned hawk-eagle) lives in sub-Saharan Africa and is limited to the eastern areas covering the habitat of the Apuk clans of South Sudan. It is a clan symbol or emblem of "lith clans" widely known since the Rum dynasty era and is the only extant participant of the genus birds in South Sudan.

Appearance: The clan language describes this bird according to its appearance. This eagle is quite large, and the upperparts are blackish. Underneath it is white but heavily streaked with black, except on the legs. There are large white windows on the primaries and the trailing edge of the underwing is broadly black. The underwing is mostly black with a broad band of white spots[67]. The head has dark grey upperparts. The breast and belly are rufous, and heavily mottled with black and white. Its wings are broad and relatively short, with chestnut over the wing coverts, and dark grey and white stripes.

With these wings and its long tail, the *lith* is capable of great manoeuvrability in its environment. The face is dark grey with yellow eyes. It has strong, hooked, almost blackish beak. The crest on the head can be raised and this gives the species its common name. The long crest is mainly above the eyes, giving a cat-like attitude to this most powerful clan symbol. It has huge sharp talons, muscular feet and feathered legs. The female is larger than the male, with a shorter crest and more barred underparts. The juvenile is paler the than the adults.

It has completely adapted to its habitat. This *lith* does not hesitate to swoop through dense bush to get its prey. Its colour is also suited to its locale. The mottled chest fits in well with the dappled sunlight of the riverine and lake forests in South Sudan.

---

67 Wing Cord, (biology)

APUK : A STATE IN WAITING

The wing chord[68] is 65 cm, the tail is 30 cm, and the tarsus is 10 cm. This is the largest eagle and is the heaviest raptor in South Sudan.

Diet: This powerful bird is reportedly stronger than the Martial Eagles. It feeds mainly on birds up to the size of a guineafowl. Francolin is its main diet. The African Hawk-Eagle also feeds on small mammals such as the mongoose, monkeys and reptiles[69].

Voice: It utters a high-pitched sound during flight, a rapid *"ki-ki-ki-ki-ki"*, and a *"kewee-kewee-kewee"* during a distinctive pendulous aerial display. Female utters a lower and musical sound *"khoi-khoi-khoi"* when on the nest. At the nest, both adults utter a shrill *"quee-quee-quee-quee"* while they bring food. The young answer in a similar way.

Where it is found: The African Crowned Hawk Eagle lives in Africa, south of the Sahara covering central Africa from South Sudan through to South Africa. They are found in woodland areas in Senegal, Liberia and Guinea in the west, and in South Sudan across to Ethiopia in the east Africa forests. It is a common resident in open plain forests close to the many lakes of the Apuk clans.

It can also be found on rocky hills and along riverine forest strips. This eagle can live from the sea level to 10,000 feet (3000m) and more. They avoid dense evergreen forests.

Behaviour: This is a noisy raptor, calling, while hidden in the forest. its aerial displays consist of series of steep dives and ascents. The male flies with few wing beats at the top of each ascent, making circles or figures of eight. It performs these at up to 5000 feet (1500m) above the forest. It throws back its head at the top of each climb and utters a display call for up to 30 seconds[70].

---

68   Wing Cord, (biology)
69   Sources: *Handbook of the Birds of the World* Vol 2 by Josep del Hoyo-Andrew Elliot-Jordi Sargatal - Lynx Editions - ISBN: 8487334156.
70   Sources: *Handbook of the Birds of the World* Vol 2 by Josep del Hoyo-Andrew Elliot-Jordi Sargatal - Lynx Editions - ISBN: 8487334156. See 'reproduction' below.

Symbols and Rituals

This bird is sedentary, and normally it remains in the same area where there are lakes and food. Occasionally, it moves some distances within a region. A pair has a hunting range of several square miles of forest, or a small area on rocky hills or cliffs, where hyraxes are numerous. The bird is often perched on a tall tree in early morning and evening hours looking for prey. It spends much time soaring over the forest, searching for monkeys feeding in the tree-tops.

Usually, it drops down onto the prey from a perch, flying silently. Most prey is killed on the ground with the exception the monkeys. It usually lifts up almost vertically carrying its victim, but sometimes simply tears them up on the ground.

It needs to kill a good-sized animal every 3 or 4 days and strikes its prey with powerful talons. The victim is paralyzed, squeezed to death, and then dismembered with its hooked bill. Any monkey caught off guard will be seized by the skull and killed instantly before being taken back to the nest for shared consumption.

Pairs are closely bonded and use the same nest year after year. They are very vocal, calling *"kwee-kwee-kwee"* during the quite spectacular breeding season displays[71].

This bird is a collaborative hunter and fighter. Pairs hunt to catch monkeys, using a clever technique whereby one bird flies above the canopy over a monkey troop, eliciting alarm calls from them which expose their position. The eagle's mate follows a short while later, killing from behind any monkey unfortunate enough to be caught out in the open. It usually strikes the skull or diaphragm of its prey with its talons in a downward motion, a movement powerful enough to kill instantly. The following foods have been recorded as their diet: Hyrax, tree hyrax, antelope, bushbuck, monkey and hare.

Traditional healers have reported seeing the African Crowned Hawk Eagle on an ants' nest, spreading its wings and breast feathers to allow the insects to climb over its body. It is believed the bird does this to agitate the ants into releasing formic acid, which kills parasites on the skin and feathers.

---

71   Sources: *Birds of Africa South of the Sahara* by Ian Sinclair and Peter Ryan - Princeton University Press Princeton and Oxford - ISBN: 0691118159

Flight: It has short and broad wings, and a long fan-shaped tail, giving it the ability to lift-off vertically when it is hunting in the closed forest. The male has more rapid wing beats than the female. They both soar very easily over the treetops.

Reproduction: Its nest is a bulky platform of sticks, lined with fresh green branches, located in a fork of a large tree. It is built by both parents. They use the same one every breeding season, adding some new materials. It may be a metre wide and several metres high and is situated at about 12 to 45 metres above the ground. They will usually breed from May to July. Both the male and female incubate the eggs for a period of up to 44 days. Only 1 chick is reared, due to Cainism (the strongest chick eats its siblings).

The Martial Eagle (Lith Apuk clans, Apuk Lith)

The Martial eagle is the largest in Africa. It is a large powerful bird comparable with the African Crowned Hawk Eagle. The adult's plumage consists of dark grey-brown colouration on the upper parts, head and upper chest, with slightly lighter edging to these feathers. The body underparts are white with blackish-brown spotting. The underwing coverts are brown, with pale flight feathers being streaked with black. The female is usually larger and more spotted than the male.

It lives in the open plains near rivers and lakes in South Sudan. This eagle may be seen when walking near Ayihow Lake. It is one of seasonal water lakes in Machuet, Tonj State. The immature ones are paler above, often whitish on the head and chest, and have less spotted underparts. It forms adult plumage in its seventh year. Martial eagles have a short erectile crest, which is often not prominent. It usually perches in a quite upright position, with its long wings completely covering the tail. The head and the breast are dark. They mark their region by circling around in flight prior to plunging on targets such as rabbits, hares, and squirrels.

The mating season is November through April in Senegal, January to June in South Sudan and Sudan, August to July in northeast Africa and almost any month in eastern Africa, though mostly in April to November. African Martial Eagles have been thought to have no distractive display flight characteristics, but they do engage in a subtle one with the males flying mildly around in circles. Rarely, the female joins him and the pair grasp talons with each other. The female will lay 2 eggs that require 45 days of incubation.

The African Fish Eagle

The head, as well as the chest of this eagle, is covered under white plumes. It is a monogamous bird. Females lay up to three eggs and incubate them for greater than 45 days. The chicks generally venture out when they develop feathers and can search for their own prey. They eat fish, small crocodiles and ducks. It is known as *kuei* in the Dinka language.

The Bateleur Eagle

This eagle has a black head and red soft skin on its cheeks. The tip of the beak is black. It is known as *acu lith* in the Apuk language. They feed upon sand-grouse, pigeons and small creatures. Females lay a single egg and nurture it for 42-43 days. It is a quiet bird but can mimic barks and many other sounds. *Acu* refers to black-chested *lith* with white feathers, brown, grey, red bill and legs.

Marchant and Higgins (1993) stated that the distinctive habitat for these eagles includes woodlands or open forests. The abundance of the species is due to hillsides everywhere there is an amalgam of wooded and open zones such as riparian woodlands, forest margins and wooded farmland. Ferguson-Lees and Christie (2001) wrote that these eagles habitually avoid large zones of dense forest, preferring to hunt in open woodland. They use trees as lookouts.

The Eagle Identity of the Apuk people

Eagles are worthy of great respect by virtue of their exceptional ability and power. The clans with eagle symbols are above all wild flesh eaters. *Lith* is the symbolic name given to differentiate how the Apuk clans are very distinctively unique and to easily identify them from among the Jieng Rek clans in South Sudan. The eagle and the clan divinity symbols have remained through times of sorrow, insecurity, and natural catastrophes. The eagle divinity emblem brought unity amongst the different clans and sub-clans. This inner strength turned the Apuk clans into one of the most powerful nation-states. It made them strong and independent of others in South Sudan in the savannah region.

Apuk Life

Homesteads were made from grass, mud, and wood with the addition of materials derived from wild and domestic animals. Both the cattle byres and cattle camps were built with the help of all the members of the clans. Each homestead comprised circular huts of wattle and blot with conical thatched roofs, and a cattle byre with a similar shape and materials.

A woman traditionally owns the hut. It has a low mud window screen for her fire and mud supports the cooking pots. A smooth shelter of stakes and millet stalks protects the woman of the household and the family *mac thok* from the sun and rain. It provides a platform upon which domestic utensils can be stored out of the way of dogs and children. In this hut, a woman feeds her family and waits for her turn (in a polygynous household) in preparing food. In the cattle byre is a cow dung fire, the *gol*, which is the centre for the men of the home when they are together in the homestead.

At the fireplace of women and the fireplace of men, the children of the Apuk clan receive their first practical lessons in the principles of Rek-Apuk social organization. The relationship between the several fireplaces of the elementary families and the central fireplace of the men and the cattle is the simple model of the different lineages which form segments of Apuk sub-clans, the *gol*, and the *wut* (cattle-byre and cattle camp and nation-state).

The items for the home or *mac-thok*, the *gol* or *wut* include:

APUK : A STATE IN WAITING

1. Clay pots for cooking, water-carrying, and brewing.
2. Gourds of various shapes and sizes. Some for serving the staple millet-porridge, some for storing oil and butter, and some for milking and drinking milk.
3. Plaited baskets in which grain is stored and plaited-grass winnowing-trays. Wicker fish-traps and baskets. And perhaps a wicker cradle for carrying babies on long journeys.
4. Simple nets for scooping fish out of the river when it is shallow.
5. Sleeping-skins of ox-hide or the skins of game, and large reed mats in which the Apuk clans when abroad roll themselves in to protect from the rain and sun.
6. Cattle-pegs and bells. Ropes of plaited grass and ox-collars, and ropes of plaited strips of hide.
7. A few hoes and simple adzes.
8. Head-rests and stools made by utilizing naturally forked branches of suitable shape, and hollowed parrying-sticks, which also serve as purses and pouches, made of ambatch.

There are also the personal trinkets of members of the household. The goatskin skirts of the married women, fishing and hunting spears of the men, and today, various small trade goods. Each household/homestead contains a mortar made from a hollowed tree-trunk, the *dong hat* set in the ground in which grain is pounded with a long pestle *lek hat* (which figures importantly in a myth). There are drums which are used by everybody but are privately owned by each family. An example is the Angandit-drum which was acquired by Malek Lungdit.

Millet porridge, groundnuts, sorghum porridges, milk and other sources are the basic foods, with roast or boiled meat and fish as they are available. These products of cattle are of significance. They do not in themselves provide a complete diet.

The form of wealth to be inherited is livestock. The equality of the Apuk clans blend with their general insecurity and subsistence. This insecurity is derived from exposure to a harsh environment.

Traditional Mourning
for a
High Priest Chief

Ceremonies of mourning as well as burial rituals and practices after the death of a priest chief are important and popular occasions among the Dinka Jieng clans in South Sudan.

Rituals include the slaughtering of the bulls and sheep with specific colours, the celebration style, the mourning period, and the cleansing ceremonies.

The 'after ritual mourning' commemoration is held immediately after the burial of a high priest or master of the fishing spear.

Introduction

Between 1991 and 1995, I was engaged in the bush by the civil war for the liberation of South Sudan, was wounded, and then assigned to the wounded soldier's program in the Kajokeji district, at the town of Kuku in Central Equatoria. I was to administer and provide psycho-educative programs for war soldiers affected by trauma, bereavement and depression caused by the fighting. Between 1996 and 2006, I initiated basic education programs in the Bahr El Ghazal Region, opened six primary schools and the Kurlueth Institute of Education (KIE).

Often during this time, the death of a spiritual clan member occurred. However, the family did not have a chance to gather for mourning rituals for burying their loved one in the traditional way due to the fear that they might be attacked or taken for labour by SPLA soldiers in the area.

Between 2010 and 2012, I was appointed the State Minister of Warrap State in South Sudan and was caught up by the death of the master of the fishing spear in the family. I presented a psychotherapy series on the bereavement, grief, and mourning for the family regarding the contemporary trends for burial rituals and mourning practices. Community leaders came to the ritual burial program to call on me and give input and opinions about these topics. This process was an eye-opener and I realised the importance of putting cultural practices into proper context.

Lonyway wut, was featured in these discussions of the ritual burial of a spear master. The ritual mourning and burial generated sufficient interest for me to learn more of the phenomenon. I believe that this practice is perceived differently by each person. People mourn their dead in many ways. This also motivated me to write in an in-depth manner regarding contemporary trends.

The Effects of Death

There is not much known about the personal experiences of the deceased. However, the powerful effects of that death become quite visible to those who are still alive. Dealing with loss of human life is a universal hardship for the ones who remain behind[72]. Among all forms of experiences that occur in any given culture, society or community, death seems to be the one that transcends them all[73]. Popular spiritual theories maintain that death is equated to a crisis

---

72 Bonnano, G. A., & Kaltman, S. (1999). Toward an integrative perspective on bereavement. *Psychological Bulletin*, 125(6), 760-776.

73 Parkes, C. M., Laungani, P. & Young, B. (Eds.) (1997). *Death and bereavement across cultures*. London: Routledge.

because it is a stressor that compels an individual to respond and adapt in many ways, or to try to formulate strategies to cope with its impact[74].

Usually, people attempt to find ways to avoid the various impacts of death. Sorrow is a normal, healthy condition and an expression of bereavement or loss. Often, when death occurs, people who are close to the deceased tend to respond to the emotions of sorrow using the same coping strategies that the person has used to deal with other powerful emotions in the past. This awareness is a basic human condition that gives significance to living. People come up with universal reactions to people who die and those people who lose loved ones. These are the things they go through in an attempt to find meaning in the event of inevitable death.

All societies have their own customs and beliefs surrounding it, and each culture has its own approaches to deal with loss. These may be more or less standardized but almost always involve a core of understandings, spiritual beliefs, rituals, expectations and customs[75]. In many cultures, the dead are venerated, and this is commonly known as ancestral worship. According to Mbiti (1975), death does not alter or end the life or personality of an individual in African culture, but only causes a change in the condition of the life. The deceased member of the family becomes an important extension of the living. Hence, they are called the "living dead" or ancestors[76].

Within an Apuk context, the dead are regarded as ancestors, while spiritual priests are agents for prosperity and continued descended lineage within families.

Mourning rituals have been a constant throughout history[77]. Different cultures perform death rituals depending on the meaning they

---

74 Frisch, N. C., & Frisch, L. E. (2006). *Psychiatric mental health nursing* (2ndedn.). Canada: Thomson Delmar Learning.
75 Parkes et al., (1997).
76 Mbiti, J. (1969). African religions and philosophy. London: Heinemann, Mbiti, J. S. (1975). *Introduction to African religion*. South Africa; Heinemann International Literature & Textbooks.
77 Rosenblatt, P. C., Walsh, R. P. & Jackson, D. A. (1976). *Grief and mourning in cross-cultural perspective*. New Haven, Connecticut: Human Relations Area Files Press.

have attached to death. Most have their bases in the traditional and religious belief systems of said people. In Apuk these rituals include, among others, cleansing, a funeral ceremony, keeping hair for years, cutting widower aprons, the wearing of mourning robes called *nai*, the slaughtering of a cow, the wearing of mourning clothes in towns, and prohibition of the mourners to play drums or to participate in social activities for a stipulated period.

It is generally believed that the funeral rites, which are the most common rituals, are a source of valuable support to the society and to those who have been bereaved. This serves as a public acknowledgement that a death has occurred. A ritual is a specific behaviour or activity that gives symbolic expression to certain feelings or thoughts of groups and individuals[78]. Rituals represent a symbolic affirmation of values by means of culturally standardized utterances and actions. From this perspective, rituals seem to perform specific functions in a given society or culture[79]. Apuk women would wear mourning robes and aprons cut both behind and in front. Everyone wore these formally in a typical funeral.

Every community has prescribed rituals that can help families to resolve their sorrow. The specifics of sorrow and rituals can also be unique from one family to another even in the same community. This is due to the influences of religious beliefs, education, and wealth status, among others. Rituals serve particular functions, but primarily they help the families to accept the reality of loss, to express the feelings connected to loss, and to relieve sorrow.

While they are perceived as celebrations, the most important aspects of these ceremonies are connected to comforting and supporting the bereaved and helping them to cope with the effect of their loss. If not undertaken it hurts the bereaved community, the descendants, and delays the chances of recovery from grief. The after-burial shrine ceremony can be an effective coping mechanism

---

78 Radzilani, M. S. (2010). *Discourse analysis on performance of bereavement rituals in a Tshivenda-Speaking community: An African Christian and traditional African perspectives*, (Unpublished Thesis).

79 Taylor, R. B. (1980). *Cultural Ways*. Boston: Allyn & Bacon.

Traditional Mourning for a High Priest Chief

because of the way it is conducted. My experiences of this and the meaning attached to it might serve as guiding principles for interested parties to explore the psychological needs of the bereaved in the Apuk communities.

According to Mbiti, death to Africans is not an event which just occurs, is handled and then forgotten. When one dies, there is a series of events which usually takes place. There is a period of at least one week of mourning before the actual funeral, then the feasting and gatherings associated with it. Evening prayers may also be conducted, depending on specific family traditions. Family members usually prepare food for friends and neighbours and inform visiting mourners of the cause of death.

Rituals play a healing role in bringing back healthy status to the bereaved members. They also enhance the expression and containment of strong emotions for family members and friends of the deceased. The repetitive and prescriptive nature of rituals usually ease the feelings of anxiety in that they provide structure and order in times of chaos and disorder. Rituals may reaffirm ethnic, religious and divinity identity. They also provide the opportunity for public displays of sorrow.

They are treated with great respect as they are believed to have a special relationship with the living, raw life spirit, the body spirit, and the world spirit. Proper rites and ceremonies performed following the death of a priest-chief in the community reflect this belief. A deviation from tradition might be taken as a sign of disrespect towards the ancestors and spirits. Bad luck could befall a clan of spiritual power, or a lineage family member who does not adhere to the stipulated traditional practices.

In traditional African cultures, funerals and bereavement rituals help in the purification of the mourners who are believed to be polluted from contact with the dead. Community members participate in ceremonies considered to be essential for the removal of a contaminated spirit and to allow the mourners to re-enter the community and return to the process of living. In addition to common rituals, many traditional African religions observe pre-burial and post-burial purification rituals[80]. This is due to the belief that death hovers over them like a shade until such a time that they undergo a purification rite. Failure to cleanse or purify as required by tradition is believed to bring bad luck, misfortune, or evil to the family and/or people close to the deceased. Rituals are believed to offer comfort and relief. Many writers like Modipa said that: "Certain socio-cultural rituals bring a sense of relief and wellbeing into communities. Such rituals may act as a psychological means of adjustment in the face of misfortune"[81].

Universally, in native Apuk religions, remedial sorrow psychotherapy is shepherded in a communal location. Soon after a death had been announced, mourners converge in the homestead of the deceased. There, neighbours, relatives, spiritual leaders and community members gather for prayers in the evenings preceding the day of the funeral. In these gatherings, there are usually traditional hymns, war songs, ritual prayers, animal sacrifices, as well as donations for supplication from the deceased spiritual leader after reaching the world of spirits or ancestry spirits.

People assist in different ways to make life easier and to comfort the family of the deceased. It is common and mutual for the sorrowing process that involves the entire community. Family members, close relatives and friends are more intimately involved due to the special relationships they had with the deceased. This is highlighted in the social, economic and political changes that have evolved the face of death rituals in contemporary communities and societies.

Consequentially, many rituals appear to have diminished in Apuk contemporary culture. There seem to be different trends emerging. Moreover, the political situation in South Sudan in the past century seems to have contributed to the way in which funerals are characterized. The political unrest of the Old Sudan pre-democratic era,

---

[80] Selepe, J. C., & Edwards, S. D. (2008). Grief counselling in African indigenous churches: a case of the Zion Apostolic Church in Venda. Indilinga- *African Journal of Indigenous Knowledge Systems*, 7(1), 1-6.

[81] Ngonyama ka Sigogo, T., & Modipa O. T. (2004). Critical reflections on community psychology in South Africa. In K. Ratele, N. Duncan, D. Hook, N. Mkhize, P. Kiguwa, & A. Collins (Eds.). *Self, Community & Psychology* (316-334), Cape Town: UCT press.

the protraction of civil wars, and the impact and damages of the post-democratic years have claimed untold thousands of lives.

In the past, funerals were initially peaceful and dignified. That changed when people started reacting against Government interference. The effect was that funerals for the victims of political unrest became political platforms and confrontations between angry communities and law enforcement agents. Funerals were polarized and became political theatre and entertainment. This sometimes left no platform at all for the bereaved families to mourn their dead. Funerals for Apuk families have become such a common feature in recent years that people tend to spend most weekends at burials.

A recent trend observed is the adoption of new rituals of mourning. Apuk clan funerals which were once solemn and sad occasions have been reinvented as stylishly riotous celebrations, replete with alcohol among the South Sudanese elite.

The celebration is called *lonyway wut* and is conducted after three months of the burial of a high priest or master of the spear. *Lonyway wut* means, releasing cattle out in the morning hours, starting from 5 am.

When they returned to the camps or byres young people started staving bulls along the way in a celebration believed to wash away the evil contamination on herds upon the death of a spiritual leader. On such occasions, girls and young men decorate themselves, and newly acquired dresses have become overly decorous, with girls in very colourful, tight skirts and young men in the newest fashions.

Family Mourning Rituals and Practices

Apuk mourning rituals reflect their beliefs and attitudes towards death. They start proceedings soon after the family member has been confirmed as dead. As mentioned above, when a death is announced in Apuk, the family is immediately considered as polluted, *pol guop*, bewitched, or cursed by the spirits offended. This implies a negative shadow, which also means that the family is thrown into a state of disequilibrium. The Parum consider a family death to have contaminated the relatives of the deceased. The terminology "pollution" in the context of the death of a family member is also used to refer to this state of contamination. In Apuk culture, death is considered as a highly intensified form of this. The family of the deceased are contaminated and anyone who touches the corpses will also be considered as such.

The period preceding the burial is to be accompanied by certain rituals that must be performed. These include the smearing of windows with ash to reflect a gloomy atmosphere. Turning pictures on the wall from sight and switching off radios and television sets adds to the gloom. The rationale behind all these efforts is to demonstrate openly the intensity of their deep sorrow and remorse and to symbolize death to the whole community, group, or clan.

In the Parum clan, it is also believed that once a death strikes in a family, the family members have been symbolically devastated by an evil spirit and need to be cleansed or purified. This evil spirit infecting the survivors symbolizes their bereavement. Subsequently, the survivors could not participate in the normal life of the community until they have been purified or cleansed through rituals.

A very long period of mourning is usually taken by the family of a deceased member of the Parum clan with spiritual powers. The amount of time taken is particular to each family and states what acceptable behaviours are and are not until the stipulated end of mourning.

As an example, there is the death of the master of the fishing spear, Deng Malek (March 12, 2012), priest chief of the Parum clan, highlighted the significant perceptions, meanings and feelings about the 'burial' and 'after burial' shrine-raising ceremonies. I have included a number of photographs of the ceremonies at the end of the book.

Their traditions governed the performances and activities that were sanctified in the Apuk community throughout the mourning period. There were rituals such as honouring the bulls with songs for two days. Speaking invocations each day in the morning and

Traditional Mourning for a High Priest Chief

evening. Losing one's temper. Talking loudly or laughing. All these things were to be conducted in moderation. Then, the new master of the fishing spear, who is a senior member of the bereaved family, slit the throats of the bulls at a time of day stipulated by tradition. Deng Malek's relatives were all there to join together with the deceased's father's and maternal uncle's families (*bi pan e wun kek panerden e man rot mat e ben*) and to mourn for their priest chief.

The role of a son of the high priest chief who died is to be designated as the chief mourner. The mourning period begins with the chief mourner occupying a sacred mourning stand erected for the purpose. He is usually crowned with the black feathers of an ostrich (called *Ajom nok wut*) and is the only one allowed to wear them for the burial period involving up to three days of funeral rites. The chief mourner stands close to the burial site where the grave is being dug, or the nearby traditional holy shrine temple site. Traditional rituals, sacrificial bulls, libations, invocations, mediation prayers, hymns, war songs etc. are performed from the stand.

A symbolic crown of spiritual leadership is worn to symbolize continuation of the lineage descending from the clans of spiritual powers. This crown, *ajom* or *ajom-nhom* is a traditionally hand-made headdress designed by utilizing natural feathers of suitable shape, and a hollowed oval helmet, which also serves as a hat, or *akup* plaited from the leaves of the coconut tree.

When the grave is dug, they kill a bull, take its hide, and cut it into strips. When the corpse of the deceased been lowered into the hole, next to it they put in live sheep tethered to pegs with a thong. They then make a platform on top of the corpse and sheep with timber, taking care all is level. Then they tie the timber together with the hide cut into strips.

After, they sing hymns, and invocation songs (*cam yai e bany bith*). When the singing is finished, they cover over the top of the hole to the level of the ground and bring his belongings to the grave.

Following this, they took cattle dung and mixed it with waste from the intestines and the stomach of the bull that had been killed for the clan spirits. They covered the top of the grave with this and burnt it so the smoke would purify the evil spirit that had polluted the family. The meat of the bull that was killed was cooked by the burning dung. Its steam was fanned around so that people could inhale it to purify all those who were near the grave. They took no pieces of meat away. Community members continued to pour in with their bulls as donations and embarked in all kinds of activities during the daytime for supplication. Invocations were conducted during the next three nights. Every day they made their feast, *a cam yai e bany bith*.

The mourners slept at the burial site together with all the children and wives of the deceased master. His friends spent night and day mourning at the Malou Cattle Camp, an area designated for holy tombs and shrines. They used them to pray to clan-divinities for the traditional masters of the fishing spear. Everyone believed in this mythology. When the grave sunk in, they made a shrine. People may then say: "The master of the fishing spear has died". More often, they will say: "The master has been taken into the earth." or "It is very good.". Nobody will say: "Alas, he is dead!"

Mourners then placed bags of clothes, mattresses, mosquito nets and poles, shoes, cooking pots, clubs, a walking stick, and sacred spears on the grave.

Deng inherited spears which were inherited by his forefathers. Those brought to the grave include:

- The Unknown Sacred Spear with the round shape.
- The Spear made by Aguelet Agei with the blade.

Tools were put on top of the grave. The spears were put on those. On the father's and on the grandfather's tombs as a symbol of Parum, all the belongings of the deceased, the Unknown Sacred Spear, spears of the grandfather, spears of the father, spirit water, milk, cow butter, *atac* or *atany*. A war shield, made from the hide of a bull of the clan divinity which had been killed in the past, was placed on the top of the bed. It was a war shield which had long been kept in the byre, and which the people had anointed with butter every spring and autumn during the 'dividing months'.

Traditional Mourning for a High Priest Chief

The widow wore a mourning apron made from goat or sheep hides, deliberately cut in half, and specifically designed for mourning in times past. Regarding the death of a spiritual master such as Deng Malek, the children, widowers, relatives and the whole community of the deceased will not show any sign of mourning their dead one but must also demonstrate a mode of celebrating their priest chief.

The fundamental principle, clear in all accounts, is that masters of the fishing spear must or should not be considered to enter upon physical death in the same way as ordinary clansmen. Their deaths are to be or appear deliberate, and they are to be a form of public celebration.

The ceremonies described in no way prevent the ultimate recognition of aging and physical death of those for whom they are performed. This death is recognized, but it is the experience of it for the survivors which is deliberately modified by the performance of these ceremonies. It is clear that this is the Dinka's intention in performing the rites. They believe that they have honoured their masters of the fishing spear by burying them with ceremonies, celebrations and rituals. The expressions used for the deaths of masters of the fishing spear are rewordings for an event which is fully admitted. In my experience, the word death is rarely used.

Rewordings replace the uncontrolled and passive connotations of the ordinary verb for 'to die' by expressions suggesting a positive act. Similarly, (though this point is not specifically made in any of the accounts) when we hear that the people 'bury their master of the fishing-spear' it is as an alternative to 'letting him die[82]'. In other words, the deliberately contrived words for death, though recognized as death, enables them to avoid admitting in this case, the unthinkable death which is the lot of all ordinary men and beasts. As we see in most of the accounts given, their intention is not primarily to undertake the special ceremonies for the priest chief's sake, but for that of the community at large.

---

82 Dinka: "Burial Alive: The Master of the Fishing-Spear," from Godfrey Lienhardt, http://www.worldcat.org/oclc/181857 Oxford: Oxford University Press, 1961, pp. 300-303, 313-314; quotations in introductory passage from 304, 309.

APUK : A STATE IN WAITING

Gifts and Rituals

The 'gathering of death' rituals have been a traditional practice in most community burial places for the Dinka Apuk. These are carefully adhered to because of the value attached.

People gather at mourning rituals and observe the practice of burial donations. This happens in the beginning when the community joins in with the family mourners. The message of the death of a family member is usually spread by word of mouth as well as by drums. It reaches the general population as quickly as possible. The first stage of mourning usually begins when relatives and friends surround the widow immediately after the death of her husband. When members of the community come to "inquire" about what happened to the family it is known as 'neck breaking', or 'family has broken neck', or 'person is destroyed', *ran aci riak*, or "Deng Malek *aci riak or ran aci nyin liu*". People are known to commit suicide when they hear of the death of their loved ones among the Apuk clans. People rush home as soon as possible to console the bereaved families and to prevent such incidents of recklessness.

In the community, the period of mourning continues for at least a year after the burial or for a traditionally stipulated timeframe. During that time, the widow and other bereaved members stay at home and are not allowed any social contact with ordinary people. They do not participate in social activities or public gatherings like dancing as they are believed to be contaminated by the death of the loved one. The widow may choose to mourn for two or three years and cannot have contact with a man during the mourning period. The end of mourning for a priest chief is usually marked by a ritual or a ceremony where the community takes part in a celebration for raising a shrine and slaughtering bulls. This symbolically restores normal life back to society.

Today, there is usually a mixture of religious and traditional practices in the communities regarding the way they celebrate the occurrence of death.

When a death is announced, the spiritual leaders as well as other leaders, neighbours, and the community at large, flock to the family where tragedy has struck to verify the news and assure the bereaved of their support. The involvement of these various stakeholders ensures holistic support. Community members provide labour such as gathering water and firewood, cooking and comporting, assisting with gathering grains, and other errands. Meanwhile, the spiritual leaders provide psycho-spiritual support. This all happens using varying forms of tradition, culture, social and religious practices including the group's interpretation of its supportive gathering.

These are the practices of community mourning among the Parum clan and the recorded performance of community rituals in the face of a death of a loved one in the Apuk homeland. Burials are among the most important and visible observances in cultural life.

Burial Ceremonies

Many traditions dispose of their dead with ritual ceremonies such as burial in order to separate the dead from the living. The Apuk clan traditions are not an exception. There are usually several ritual ceremonies accompanying the burial of priest chiefs. These vary according to ethnicity, clan, and kinship and belief system.

In traditional Apuk clans, as soon as the person is dead, the body is prepared by the immediate family mourner helped by other married women. Burial usually takes place on the day after death to avoid decomposition and the spread of disease. There were no mortuaries in the countryside in the past. The corpse was then covered with the hides of bulls. In present times it is taken to the mortuary where it will stay for a few days while the family is busy preparing for the burial.

On the eve of the burial, the immediate members of the deceased family sleep next to the grave and pray from the bottom of their hearts to appeal to the spirits, ancestors, *yath, agoloong* at this overnight wake.

The gathering of the night wake is enacted to appeal to the divinity spirit and allow the community members to say their last goodbyes. They even testify about the deceased by saying in prayers what the deceased person did in life. Ritual killing in the form of slaughtering a sheep or bull also takes place on this night. This will be for the provision of a blood sacrifice for the spirit and the ancestral spirits attending the burial, and the 'in the world' spirits. The hide of the bull is usually used to tie the wooden branches on top of the corpse and sheep for burial since there were no coffins in the past.

Burials in Apuk are heavily influenced by spiritual and traditional practices. Many such rituals are still observed and many of them are evident in burial services. As an example, a Padiangbaar clansman at the breaking of dawn on the day of the burial provides a ritual compensation gift. As soon as the corpse is carried out of the house, traditional praise-making is done by a close elderly relative. This eulogy serves as a means of honouring the deceased and serves also for psychological relief. Tribute or praise is supposed to evoke a response from the bereaved to sing for a priest chief as it is believed that songs of warfare and spirituality may relieve them and is considered therapeutic. Ceremonial songs continue at the gravesite and during the burial where the bereaved sit at one side of the grave and take part.

The spiritual high priest chiefs, war leaders, and community members usually participate in the burial process. The people attending the mourning rituals and burial ceremonies will be expected to sing songs and hymns.

There are symbols used to commemorate loss and there is complete silence at the home of the deceased. The lighting of candles, parties and celebrations are normally prohibited as a sign of respect for the deceased family member. The bereaved would also continue to engage in cleansing rituals for purification with special ritual sacrifices using animals during the mourning period until death 'fades' away. This is contrary to the Western cultures where it is presumed that life will continue after the burial, and people are encouraged to get on with their normal lives.

Apuk clans have traditionally used their homesteads and cattle camps as a final resting place for their dead. As an example, the master of the fishing spear, Deng Malek, is buried in the centre of the

Traditional Mourning for a High Priest Chief

Malou Cattle Camp. This was done because his Grandfather Agei Aguelet Agei, his father Malek Agei, and Paramount Chief Uncle Agei Malek Agei are buried there.

This explains the concept of identification with a historical place. There is often an attachment to these spots and has become woven into the communal identity. Every person has a knowledge of their historical past that consists of places, spaces and their properties which serve instrumentally in the satisfaction of one's biological, psychological, social and cultural needs. They also serve as part of the socialization process during which self-identity is developed. Having an Apuk homeland captures this identity effectively.

I contend that to die in a culture of historical belief is like going back home where you belong. Hence the use of words *ta ci ran thou, ka la ten werkan dit ci thou theer*. In Apuk clan thinking, this implies that when a person dies he or she joins their ancestors who died before and are in the world of spirits. As such, one needs a proper burial where there will be all the elements of respect and dignity. From the most ordinary person to the most highly respected Parum clan members, each has been buried either at home at the middle of their family's huts under the shrine or at the cattle camp just like Deng Malek.

Recently, people from the Apuk clans living in towns or in South Sudan's urban environments, have been abandoning the practices of burying their dead in their homesteads due to political and other reasons. Technological advancement and a shortage of burial spaces in metropolitan areas have contributed to popular practices such as burying in graveyards etc. Other forms of disposing of the dead are emerging such as cremation. Some consider this progress, and some do not.

After the burial of a priest chief, people go together as a group to mourn with the family members. Then there is a celebration or ceremony at the burial place, in a cattle camp, or the home of the deceased. The people bring gifts such as bulls, or sheep to attend to the needs of the burial rituals and ceremonies. In some cases, they can also end up being too aggressive while displaying war games.

These often lead to incidences involving injuries or even death.

A mixture of noise, war songs, and drumbeats characterizes these ceremonies. Many first-time outsiders are shocked at what happens, as it is vastly different from their own customs.

There is an overwhelming acceptance among the community that celebration can replicate spiritual blessing, spirit forgiveness and harmony in mourning rituals. They are more about the people remaining behind rather than for the deceased. Thusly, people go there to give gifts and celebrate. The burial is very painful for the bereaved. This is the reason it is followed immediately by a celebration. In many cultures, this might be controversial. The general feeling among newcomers is that people who attend burials should not celebrate. However, some of them felt that it was fine to celebrate the life of someone that had just gone.

How the Young and Old View Burials

Often, older people feel that death of high priest-chief is a punishment from the *Jak*, *Yath*, ancestry spirits and *Agoloong*. They pray and make ritual sacrifices for the death of their leader and appeal to the divinity and spirits to forgive them for their sins and to take their offer that will be conveyed by the spirit of the dead which is joining them in the spirit world. They consider the death of a priest chief as a disgrace to the family clan, culture and tradition and are hurt by what they see occurring to this family of spiritual powers. Elders believe that celebrations after the death and burial of priest chief are a proper way to offer spirits gifts in sacrifices to support the spirit of the dead person and to support the ancestry spirit for the return blessing.

However, they know that it is also a form of socializing because people may attend these celebrations even when they did not attend the burial. Young people who had not seen one another for a very long time meet to catch up and new friendships or associations are formed. They may even end up marrying. Some felt that the priest chief celebration is also enacted since relatives live far apart and a

Traditional Mourning for a High Priest Chief

burial is a good chance to see each other.

The after-burial shrine ceremony can be an effective coping strategy because of the nature of the way it is conducted, and types of donations collected for ceremonies. The experiences of this writer regarding it and the meaning attached might serve as guiding principles for interested researchers to explore regarding the psychological needs of the bereaved in the Apuk communities.

Politics and History

The Dinka were one of the Nilotic ethnic groups of the Republic of South Sudan. There is very little known about the background and historical development of Dinka Apuk clans as an offshoot of the semi-nomadic Nilotics. Their history is one of struggle. That struggle may be moral. It may be physical. It may be both. No change, great or small, comes without demand and the voice of the people speaking as one. The demand for freedom, dignity, political social equality and social justice has echoed throughout the savannah region and beyond the clans of the Apuk of Rek Dinka.

The Apuk historical development era derived from Egyptian through Sudanese sources, which described the land downstream on the Nile as "miserable". It is believed that the Dinka or Jieng, from where the Apuk clans branched out, was part of ancient Egypt jointly with Sudan. Therefore, South Sudan is considered the most likely location of the land known to the ancient Egyptians as "God's Land"[83].

Egyptian excursions proceeded from the savannah land to the interior to the swamplands. This marked the limit of penetration into the southern Apuk land mass from the river shores. It was inhabited by the "fish eaters" living in scattered caves in the narrow savannah lands. Beyond them, lived the "wild flesh eaters" and "calf eaters". Each nationality of clans was governed by its chief[84]. This

---

83 Encyclopedia Britannica, "Sudan".
84 "The Island of Meroe", UNESCO World Heritage, Retrieved 2012-09-06.

Politics and History

area extended over swampy wetlands to the east of Apuk. However, that form of clan began to fade away. It was shattered by war and they passed their rule and domination over to the Apuk.

Since independence, the development of the Apuk has been beset by inter-ethnic/clan violence and wars of conquest for the land.

Whether we go back a few centuries or even a few of decades, the Apuk clans were not united but were independent and warring. Many studies have defined a clan as a tribe, and tribe as a clan of independent states loosely united for social security. I feel that each clan has its own unique composition.

The subjugation of weaker clans was a significant issue. The clans of the Apuk had a long list of bloody civil wars. They were governed with the attitude of "the strongest have it all and the weakest nothing". Peace between neighbouring clans regarding water and grazing rights seemed an unattainable goal.

Apuk villages today are backward with the poorest health and education services, and lowest standards of living in the region. They have endured years of conflicts, enslavement, and forceful conscription of young clansmen sent to fight in the World Wars of the last century.

The wars of conquest brought Arabic and English languages into their lives. Those languages are spoken only by the elite and are the official languages used in offices in the various towns. The Dinka Rek clan language is used by the general public to this day. The tradition of oral literature remains to some degree.

Our predecessors confronted external threats dating back many centuries. This includes the Deity, descendants, Atany and Rum Ateny, who neutralized Bantustan predators, stock stealing nomads, and salvaged the lives of the people in the historical past. Bantustan nomads had massacred, abducted, tortured and terrified the Pabuor, Patiir, Padiangbaar and even the Parum clan and forced the people into hiding. Rum began his dynasty reign by instigating a horrific war that forced Bantustans to negotiate a peaceful end to their insurgencies. The Apuk emerged as the dominant regional power.

APUK : A STATE IN WAITING

The Turkish Regime in Apuk

The Turkish empire annexed portions of the Nilotic peoples and interfered in their dynastic sphere of influence. Over the years however, trade developed. The caravans of the Arab merchants carried grains, ointments, charms, jewels, necklaces, earrings, costume, jewellery, ornaments, bits and knick-knacks to the Machar Rek River. They returned with ivory, hides, jewellery, and arrowheads for shipment downriver. These Arab merchants valued gold, ivory and the slaves they captured from clans living along the river and lake banks in the Nile valley.

There was a war of heroic confrontation between the Apuk and the Turkish regime near the end of the 18th century. The Arab slave merchants were defeated and driven out of Jak and the slave trade camps. This was accomplished in spite of the death of a martyr/hero who sustained his fatal gunshot wounds on the battlefield. The pro-Turkish forces had been fighting their way inland to reach new markets and tap into fresh sources of natural resources. However, they were slowed and weakened by the pestilent swamps of the Sudd which expanded deep into the savannah forests and muddy valleys.

It is somewhat anachronistic, to refer to the diffuse concept known as a dynasty along the lakes, and rivers. However, it was a dynasty as it had a dominating, significant influence over its neighbours in every direction. Even after its time, the legacy of clan divinity culture and dual control of war leader and master of the fishing spear remained important.

This dynasty controlled the Apuk homeland in the southwest of Rek. It comprised much of the Toch swamp wetlands portioned to cattle herders in the extreme east, the Maluil Tarweng clans of the southeast along the Wanhalel river, and the Angol clans of the extreme east. It also managed the clans of central Apuk, the Malony clans of the southwest, the Aliai clans of the central-northeast and the Machuet clans of the "Oldest Motherland" in the northern frontiers. This is to where Apuk people expanded!

Politics and History

Resistance to foreign conquest was an ongoing affair. Enemies constantly tried to put their greedy hands on the Motherland. The Apuk survived these assaults on its sovereignty in a series of desperate battles against the stronger Anglo-Egyptian Sudan forces and Arab slave merchants attempting to invade, conquer, colonize and control them.

The War Between Anglo-Egyptian Sudan and the Clans

This war broke out during the early part of the last century. It expanded into the southwestern Apuk Rek Dinka clans in the Tonj District.

During Colonial rule in the Tonj District, fighting went on between slavers and British patrols. The slavers were attacking clans in the chiefdom, which led to the death of master of the fishing spear Malek and more than 200 people. Over 30 clansmen and women were reportedly kidnapped and enslaved in the battles, including family members with supernatural spiritual powers. Although the Tonj District was created to further the policies of Colonial rule, they were unable to establish effective control over the area.

Malek Rum Wol was the first traditional chief and spiritual leader to cooperate with the Government. When Agei ascended to the throne to replace him, he consolidated his leadership through spirituality and political influence. He also organized a powerful military foundation and introduced modern weaponry and tactics to match the adversaries he faced. He led attacks of retribution, fought major battles and gained a heroic victory that cemented the dynasty even though over 400 lives were lost.

Chief Agei mobilized forces that defeated the ineffective representatives of the Anglo-Egyptian Government and overran the Jak Patrol Base in the middle of Machuet Apuk. The Colonial Governor sent troops northwards to the Jak base in an attempt to regain units lost and heavily routed the Apuk. However, Agei's forces broke through later and retook the region.

With the victory at the battle of Thon Gai Base between Jak-Rom Base, Alach Miok Village and Akon-Agiu Village in hand, and the British colonial patrol contained between the Machar-Arol Village connected to Git Village in the Maluil Apuk section and Akuwei village way to Paduer village in the Machuet Apuk Section, Chuei Ajai Base was left for the taking. Jak Rom Base was commonly known as Jak-Gathering Center. But no order to attack was given by the Chief Malek Agei Malek Rum at the military headquarters in Jak-Rom Base of Apuk Clans Chiefdom. It appeared that he was wiser than the British had given him credit for. Realizing that the Government would bring all their forces to bear on chiefdom if attacked, he instead sought to restore the peace.

Agei adopted modern methods of rule and exerted tremendous influence in the region. He committed resources to protect the minority clans from adversaries. He made peace along the borders in every direction. Agei was a most feared leader, fighter and a respected spiritual master. He and 51 others were killed while fighting government troops. Agei died a heroic death while protecting the lives of his people.

The first in line descendant was Aguelet Agei. His mother was the first wife Athulueth Deng Thou of the Padiangbaar clan. However, Aguelet was a great fighter and refused the throne in order to lead the fight for revenge. He instead nominated his younger step-brother, Malek Agei from the second wife, Ajok Mathiang to replace their father.

Chief Malek ascended to the throne while still a young man. Because he trusted his elder brother's abilities, Malek dispatched him to organize the fighters that defeated and ejected the Arab slave merchants from the interior. Unlike his father, Aguelet Agei survived the wounds he sustained in the fighting.

According to accounts, Chief Malek and his deputy Ayuel Baak were kidnapped and taken to the Chuei Ajay detention centre by a government patrol in 1941 and were brutally murdered there. It seems this was because the two leaders opposed any forceful conscription of young men to be trained and taken to fight in World War II.

Aguelet Agei continued fighting and appointed another named Agei Malek to the throne. He was the son of his stepbrother Malek Agei Malek Rum (murdered with Ayuel Bak). Agei ascended to the throne at a very young age. This chief Agei became an influential political figure who emerged as a modern leader.

He managed to diminish government interference until he retired of old age. He then transferred the clan throne to Mathok Malek, his half-brother from the last wife Ajak Ayom Arou.

Chief Mathok Malek Agei Malek Rum died on the throne in December 1959. His elder son, Malek Mathok ascended to the chieftaincy in January 1960 and reigned as clan chief until 1976. At this point, there was a tragic crumbling of the Apuk nation. This was the result of political and social upheaval and betrayals that divided the state.

A new chieftaincy was carved out of the Malony, Tarweng, Angol and Manging clans. It was combined under the newly appointed Chief Akot Makuach of the Pabuor Clan. He was descended from the Bol Chiirial clan. This was the first time this had happened since Rum Wenkook or son-cave unchained clans from Bantustan attackers many centuries ago.

In the very early 1920s, the Colonial Government passed the Closed Districts Ordinances. This permitted Christian missionaries go into the Southwest. Thereby the Apuk were converted.

Clan Divinity and Political Changes

Little is recorded about the tradition that the clan divinity and political authority systems began with clan the Pabuor and the priest Bol Mel. They grew to the Patiir clan of Aguet Lokbaithok, and the Padiangbaar clan of Bek Amuuk. It was then followed by the Parum clan of Rum, master of the fishing spear (divine priest chief, *beny bith kec apeei*).

In the southwestern Rek region, clan divinity, social, political and military mastery was established. The clans, clansmen, officials, priests, merchants and artisans were settled in new homesteads. The Jaang language became widely used in everyday activities. Wealthy clansmen and priests with superior spiritual powers took to worshipping gods and built temples, holy shrines and tombs for them. They remained the official centres of worship for clan divinities until foreign religions such as Christianity entered the arena. Influential clans with spiritual powers like Parum did not decline in power or succumb to Christian domination. Rather, the traditional priests regarded themselves as central social, political and military authorities and believed themselves as idols of culture and religion for the clans concerned.

Christian missionaries came and converted some members of the clans. They observed them practising their traditions and had their traditional literature documented between the 18th and 19th centuries. The spiritual masters appear to be recorded between 19th and 20th century AD.

Wunriir Villages and Cattle Camps

Wunriir became a dominant centre in the middle ages. Much later, its mud wall villages were extensively expanded into multiple mud-wall villages, cattle byres and cattle camps. Further expansion took in hunting forests from northern Machuet to the western Malony of lake region. It included the rivers and swamplands in eastern Apuk, and extended into the southeastern wetlands of Madol Island, Aguudi Island, Diang, Ju, Madhol and Lietnhom. There, clansmen in armour rode barefoot and the leaders were fed fish, wild meat and cow's milk in reclining cow dung chairs.

Real life in ancient Wunriir though, was quite a bit less glamorous. In a time before modern sanitation and modesty, getting through an average day was a difficult disgusting task, and far more than one could ever imagine. There were people who made their living just from fish, wild foods and/or hunting.

Politics and History

When a succeeding clan leader failed to assert full control, individual members organized forces from several clans and sacked Lwalla bases, compelling them to move further east and southwards, and pushed Lwalla away across to the western river bank of the multiple waterfall sources in Bantustan border of Tombura State of Western Equatoria. This waterfall river source is commonly referred to as" Toch bot yi cin" in Dinka Rek Language or "Toch in Licking Hands" because there are different types of foods in wildlife games there. Toch-Bot-Yi Cin will be explained later. They proceeded to areas occupied from Malony in the southwest bordering Luo (Jurchol) to Maluach in the west and all the way to Akon Agiu and Ahech-Loch in Machuet on the Apuk borders of the northern frontiers.

A Rum descendant took over as supreme master of the fishing spear and war leader through the use of the deity spirits present in all. He is the ruler of all the spirits and his duty is to give life as the holder of life itself. He was the master of the fishing spear, and the guardian of the shrines of ancestors, holy tombs, and Ateny Wundior.

During the time Rum was controlling the Apuk Juwiir, the Chiir villages at Maluach in the Machuet homesteads extended over a territory stretching from the upper streams in the southeast of Madhol to the river Wanhalel, to Tarweng in the south. Rum influenced the succession system and moved from the old Wunriir villages to the new base in Jak. There he established the dynasty which persisted along a lineage of the powerful clan divinities with dual power.

Pabuor descendants retained their clan priesthood. They were the guardians of the clan shrines at Wunriir, Adoldit and Madhol. Parum clan descendants continued to be the divine priests, and the guardians of the holy shrines of ancestors, and grandparent tombs at Wun-Ngap and Lietnhom, the MadolAliaiRiver and the Jak Holy Shrine. They raised spirituality to record the accomplishments of their reigns and erected temples at Jak centre to contain their mausoleums. These objects and the ruins of the fortifications, and temples at Jak, Madhol, Ju, Wun-ngap, Machar, the Holy River of Madol Aliain Apuk, Panakdit and the Jak holy shrines attest to a centralized system that employed skills and commanded the labour of a large workforce.

The succession system by necessity favoured the clansman of superior priestly heredity who was a heroic family member and was deemed most worthy. He often became the leader and was deemed to possess the divine spiritual powers to give life, to protect life, and to love the people he guided in war. The role of the master of fishing spear and guardian in the selection process was crucial to a smooth succession. Priority was always placed on distinguished military experience.

How Change has Affected the Clans

In addition to the work of post-independent writers and their revisionism, what can be observed is much of it does align with a shift in theories. They represent all conflicting opinions as being false, whether it be on religion, spirituality, the perpetual conflict between religion and secular governance, the impulse of imposition, the denial of action, the continuous over-generalizations, and the lack of trace studies.

The winners from the conquest era even today are still dominant. The history of South Sudan by South Sudanese people still has this 'side-line versus the middle' attitude which justifies itself by binary opposition and negation, rather than affirmation.

I have an obligation to write about the overlapping history of the Apuk clans and the Jieng-Dinka clans within the overall history of South Sudan. The wish is to enlighten readers regarding this subject of which is very little is understood. To bring into the light those many people who endeavoured to twist the identity, culture and custom of our diverse ethnic clans and their way of life in South Sudan.

The history of South Sudan overlaps history of Apuk clans. The term "South Sudan" is only used gain contemporary approval of the histories regarding people who today are victimized because of their birth origins. Historically there was no South Sudan 'identity'. It is a country whose borders were 'drawn' by others. The history and politics of "South Sudan" is a contemporary thesis of an identity that is barely a few years old.

When the history of the Arabs was in the making, the history of Azande clans or Jieng-Dinka clans was 100% on the line. When the history of the Christians and Muslims was in the making, the history of the clan divinities was on the line. Therefore, the history of Sudan and of South Sudan is also the history of clans and clan divinities.

During all the major development eras of the Islamic and Christian kingdoms, there were clan chieftains in the Cushitic kingdoms, even before Christ. In Khartoum for hundreds of years until present a clannish quarter is still visible. The people of Nilotic stock were there around the 8th century AD. The Red Sea was not just used to transport slaves, ivories, jewels, ornaments, gold, other trade materials. Ideas were traded as well.

History and Politics in South Sudan

There is history, and then there is the politics of history in South Sudan. History is an account of what happened. The politics of history is explaining a process for those events to serve a specific objective. Clans versus South Sudan is not history. It is only a recent consequence of the economic drivers in the country.

Regarding oil revenues, a system of violent competition has played out in political circles. The awarding of non-competitive agreements, agreement inflation and the manipulation of payrolls became common in services spending. Public servants were provided with powerful means and the revenues required for purchasing or leasing the loyalty of armed and/or established parties.

South Sudan was engulfed in a mutually-reinforcing state of war that involved more than the two principals: The government and the opposition[85]. Several drivers of the conflict, some new and others

---

85 East Africa Report, (Issued 9, January 2017), Institute for Security Studies

APUK : A STATE IN WAITING

accentuated by it, have emerged. Badly managed decentralization, exploitation, marginalization, clan rivalries, exclusionary politics, socio-economic non-development and unaddressed local grievances have fed the fire for paramilitaries and insurgencies countrywide. These blights were enabled when conflict mitigation and prevention mechanisms were not created and integrated into agreements. Oil revenues employed and fed a powerful support network of individual parties and political marketplaces, particularly if such a network received inflated, lucrative service agreements for food, fuel, armaments and other substantial equipment.

South Sudan is number 193 among the members of the United Nations. It is a member of the African Union, The East African Communities, The Intergovernmental Authorities on Development (IGAD), and The Arab League. Juba is the capital for political and commercial activities on a temporary basis. Ramchiel is proposed to be the future capital for the young nation. Development began in 2017 to shift some administrative units there. South Sudan has a federal administration with a presidential system of government. There is a parliament known as the National Legislative Assembly operating side by side with upper Council of State Coordination. There is also a National Transitional Constitution.

For decades, what is now South Sudan fought protracted wars against Sudan. Many international players perceived this as a legitimate liberation struggle. However, the peace agreement signed in 2005 made no provisions for easing clan tensions that originated in the early 1980s when people of ethnic clans of Dinka origin were singled out in every city across the country. They were frequently arrested, tortured, ambushed and killed by their adversaries wherever they were seen moving towards areas controlled by rebels, or before reaching the rebel training camps.

The Dinka population living in Wau town were in constant fear and anguish created by the state security agents that mobilized and armed forces against them. All those identified to be against the Dinka were armed mainly to liquidate Dinka elites and pro-movement groups around Wau Town. This led to the disappearance of Director

Luka Ngor Bak Matik, murdered in August 1985 in Wau in the Bahr El Ghazal Region. The Fartit, Balanda and Falata paramilitary forces were responsible for his kidnap and murder. It was an act which brought Wau city into a very dangerous security situation and resulted in the division of the city into two warring zones. A zone for the Jieng groups on one side and another for the government militia alliance including soldiers of Islamic Jihad, *Mujahideen* who were receiving arms from state security agents.

Road Contracts: Criminal Enterprise?

The history of roads project contracts, dirty money and dirtier operators was discovered when revelations regarding previous contracts were made public. It rocked the overpriced deal cartel in South Sudan. From 2006 to December 2015, the government paid enormous amounts of money to phantom companies, with millions more erroneously being spent. This practice continues to the present day.

The big question must be asked. Did the people of the counties of Tonj State pay with their precious blood and labour only to enrich the principals of these phantom projects? Would the judiciary of South Sudan be brave enough to order an investigation into this fraudulent behaviour? Or should the judiciary be mandated to create public judicial corruption resolution laws with retroactive powers? What is needed by South Sudan is an effective action plan to recover the stolen money (locally and internationally), apprehend the culprits, and eventually put an end to the looting and racketeering.

Another classic debate about the history of roads projects is the issue of the foreign companies which were awarded contracts in Central Equatoria State, Kapoeta State, Tonj State, Gogrial State and Gok State. In fact, it would be unfair to call any such companies 'foreign companies' because if they were real foreign companies, there would be functioning roads across those states today. The fraudulent activity is most painfully felt in various Tonj counties. What should have been some compensation to community victims for their efforts in blood to fight a civil war in solidarity with SPLA movement for over 20 years has turned into an international joke.

There are many international companies renowned for their technology and perfection in building roads, schools and hospitals. No one can, therefore, be fooled that any such company awarded costly contracts for road construction would not actually do the job. The truth is that the contracts went to phantom companies run by a home-grown patronage racket. They were, in the words of Western countries, 'shell' or dummy' corporations. The money went into them and then disappeared.

And at a time when roads project stories were on lips of every citizen in Juba, Malakal, Wau, and Kuajok, two remarkable developments happened:

One: In response to public outrage over the previous failures, those in power instead sub-contracted Juba-based companies to implement the construction of roads in the Bahr El Ghazal and Equatoria regions. Who is behind these Juba-based and Wau-based companies is there for every citizen to guess!

Two: The biggest shock was this: The dirty money was now being loaned to and laundered by government institutions. Those victimized by our wars have questions to ask. What is so magical about the dirty money and those criminals responsible for its acquisition? Could it be that their smooth appearance and language makes their 'mates' in government forget the widows of our fallen comrades? Are these mates not aware that our widows, orphans, widowers, victims and silent heroes have been marginalized without compensation or reparation? Or are these poor people just not nefarious enough to get their compensation?

These contracts are typical of how South Sudan is nowadays manufacturing dirty money and cutting its own throat. They were awarded without any tender process, public bidding, competition, or even a window of transparency. It was well known in East Africa what road construction companies generally charge per kilometre. The contracts handed out overcharged and cheated South Sudan to the fullest. It was only natural for the phantom companies to charge a million dollars per kilometre. Hence, according to their warped calculation, the 500 kilometres of roads identified by GoSS between Lakes State and Warrap State, mainly to link Gok counties, Tonj counties, Wau counties and Gogrial counties would cost a total of half a billion dollars.

In a political marketplace such as ours, corruption and patronage ARE the system. These roads projects were a major source for siphoning millions of dollars from the coffers of South Sudan. The project to link one state to other state was dreamed up by the patronage racket, while the chief felon of the group, acted as the distributor of the funds. A great deal of money has been spent on phantom projects such as this that do not exist on the ground. This frustrated President Salva Kiir Mayardit, and to use his own words in one of his recent speeches, he stated that there are many such phantom projects and behind them, there are many "hidden cows".

As things stand today, those counties are still without roads because the companies have failed to deliver. It is not expected that new road or hospital construction will be initiated in the near future because the same crimes will simply be committed again. In South Sudan, "anything goes", as per the rules of no transparency, no accountability and no judicial mechanism is in place for the law courts to bring corruption and patronage charges to trial. The World Bank has refused to fund construction activities in South Sudan due to rampant corruption. (The USA recently took the same steps.)

South Sudan ranks 169th on United Nations Index. When conflict is considered, the score becomes even lower. This shows that countries cannot develop unless there is peace and good governance. The South Sudanese today barely have any basic services due to poor infrastructure and a lack of trained personnel. It languishes at the very bottom of the exploitation and quality of government indicators. There is no political will to implement reform or transparency measures. This is particularly striking when taking into consideration that each year in the period since 2005, oil revenues have provided funds for public spending equivalent to USD 340 per capita. This is eight times that of Ethiopia and five times that of Uganda.

Decades of neglect, war and bad administration have made the population in Tonj State one of the most deprived in the world. The people of Apuk who had accommodated the SPLA rebels, have been left impoverished and go through the painful experiences of intimidation and daily harassment.

Unequal Wealth Distribution

Regarding the culturally diverse clans of South Sudan, the historical logic of distributing influence and wealth on a regional and clannish basis has seemed rational for most South Sudanese people. This system began to break down during the leadup to independence. When changes to statehood began to be implemented, political loyalty, not ability, became the basis for political appointments and positions of power. They held the reins for distributing wealth and influence as the state institutions were developed.

This classification system reinforces the inefficiencies that encourage fraud. It expels the honest players who threaten the criminal classification system and rewards the bad actors who perpetuate and sustain that system. Those who received state positions also sought to settle scores with old rivals. There was constant jockeying for power among various political loyalists. Part of the prize for this competition was control over a share of the state's financial resources, a role in the state services, and a new power structure which many used for feeding their patronage networks.

The history of the clans shows that anytime they and the government players get together, the relationship is that the clans are the defeated and the government is the conqueror. Clans have neither rights nor institutional protections. We must also factor in that South Sudan as a nation places the people's interests far below that of the interest of the political parties. Those parties then state that each clan only had its community interest at heart and weren't considering the entire country.

Politics and History

Who was it that had to face down the 'Weapons of Mass Corruption' and the dynamics of profit and power fuelling the war inside the country? It was the clans. During the protracted conflicts marked by the violence funded by state and non-government players, only the people suffered.[86] For the leading political parties in pre and post-independent South Sudan, battlefield alliances and loyalties all contributed to a system of violent kleptocracy[87], and the formation of a powerful and unchallenged patron-client network.

Violence or the threat of violence is used as a bargaining chip for a greater share of power[88] The rivalries and disputes among parties quickly turns deadly and pits the clans against one another. This mostly involves young fighters from such clans as the Jieng, Nuer, Jurchol Luo, Shilluk Luo, Mundari, Bari, Fertit, Pojulu, Kuku etc. who are loyal to their rival parties and leaders. The fighting in South Sudan disproportionately targets civilians; particularly women and children. This horrific conflict of power and self-interest has taken a heavy toll.

---

86 Enough Team, Edited by Jacinth Paner, (January 2017, page 4 -8)
87 Enough defines violent kleptocracy as a system of state capture in which ruling networks and commercial Partners hijack governing institutions for the purpose of resource extraction and for the security of the regime. Ruling networks utilize varying levels of violence to maintain power and repress dissenting voices. Terrorist organizations, militias, and rebel groups can also control territory in a similar manner.
88 Alex De Waal, "When Kleptocracy Becomes Insolvent: Brute Causes of the Civil War in South Sudan," African Affairs 113 (452) (2014): 347-369; see, in particular P. 348.

Fighting Corruption

The struggle for political power and control of natural resources, revenues, corruption and nepotism appear to be the key factors underlining the breakout of the civil war that ravaged the entire country on December 15, 2013. It is sickening to note that even the names of powerful political leaders are being used to fleece the flock left, right, and centre. This is being done mainly for the prospects of a cheaper and more manageable political landscape.

The tragedy of the cancer of corruption is the fact that it is firmly entrenched in the higher echelons of establishments. Individuals tasked with tackling the malady are the very ones who actively engage in it. It is pointless to expect the police, judiciary or politicians to lead this war. Any person who got his or her position in a corrupt manner will never spearhead this fight.

The institutions that are mandated to deal with this dragon called corruption are always incapacitated by it and are rendered toothless, barking dogs. Indeed, corruption as a trap is identified as the single biggest threat to advancement and it must be killed off in Apuk society. Corruption has killed our past, our present and is rapidly killing our future. Corruption should not be allowed to turn Apuk or any alliance, into a man eats man place. It should be eradicated.

The prioritization of the challenge with respect to addressing corruption should focus on institutional strengthening, policy, public-sector reforms, financial management, public procurement systems, devolution, good governance and democracy.

This administration should enhance the monitoring, investigation, prosecution, restitution and reduction of corruption opportunities and incentives. The state equally must make a tremendous effort in putting in place a clear institutional framework for public sector reforms, including the establishment of sectoral reform committees, defining the core functions of each state department, issuing guidelines on the rationalization of institutions, and right-sizing for employees. There should also be an institutionalization of performance appraisal criteria and a code of regulations to address work ethic issues. Effective management of public finances should be provided and enforced. This will create oversight responsibilities that will address the problems of the inadequate planning and project prioritization that has been a recipe for corruption and disaster to date.

A procurement system and a public procurement and disposal act, as well as other legislation and administrative measures, will provide a response to the many corruption-related complaints emanating from the procurement sector. Moreover, the introduction of an integrated financial management information system will help in facilitating efficient and effective electronic procurement.

Wrong Role Models

Young persons are seeing their fathers making money in the way most rich people made money in this country; through corruption. They just want to be rich, and they want to be rich now. It does not matter to them how they get the money. Imagine, if these young men had come from poor families where putting food on the table was a real problem, and where rent and school fees took up a significant proportion of monthly income, one would understand their desire for riches. But they live a comfortable life in a neighbourhood where having a nice house and more than one car is the norm rather than the exception.

The phenomenon of celebrating those who have made their money through fraud, corruption, or other illegal activities, came to the forefront when the alleged mastermind of a scandal developed a fan base. Was that the turning point in South Sudan and in the Apuk community, when a man who nearly destroyed the whole economy was lauded and treated like a hero?

Corruption permeates all sectors of the economy and all levels of the state apparatus. It manifests itself through various forms, including grand corruption networks along tribal lines in the country. Corrupt practices and rapid self-enrichment are alien and observable among the powerful politicians inside the political establishment. Against this background, the young people want to emulate these wrong role models to enrich themselves as quickly as possible to be on a level with their wealth making mentors among prominent clans. But they are fragile and subordinate to the kleptocratic operation of the broader clan principles. That is why these young clansmen have resorted to corruption as the quickest way of acquiring money. Above all, corruption and patronage are distortions of clan principles.

It is not too late to guide young people away from choosing wrong role models. This can be done by discrediting and shaming looters. Shame the ones inside the financial patronage networks where political life is so personalized that everything revolves around corrupt individuals who promote corrupt practices. They do this to finance and fortify political market networks aimed at self-enrichment and brutal repression of dissent. This culture of false pride and values that creates corrupt individuals must be eliminated by the truthful clans and by the mighty divinity of Apuk. Young people should be persuaded and guided to choose good role models rather than become evil and face disgrace.

These corrupt men have only one interest; to ensure the corruption remains undisturbed, and optimally to govern for life. They weave decisions around this perception of the tenured-for-life politician and view themselves as life members. This enables the government to act as it wishes. Government officials should be called to listen and advise but the decision of the members of the public should be what counts in the end.

Fighting Corruption

Fixing the Problem

A new tough anti-corruption team could carry out a lifestyle audit of public institution employees deployed in lucrative departments and state agencies as part of the fight against corruption in Apuk State.

Apuk is our homeland but it is being devastated by human impact. Native clans and subclans have a great deal to teach our contemporary Apuk homeland about sustainable life. <u>Only take what belongs to you or what you need is the Apuk philosophy.</u> The Apuk can live comfortably without waste or excessive indulgence. Competitive corruption, violent conflict competition, deforestation, greenhouse gases, the destruction of animal habitat, poaching, endemic diseases, unsustainable exploitation of the natural resources and ultimately the large-scale economic collapse are a disaster for everyone. We all play a part in propagating this evil. And we must not distance the rule of law and conservationism from the broader issues of poverty reduction and education. It is all interlinked deeply. We must create consequences for these predatory actors that harm the Apuk people. Fixing the wealth disparity in the Apuk homeland will restore communities who turned to these destructive, disintegrative habits to feed their families in the wake of economic collapse

Prevention measures must be put in place with fresh strategies to ensure an effective war on graft, dirty money, and to deter wrong role-modelling and collaboration with corrupt fat-cat mentors.

The message must be made clear to our young people. You steal public resources or monies and there will be nowhere to hide.

The Problem with Judiciary Revenues

Judicial Court cases have mushroomed following population concentration changes in Apuk. They reflect changes in the economy over the period. Thiet town has swelled with the arrival of SPLA soldiers, internally displaced persons and the incorporated judiciaries attached to them. During the civil war the town was controlled by a military administrator (MA) in the SPLA barracks at the Mayom Abun and Yinh-Kuel bases. People flowed in as employment opportunities presented themselves with non-governmental organizations (NGOs), and other international and national organizations.

The difference between traditional courts and the SPLA courts in Thiet Town has added a complicated economic dimension, replicating more division between 'money' and 'non-money' spheres. This is much like the 'bride wealth' amounts or compensation amounts as social capital, in forms of marriages and the exchange of cattle and livestock. It has been through this social interaction between both spheres that some of the additional significance of the judicial trials skills lies. They were introduced at the same time as the money economy began to impact on people and played an important role in resolving judicial disputes for both money and non-money economies, and in mediating between the values of the town and of the traditional village. The traditional chiefs' courts became closely linked to the money economy, especially as many of them were forced to operate court trials inside a town that was controlled by SPLA

The Problem with Judiciary Revenues

officers who collected tax revenues from chief's courts and livestock market centres.

SPLA commanders have appointed their court agents from amongst the local people as their judges to trial cases within their jurisdiction since 1985. Traditional chiefs' courts were moved to Thiet Town to deal with financial debts and disputes arising from generating revenues in emerging markets.

The SPLA officers attached to traditional chiefs' courts collected court fee charges and most penalty fines in the form of cash. Judiciaries created by individual senior SPLA officers were there to support the separate military services. These judiciaries were the main sources of cash revenue for the military authorities, so the chiefs resorted to penalty fines which must first be paid in cash. However, appointed judges in separate judiciaries were dispensing fines of cows ranging from three cows to eleven cows[89], so that the persons judging cases got paid with one to two cows each per trial collected from the accused persons that pleaded guilty in those proceedings.

The Wanhalel Dinka laws agreed to in 1975 established the "right" of parents to a minimum number of bride wealth cattle. "Thirty-six cows would be written down and known as the Wanhalel law of marriage, to give the family of the girl the power to collect those cows from the family of the boy"[90]

There are people who translate court trials known as *agamlong* (interpreters) in the Dinka language, and who get paid for their work. Meanwhile, the chiefs were disarmed of their 'traditional' work. Policing by the chiefs, like *nhomgol*, and *baziger*, or *banyriel*, was replaced by military officials or soldiers. Authorized by the chiefs, they were sent to collect the cows as penalties from the guilty persons using force and brought to the courts. These practices and operations went on until the CPA was signed in January 2005.

---

89 Akok Wol had eloped with the girl and was charged in the Court President held outside Thiet Town for trial and was punished to pay five oxen, and six cows distributed; five cows given to the parents of the girl, one to the soldier sent to the collect cows, and all five oxen were reported to be fines paid to the court, and the rest to the military, as per government edicts in the liberated areas.

90 Interview with County Court Judge, Thiet Town

The code of SPLA/SPLM Laws was used in the courts to reflect the principals of their financial regulations, in terms of trial sentences, fines, or compensation amounts. Wanhalel Dinka law is about the resolution of judicial disputes, process and outcome, but it was not operational during the SPLA military administration. The judicial trial courts in Thiet town refer to the norms that might explain and justify court decisions, but which are not and were not the same as laws. In fact, in Thiet, the Arabic word *ganun* is used much more commonly.

If one was asked to explain what *ganun* are, people would say that it came from the SPLA government, and then explain the different amounts of penalties and compensation, interpreted as *apuk* in the Dinka language, which the various courts are able to award. The amounts of bride wealth and/or other compensation for pregnancy and blood wealth payable in court cases is accepted as being set by the Wanhalel Dinka Customary Laws. However, in some court cases, blood wealth payable influenced by the SPLA was ranging from 55 cows to 90 cows beyond the 'real law'.

These judiciary fines, *garama* or *hakarama*, are understood to be the 'Government's share', and sometimes referred to as 'money for the court'. This is a case of court members participating in the resolution of judicial disputes that has been key to the courts of traditional chiefs, which are different from individual chiefs simply appointed by unknown rebels or militants for income generation. Therefore, the resolution of judicial disputes was fully understood to be a kind of social development service where revenues for the government must be paid, or as a means for the government to be able to insert itself into, and to appropriate from those generating revenues for the local economy and social economic development.

Regardless of all these challenges, the judicial trial courts of traditional chiefs continued. Their function in non-money terminologies was to award compensation including fines in the form of cattle and livestock. Practically all compensation connected to Dinka clan homicides or minor injury offences takes the form of cattle. But for fines for offences in Thiet Town courts the application of money is much beyond prevalent. Payment of money in marriage is usually

The Problem with Judiciary Revenues

considered as money for the 'tobacco of the old man or old woman', 'buying the clothes', 'purchasing the bed sheets', and so forth. In addition, cash payments in Thiet Town courts symbolized compensation or restitution of unfulfilled obligations. This is important because of cash values in rural cattle keeping villages, where conditions are different when converted into monetary payments in the courts and may be far below or above the market rates.

In the resolution of judicial disputes as supervised by the traditional chiefs' courts, and the individually appointed chief's courts operated in judiciaries at Thiet Town, money was sometimes combined with livestock. This often occurred at times where a goat or chicken was needed for traditional purification purposes. Money paid to bail people from jails was sometimes exchanged by using cattle and livestock. Money inevitably symbolizes something else, and hence monetary application in the law courts is a system of exchanging or converting between financial wealth and the local livestock based moral and social wealth. Some law courts have gained cash wealth through bribery and corruption, making them less accountable than the traditional moral wealth, and bringing privilege to the selected and appointed chiefs with access to money in the court of laws. It was observed that the judiciaries have become more concerned with extracting the financial payments of fees and fines than with ensuring that compensation or *apuk* is paid.

Few traditional chiefs distinctively link these emerging trends of 'hakuna' with the new military administrators or the government. "When the military government came here with their new laws, they changed our old laws, and until today in this war, they have not returned to the old laws of the *apuk*. They are working with the laws of the SPLA. The laws of war. Military laws are only good at charging people money."[91]

Still, the misuse of the law courts by some chiefs vulnerable to 'money' is an extension of the tensions of the changing social wealth. People having an education or relatives abroad will have access to

---

91 Traditional chief explained to the writer, while teaching in Kurlueth Institute of Education, Thiet, 2002.

cash, while other people will remain dependent on wealth in cattle and livestock. I discovered that there was not a single elite, although there were relationships with different types of local elites that came out to condemn these practices. On several occasions, this writer has witnessed that the traditional chiefs appear to be defending the traditional social wealth and social moral order against the exploitation and abuses of politicians and militancy. The new cultures brought by the younger generation and those young returnees and their close relationship with military control and Thiet Town local elites are evident everywhere. Many people in the Apuk homeland believe that those taking a complaint to the court have done so because it is imperative to regulate the economic wealth of cattle and is also viewed as a means to access cash. People have reported that they going to court simply to 'get cash money'.

From 2013 to 2016, the coalition government began to increase the number of counties, *payams* (jurisdictions with a minimum population of 25,000) and states falling under centralized administrative and judicial control. The last two years have witnessed a rapid proliferation of new and subdivided units as each clan or section has been convinced that their access to government resources depends upon being recognized as such. The number of judiciaries has increased exponentially, and they have established themselves in the newly created units or towns. Tonj State, for example, now has scores of judiciaries sitting within its boundaries. It even represents some units of neighbouring states. In general, the increase in the numbers of judiciaries and the erosion of a rigid order means that there is virtually a type of judiciary job market whereas everyone is carving up a piece of the pie for themselves. These additional states are described as 'tribal' or 'clan' states. However, people also have considerable latitude as to which clans and subclans are to have a 'state' of their own in place.

Judiciaries that have gained a reputation for favourable judgments are attracting large numbers of cases. People have been going directly to higher law courts like the county magistrate. The creation of around thirty-two states, counties and *payams* have provided a

The Problem with Judiciary Revenues

betting mindset of sorts that the higher the judiciary fee, the higher the potential reward. There is also a desire to conduct the case in the most prestigious or authoritative court. For example, the chief's courts in rapidly expanding Tonj Town, the capital of Tonj State, receive multiple cases for hearings from a variety of ethnic groups. This court has gained a reputation for swift judgement and frequent floggings. This reputation has attracted cases from displaced persons from Tambura State, Gbudue State, Wau State and other urbanized communities. The popularity of flogging as a punishment might appear to reflect the former Sudanese penal codes. People consider it to be satisfying to see immediate justice.

These rulings make the dominating aspect of the judiciary particularly evident, such as flogging teenagers for petty offences. However, the actual traditional chiefs are distanced personally from such punitive justice, reflecting a noticeable desire to abstract and depersonalize the use of force.

This is exactly the notion of impartial, official, government power that people have long sought through the chiefs' courts. It reflects the need for both justice and punishment to appear both collective and impersonal. This is also noticeable in the role of the *agamlong* in traditional chief's courts in Thiet Town and may also lie behind the widespread use of oath-taking in the judiciaries using spears, sheep and/or cow sacrifices, or a Holy Bible or Quran.

The traditional chiefs use police and court bailiffs in Apuk to serve the purpose of equal justice. The chiefs' courts combine the notion of a collective will with an impersonal power of enforcement.

"The Court Bailiff, bazing-ger bany, is the one given power by the Government, hakuma. It is not his own power. When a person is in a position like this and decides about collecting cows and then is asked by someone to carry out that collection of cows, he is undertaking bazing-ger bany (or beny-riel). Traditional chiefs have given him power and have authorized him to use that power to collect cows from us, so people have to accept it"[92].

---

92 Traditional chief of Court President reported to the writer in Thiet in 2003.

Since the coming of the Anglo-Egyptian Sudan Government, the police have been present. However, they represent entirely alien forces. Even after a history of arbitrary and often abusive police behaviour, and their continuing overlap with the military, the Apuk clans were taking cases voluntarily to them. They are also closely connected to the chiefs' courts. From around 1990 to 2004, when contacted to explain what they would do if someone wrongs them, people said they would go to the military administrative police, who then would send them to the appropriate court. The military government have clearly changed the way the police have affected the lives of people as opposed to a time when they were largely restricted to maintaining law and order.

Sometimes the military police settle the offences or disputes themselves without even sending the case to the judiciary or court. They also have other cases directly sent to their paramilitary established courts in the barracks, or in Thiet Town. Chiefs could formally request that the military police arrest or imprison someone. This practice changed in 1987. The chiefs must now obtain warrants of arrest from the SPLA military police attorney. That was the cause for the complaint by the traditional chiefs that they have been made powerless. They stated that: "Our powers have been taken over by the SPLA military police! Military personnel are doing our job!"[93].

This rule spread wider when accusations involving any 'blood' must be taken to the military police. It became crucial for obtaining compensation of *apuk* according to the number of penalty fines and fee charges under the military police code. As a result, even relatively minor injuries or bruises were reported to the military police. Women in general pursue this avenue if beaten by their husbands, or other women, or if asked to help soldiers to carry ammunition and become their wives, not to return to their legitimate husbands.

---

93 Since Thiet was captured by George Kuach on October 22, 1984, SPLA established its Military Headquarters in Mayom. This gave them opportunity to enter into the affairs of the community. Community members who were not seeing their cases resolved according to their wish, prepared to go to the officer in charge and have their cases settled by the use of force, which encouraged unscrupulous people to settle their cases through militancy.

Reckless military officials have broken many marriages and lured married women to leave their children behind, while other girls and women were commandeered into new marriages. There were widespread complaints that the military police involvement made these disputes escalate more quickly.

"In my opinion, people should try to resolve things before 'rushing' to the SPLA military police officials and their guns, because jail or fines will damage social relationships. This use of a military government force from the SPLA should be a last resort." said an elder to this writer, while I was teaching at Kurlueth Institute of Education (KIE), in Thiet.

Clearly, the military police officials have successfully inserted themselves between communities and judiciaries and have taken entrepreneurial advantage of the space they inhabit in Apuk, especially in Thiet Town. But more importantly, there was also a popular desire for that militarism because communities feel that military uniforms and armament adds authority to their claims. The paradoxes of the contradiction with which the power of the SPLA Military Government was viewed were particularly noticeable in the attitudes and practices towards military police officials. They were much more a part of the military government, than were the actual traditional chiefs, descended from recognized chiefs by the former British administration.

The Lack of Social Justice

It was easy to understand why there was an increasing number of people appearing in judiciary courtrooms or judiciary under the trees and police stations. Essentially, they were requesting access to the government of the day as a source of equality, social justice, and a neutral and effective resolution of judicial disputes. There was a widespread awareness that government power was no longer as obscure, faceless and/or depersonalized and that it was interpreting that the government was more effective in settling grave disputes. In reality, the coercive power of the government and its institutions was usually limited. On the other hand, views regarding the usefulness of government in the past years do reveal specific concerns with the way that the current government has been appropriated in divisive ways by corrupted leaders and politicians.

The regular police, for instance, are deemed to be powerless in relation to the military police. Sometimes, military officials are understood to follow 'jungle' or 'bush' law rather than obeying government authorities. A good example is the soldiers who had forced civilians from Lietnhom and Atot villages in 1992 to carry arms etc. up to Waranguoth village in the Malony Apuk section and shot dead Malou Wiir among those civilians. They claimed that: *"We have suffered in the bush, fighting for your freedom, you must carry ammunition up to the barracks or you die."* One reckless soldier seized two civilians who were carrying milk to a sick person back in March 1993 and shot one dead at Maluil Apuk village. The soldier declared:

> *"We don't have mercy with people disobeying our orders because we are here fighting for this land. Even my own father, if he refused to obey SPLA orders, would eat the bullets in my gun."*[94]

Indeed, Deng ate bullets and was found dead by the community. Mistreatment was rampant in the Apuk homeland, but the nonappearance of the discipline and coordination of the military police undermined the connection of the government to the judiciary court.

The failings of the court system are mostly deliberated in cattle keeping areas like Toch Apuk, where inter-clan, subclan and regional disputes between young men of different sections have occurred frequently since the colonial administration in the 1900's and resumed from 1970 onwards. Such disputes have been fuelled by the proliferation of small arms in the region. However, some local

---

94 Elder person of Apuk community interviewed narrated the actions to the writer, while teaching at Kurlueth Institute of Education (KIE). This elder also lost one eye as he was being tortured at Mayom Abun in Apuk Juwiir.

The Problem with Judiciary Revenues

communities elaborate this threat in order to blame elements among SPLA officials for interfering in the disputes and supplying weapons for their own personal profit.

Local people then focus the failure to attain dispute resolution through the judiciary courts for several reasons. The judiciary courts that have largely heard the homicide cases resulting from fighting are largely corrupt and deliberately delay hearings. They are also seen to prioritize the extractive aspect of court penalties, such as the fees and fines, rather than the execution of compensation for *apuk*, awards. Due to these practices, the value of the lives lost can only be reclaimed by revenge and further cattle rustling and looting.

The traditional chiefs and others agree that they are unsuccessful because they are no longer effectively backed up by government power. Instead, the military and police officials release prisoners and interfere in court cases. It truly reflects a further fundamental shift regarding the politicisation of traditional and local justice systems together with local government administration. The confused and eroded chain of command from the lower to higher judiciary courts was and still is an exceptional challenge. This reflects the loss of a clear, official, and progressive avenue to accessing the power of government. A number of these challenges were deliberated as early as 1927 during the historical Wanhalel Dinka Customary Laws Conference and then again in 1975.

These discussions revealed the apparent effectiveness of payable *apuk* of blood wealth to be collected by the parents of the victim using local justice regarding homicides in tribal or clannish dispute cases. They lamented the resolution of fighting through the payment of compensation, for *apuk*.

This has also become apparent in the continuing conflicts since 2008. The fact that we are homesick for both an effective enforcement of compensation (*apuk*) and for the capital punishment of the colonial period, reflects a desire for the governmental 'power' that used to back up traditional judicial dispute resolutions of the chiefs. On the other hand, it has become too sensationalized and politicised to do so commendably any longer.

According to the statement of an elder in the area: "Traditional chiefs do not have power at all. Nothing can go smoothly until those powers are returned back from those who robbed them". This is a statement which implies a similar notion of power regarding the police, or the *bazing-ger* of the chief that people have sought to access through the chief's courts.

The current government is no longer comprehended as being indiscriminate. It is understood to have become more divisive and sensational, and seemingly sides with one person or party in disputes. There are rather longing local memories of the previous success of the colonial government in ending disputes by a combination of government law enforced with equal justice with the further traditional endorsement of sacrifices performed by the high priest chiefs. Before, there were clear differences between the government and the people. Today everybody has a gun. Truly, the gun itself does not cause the growing fighting. However, it does symbolize the view of a government that is broken. This reduces the functions of government to a less effective role in the judiciary courts and police. The writer met community leaders who argued that the government can be unfriendly and disconnected with reality.

The government of South Sudan has been pursuing a greater increase in control over the chiefs and their courts, as well as over harmonization at the grassroots level in the local governments. The Ministry of Justice has encouraged the recording, codification and harmonization of customary laws since 2008. Local government acts have all focused on governmental intervention in the judicial system.

Traditional chiefs have been attending conferences, workshops, rituals, and practices. The government wants to record customary law to bring traditional judiciary courts into a statutory set of codes that restrict the chiefs' autonomy in decision-making, which is not actually based on a particular body of rules but on particular practices and logic. The government links customary law with certain ethnic groups, partly revealing a serious tension over cattle keepers who have moved into agricultural areas, and whose cattle-based compensation they consider to be incompatible with

The Problem with Judiciary Revenues

other forms. Yet in individual cases, the courts are quite capable of finding a suitable exchange between the different economies and currencies.

This is really a political issue, reflecting the inherently political nature of justice. Politics have become increasingly 'tribal', so the law is held up as an aspect of ethnic culture to be defended. Defended not so much against a homogenizing government, but against a government perceived to have been appropriated by other ethnic groups.

The Corrupt Judiciary

A political appointee may tribalize a socio-political conflict, in an effort to mobilize a constituency cheaply and divert attention from the real political issues. He realises that the best approach to creating loyalty among individuals is to flame a tribal clan crisis to marshal one set constituency chiefs against others. However, in doing so his actions diminish and corrupt the customary courts of tribal chiefs whose power is legitimated by custom and who may in turn find themselves appreciative of the original customary chiefs. The most powerful and subversive demand is for equitable access to justice and rule of law. The logic of the unregulated political marketplace network reduces social relations and people to commodities that the judiciary and customary court corrupts and ruins.

People must resist the corrupt judiciary and customary courts because it is a fundamental violation. The language of increasing security in communities and the promotion of substantive legal reforms that hold perpetrators to account for crimes is a powerful way of asserting basic human dignity and a demand for government in the public interest. Evidence suggests that vulnerable communities want to regularly address economic crimes and atrocities.

The Apuk recognize the interrelated nature of these violations. There cannot be peace without justice and equality because peace is linked to justice and truth. Both justice and peace have encirclement and when justice is done, peace is achieved, and truth is attained. If you look at some of the frustrations of today, we have a leadership that has failed. We have 'for life' leaders who have no vision. That is why our communities are in chaos today. There is tribal fighting on many fronts. All those hopes which the Apuk had when supporting civil wars with countless numbers of cows, goats and human resources for decades, have vanished. They found themselves losing everything. The Apuk got nothing. It continues to be a marginalized community and is denied the right to basic social services.

In fact, corruption is the system everywhere regionally. Anyone aspiring to anything in government or public service must join that kleptocratic club. Much of the public wealth has been stolen or recycled into the patronage system. Administrators are at the top of the system, but not in control of it. As local administrator remarked, "Once there is corruption, there is insecurity."

Political life is so personalized that everything revolves around them. These witty individuals had humorous moments in their governance. These moments of humour, possibly more than anything else brought down the functioning criminal justice system, customary courts, the police, army, prisons, and confidence in the rule of law. Around each self-interest based political head is a cadre of trusted men. Most of them are illiterate but enterprising and witty. Their sensitivities about political life make them well versed in the making of key political decisions. Whatever they said was acted upon with speed. No brakes needed!

This self-interest corrupts the judiciary including the customary courts. There were a few judges and customary chiefs who decided to stick their heads out by giving independent decisions on a number of case hearings. This caught the attention of the corrupt leaders. Upset by the manner in which these traditional chief judges were acting, they arranged for the removal of the security of tenure for these same judges.

If you have a situation of insecurity arising out of weakness within the state and a proliferation of small arms, then you have very weak

The Problem with Judiciary Revenues

police, army, prison, judiciary and even customary court. There are so many cases that are not seen, and communities that see criminals walking free. As a result, they decide to take the law into their own hands. In some areas, the government established special bench courts for severe crimes case hearings. Others did not and said it was not their responsibility. Now we see the resultant crisis. Politicians also insist on appointing the members of the court and constituting judiciary and customary service courts on their terms. With a stroke of a pen, the power of the judiciary and customary court was corrupted and ruined.

Geographics and Boundaries

Several outstanding traits in the Dinka's overall character may be said to be consistent with ancient Egyptian and Sudanese knowledge acquired via food supply routes. These originated along the Nile valley in the sub-Saharan region.

The Dinka are a combined group of several closely related peoples living in southern Sudan located along the western, eastern, and southern sides of the White Nile River. They are the largest clan in the region with an estimated population of 5 million people.

Their range extends from the northern border with Sudan and Ethiopia down to the southern border. The Rueng and Padang Dinka clans inhabit the northwest and northeast of the White Nile River on the extreme north and northwest border of Sudan, as well as to the extreme southeast in the Upper Nile region.

The Dinka of the Bahr El Ghazal region are concentrated to the west of the White Nile River. They once inhabited vast lands from the Chad border to the extreme west, the Sudan border to the north, and down into White Nile River section bordering Equatoria in the south.

The Dinka Ngok clans settled along the northern border of Sudan, sharing it with the Mesiria Arab tribes and the Dinka clans of Twic and Rek Malual.

With the exception of the Jurchol-Luo clans, the rest are Rek Dinka.

Geographics and Boundaries

The location of Apuk lands is in the general (not specific) area inside the oval.

APUK : A STATE IN WAITING

According to traditional accounts, at its heights, the Clan of the Deity Rum was one of the leading clans of the Apuk state during the chiefdom dynasty. It occupied most of the territory, except for an enclave towards the southwest which was held by Pabuor clan divinity descendants in the Adol area and Pagong clan descendants that came later from the Muok clans of the southern parts of Tonj State and were welcomed to settle in the Machar area. Also, a region in the northeast became occupied by the newly arriving commoner descendants of the Pakuieth, Padiangbaar, Payuom, Padolmuot, Patiir, and Paluet clans amongst others. Their linguistic and cultural homogeneity is noticeable, and their customs and social structure can be treated as that of a single people. Those who know the Machuet will observe that their historical development, growth, and change of cultural possessions aligns into the establishment of the masters of the fishing spear and the first Apuk country based in the Wunriir homesteads of the Machuet section.

Machuet lies in a vast curvature of the equidistant Apuk homelands interconnecting clans in the Malong section of floodplain lowlands with many lakes in the southwest with those in Aliai section of savannah forestlands in the northeast. It is also connected with the clans in the Maluil section of thick green forest drainage land, which slopes down into the Toch swamp rivers and the Wanhalel River in the south of Tonj State. It is a flat country of sweeping savannah, and savannah forests, in the midstream of all the clans converging upon the central mainland.

For four months of each year, heavy rains and flooding render most of it uninhabitable and impassable. Transport becomes extremely difficult between the higher stretches that remain above the flood. It is only there where it is possible to build permanent homesteads and cultivate lands around them.

The Apuk region is relatively poor, but the culture of the people is rich. Stone is rarely present and natural iron may only be found on the fringes of the territory. The Apuk clans in Machuet and elsewhere are not iron-working clans. Iron hoe-blades and spearheads of foreign make were acquired from Greek merchants and later Arabs who began to trade with it. The Apuk in the western areas say that in the past they obtained them from the iron-working Luo (Jurchol) to the west and southwest and that in the centuries past, they used weapons and other tools like digging sticks, created of horn, bone, and wood. The Apuk of the past were dependent on their cattle because agriculture and fishing were so difficult for them.

Wetland Islands

The Apuk clans have some of the best wetland islands in South Sudan today. You will find many of these in and around rivers and wetland shores. They are often referred to as 'Toch' of the Dinka Apuk.

The Madol Aliai Holy River

This is a divine place where fishing rivers and springs are managed and controlled by the spiritual priest descendant from the Akuin branch of the Parum clan. Catching fish, drinking spring water and using river resources can be authorized through a spiritual blessing by the high priest who inherited divine resource authority for this specific wetland.

Madol Akuien Island is also called Madol Aliai. It is further up the river on the extreme southeast where there are other rivers that branched out from the Wanhalel River connected to the Wanhgoi River and stretch up to the Akarap tributaries on the border with the Dinka Rek clans and the Luachkoth clans.

Lochpiny Island

Lochpiny Island is between Aguudi Island to the west and Awan-gorool Island to the north in the middle of the wetlands. Cattle herders and fishers come here during the dry season for fishing, grazing and access to drinking water from Apung Machuet and other sections. Lietnhom is a gateway west of Lochpiny Island to those travelling from villages in the extreme west towards Aguudi Island. Lochpiny Island is used to pass through the surrounding wetland islands to Toch Apuk.

Aguudi Island

It is in the middle of the Toch wetland which is the area's most popular attraction. The fishing camp itself has its own star figure: Bol Mel, one of the high priest chiefs of Pabuor clan.

He was reported to have been the first fisherman to erect thatched shelter there many centuries ago.

The river there produces a sturgeon type fish weighing in at over 200 kilos, Bol Mel was said to be one of the most excellent fishermen of his day.

He is perhaps the region's biggest celebrity.

Bol spent much of his life fishing in the river nearby. The island is flanked by indigenous trees and offers an abundance of tributaries for fishing, drinking, domestic uses and strategic settlement camps.

It was here that Bol's fearsome reputation was made.

Oral tradition traced Bol Chiirial as Bol Mel Madut Anei. The Pabuor clan he first founded settled in Maluach region and expanded from there. Other members moved to the Maluil Apuk division near the Wanhalel River. Their spiritual masters were buried at Madhol, a tomb shrine celebrated annually by people who traverse from the Manging sections to bring their herds to Aguudi Island during the dry season for grazing. Others used Madhol for fishing and hunting purposes in the dry season until it developed into the high priest temple village for the Pabuor clan as it was closer to the Toch Bol Chiirial shores.

The Apuk has four distinct regions:
1 The Toch (swampland): The eastern portion is highly suitable for pasture, with drinkable water for humans and animals. It borders the

Geographics and Boundaries

swamplands of Thony to the southeast and Luachkoth to the east.
2 The Liil (lowland): The wet region between the highlands and the Toch, is used for agriculture, particularly for grain. It is near the Wanhalel River adjacent to the swamplands. It is bordered by the Thony and Yar territories to the south and extends to Malony lands bordering Yar to the extreme southern reach of Apuk territory.
3 Forest Wilderness: The barrier areas. It is wild, and barely inhabitable to the extent that the animals and people which are unwelcome elsewhere, such as lions, leopards, and outlaws, make it their home.
4 The Sandy Lands: This elevated plateau is situated in the Machuet and Aliai areas between the wildernesses. It has rocky slopes but very fertile soil. It is bordered by the Jurchol lands to the northwest and by Kuanythii to the extreme north in the Machuet region. They are bordered by Kuac Akeen and Luackoth to the northeast. The soil produces grains, groundnuts, sesames, millets, beans and a variety of fruits. Oils and wine are also produced here.

South Sudan's Geographic History

South Sudan in Arabic is 'junub as Sudan'[95]
South Sudan is a young country in East Africa which gained its independence on July 9, 2011. It inherited its borders from those of Anglo-Egyptian Sudan in 1889, and Sudan in January 1956. It is now bordered by Sudan to the north, Ethiopia to the northeast, Kenya to the southeast, Uganda to the south, the Democratic Republic of Congo to the southwest, and the Central African Republic to the west.

The British colonial administration took the direct control of Sudan in 1899 and divided areas according to tribal and customary beliefs, racial, identity, traditional and clan identities. By 1925 this

---

95   Wells, Jonh C. (2008), Longman, and Roach, Peter (2011), Cambridge English Pronouncing Dictionary (18th Ed.), Cambridge: Cambridge University press, ISSN 9780521152532

had changed, and closed districts were created on cultural, racial and clan-based identity lines.

The provinces were comprised of Darfur, Bahr El Ghazal, Mongalla (Juba), Upper Nile, and all of Kordofan. Sections of the provinces of Halfa, Dongola and Kassala were also established. The closed districts covered an area of about 717,225 square miles or two-thirds of the country[96]. The Governor-General of Bahr EL Ghazal Province in Wau directed that the main features of the approved policy of the government for the administration of the southern provinces should be restated in simple terms:

"The policy of the government regarding southern Sudan is to build up a series of self-contained racial identities with units of tribal or clannish identities and the structure and organisation should be based on whatever extent the requirement of equity and good government permits upon indigenous customs, traditional usage, and beliefs.[97]"

The Anglo-Egyptian Sudan Government adopted the Closed District of South Sudan policy in 1930 that separated 'South Sudan Regions' and treated them separately on recognition of the wide difference between the identity of black people and the Arab Muslims in Northern Sudan. Sir James Robertson reversed South Sudan identity policy in April 1946 in Khartoum when he declared black people from the south would be united with Arabs from the north.

The present-day boundary between South Sudan and Sudan is principally the result of the 1889 and 1956 Turko-Egyptian Sudan and Anglo-Egyptian Sudan Condominium delimitation treaties. At present, there is confusion and controversy in South Sudan, regarding the separation policy reversed in 1946. There is also the question of the Ngok clan of the Padang Dinka of Abyiei who were denied their rights in 1956 to reunite their ancestral lands, and of the clans separated in 1905 from Jur River District of Tonj and Gogrial on a voluntary basis.

---

96   Study note by Dr. Dar-es-salaam on a brief history of the Sudan (1979), page 7.
97   Beshir, Muhammed Omer, The Southern Sudan: Background to Conflict, Billing and Sons Ltd., Guidford and London, 1968, page 115.

Tensions increased when a secret bill of re-demarcation was passed by the ruling regime in November 1980 in Khartoum resulting in borders being moved fifty miles (80km) deep inside South Sudan and cutting into oil-rich areas in places such as Hafra el Nahas, Kafia Kingi, Panthou of Heglig, Abiemnhom, and Kaka. They were eventually annexed to the North.

The Ngok clan identity provides grounds for a potential conflict regarding border challenges between South Sudan and Sudan. This is because of the denial of Ngok clan birth and origin rights and their right to decide their fate regarding whether to return to their ancestral homeland in South Sudan or to remain with the Misseriya Arab clans of the Southern Kordofan region and Blue Nile region in Sudan.

1956 Boundaries

South Sudan and Sudan share a very long colonial generated boundary of over 620 miles (1,000 km). Apart from their connections as neighbours, they have many common features. Clans like the Jieng Ngok of the Padang clans and the Fartit and Falata clans live in both South Sudan and Sudan along the border areas. Many rivers such as White Nile, Lol, Kiir and Sobat flow to Sudan.

The border has two distinct sections:

From the Sudan border to Kiir River where two regions of South Sudan, Misseriya and Rezigat of Southern Kordofan lie, the international boundary manifests a genuine ethnic divide. No major Rezigat and Misseriya nomadic tribes live on both sides of the international border.

The second part of the border stretches along the White Nile River to the borders where South Sudanese regions like Renk, Kaka, Ruweng, Panthou, and the Northern Nations have many ethnic groups living on both sides of the border.

APUK : A STATE IN WAITING

On the border down to just north of White Nile River, the international boundary represents a genuine ethnic divide with only the Misseriya, Rezigat pastoralist descendants of Arab clans traversing the two countries. Major clans of the Padang Jieng live in on both sides of the White Nile River and the border. However, the Comprehensive Peace Agreement provided for demarcation of the borderline between the two regions during the interim period (and is ongoing) based on the 1956 border. At the date of writing a technical team has been consulting with local chiefs and elders inhabiting the Abyiei areas around the border. They will consult with local and state governments with common borders and use internal and external sources of information from individual experts and historians.

The White Nile River passes through the middle of South Sudan. This has divided various clans living along it into two: There are Padang and Nuer clans on both the eastern and western banks.

The Ngok Jieng of the Padang clans of Abyei are among those located along the western White Nile River including the Padang clans of Ruweng, Abiem-Nhom, Panthou (Heglig), and Abyiei Ngok.

Southwest Twic, southwest Malual, the other Reks of Aguok, Awan, Kuac, Apuk north, Lou, Kong-Ngor, Abiem, Nyang, Apuk Padoch, Lou Paher, Awan, Kuac-Leer, Ajak, and Luanyjang, Gok, Agar, Atuot, and Ciec live in the Nile valley as well as the Western Nuer.

Other Nuers and Padang Dinka Jiengs are on the eastern White Nile side.

South Sudan shares history with Sudan in the Nile valley, such as the ancient kingdoms which flourished there during the dynastic era when there were identical systems of kingships.

From the White Nile River to the border with Sudan and the Sobat River to the border with Ethiopia, many clans live on either side of the frontier. Notably the Padang clans of Jieng, Anyuak, Nuer, Murley, and Maban.

Along the border with Kenya, the Toposa clans live on either side.

Likewise, the Acholi, Madi, Kakwa and Kuku clans live on either side of the border with Uganda.

Geographics and Boundaries

The Azande, Balanda and other Sudanic speaking peoples are based in Congo and Central Africa but cross the border into South Sudan.

The Sudanic, Bagara, Mesiria, Rezigat, and Falata from Nigeria are based in Sudan but cross the border.

Clans like the Nuer, Anyuak and Berta live in South Sudan and Ethiopia along the border areas. Similarly, they and the Padang Jieng-Dinka and Falata live in both South Sudan and Sudan along the border created when South Sudan separated in 2011. Two rivers from Ethiopia, the Blue Nile and the Sobat flow to South Sudan and Sudan, while the White Nile River flows from its Lake Victoria source and passes through South Sudan, Sudan and Egypt where it joins the Mediterranean Sea.

The Murley are based in South Sudan but cross the border to Ethiopia and back.

The British Colonial Government signed treaties with Ethiopia to demarcate the Sudan-Ethiopia boundaries. They also signed treaties to demarcate the Sudan and Kenya, Uganda, Congo and Central Africa boundaries in the 19th century. The writer will not investigate these various agreements and treaties at this time.

The boundary between South Sudan and Sudan has been very important regarding its political history since its inception. Both countries shared the colonial consequences of rule by Turkey, Egypt, and the British, as well as the boundaries demarcated by treaties agreed to by them.

The Abyei territory of the Dinka-Ngok Padang was transferred from the former Jur River District of Tonj and Gogrial in 1905 at the request of the people of the area for administrative reasons under the chieftaincy. However, it was later annexed in 1956. When they wanted to return to the south, this had to be resolved by referendum. This argument denied the Ngok clans their identity as they were only considered political territory and an artificial nationality. Pledging allegiance by individual Ngok was brushed aside because it is on rich territory. That is why the Padang people of the disputed Abyei areas have had their calls been denied by the Sudan government to determine their fate of ancestral land. The people of Dinka Padang through referendum were supposed to vote regarding returning to their original ancestors by the end of the transitional period. This was in accordance with the Abyei protocol which is part of the Comprehensive Peace Agreement (CPA) that led to South Sudan's secession from Sudan in 2011. Abyei remains part of Sudan until the referendum has taken place.

Many clans existing in both countries have had their way of life influenced by cultural assimilation. Even so, the people born on either side still consider themselves as one people.

Some clan members chose either Sudanese or South Sudanese citizenship when the two countries separated. The border area has major effects regarding social, economic and political developments in South Sudan. It is also important to note that South Sudanese opposition forces use Sudanese soil as a launching pad in their war against the Government of South Sudan. Similarly, the border area between South Sudan and Ethiopia was used by the liberation movements of 1955 and 1983 as a launching pad in their two civil wars.

The Challenges of Boundaries

Boundaries, frontiers and borders are always the most delicate challenges between any two countries with territorial issues. Most of the time it is a painful process and has a great impact not only on the individuals and communities that inhabit the areas involved but also upon all concerned. The international community views some boundary disputes as more important than others for various reasons[98].

The main ones include:

- The size of the disputed area.
- The magnitude of the antagonism of the claimants.
- The involvement of ethnic conflicts in the disputed area.

---

98 Dzurek, Daniel J. (Winter 1999- 2000): "What Makes Some Boundary Disputes Important?", IBRU Boundary and Security Bulletin, 83-95

Geographics and Boundaries

- The historic animosity between the disputants.
- The occurrence of recent violence in the area.
- The weakness of the disputants and their inability to control activities on their frontiers.
- The size of the area involved.
- The number of inhabitants at risk.
- The resources of the disputed area.
- The strategic nature of the disputed area.
- The number of people killed in the area.
- The number of claimants.
- Third party involvement.
- Religious differences in the disputed area.

Definitions

Academics studying boundaries have recently tried to classify the changes and comparisons between the terminologies; boundary, frontier, and border. Most of the time they are used interchangeably. They have come up with theoretical changes and comparisons.

Examples are such as 'frontier' loosely defines an international boundary, 'boundary' designates divisions at the sub-state level but may be used for larger divisions. For simplicity's sake, I will use either as I see fit.

An international boundary is defined as a line dividing territory over which states exercise full territorial sovereignty[99]. International boundaries fix permanent lines, both geographically and legally, within the full scope of the international system and can only be changed through the consent of the relevant states. Such boundaries have important consequences regarding international responsibility and

---

99 Caflisch, Lucius (2006): "A Typology pf Borders," International Symposium on Land and River Boundary Demarcation and Maintenance in Support of Borderland Development Bangkok, 7-9 November 2006.

jurisdiction[100]. Boundaries are divided into "general" boundaries, and "fixed" boundaries[101].

For a general boundary, the exact line is left undetermined, whereas a fixed boundary is the one that is accurately surveyed and certified.

There are two types of borders: bona fide borders, and fiat borders. Bona fide borders are physical boundaries like river banks, lakes and coastlines. They exist in the absence of delineating activity. In other words, they exist independently of all human cognitive acts. On the other hand, fiat boundaries are the creations of humans and hence involve human decision.

There are also natural (geometric), and artificial boundaries. Natural boundaries involve hydric boundaries (on swamplands), water courses, and dry boundaries are mountain ranges etc. Artificial boundaries are marked by monuments or marks that are put on it. Artificial borders "depend neither on physical characteristics nor ethnic characteristics[102]". They are also the cause of many border disputes. That is why there exists a belief that "natural" boundaries are good while "artificial" boundaries are bad. However, we should keep in mind that at present "there is no rule of international law under which natural boundaries enjoy priority over artificial ones[103].

Borders are established by historical precedent, allocation, delimitation, demarcation, and characterization or management. In boundary making there are:

- Political decisions on the allocation of territory.
- Delimitation of the boundary in a treaty.
- Demarcation of the boundary on the ground.

---

100 Shaw, Malcolm (1997): "People, Territorialism and Boundaries", In: European Journal of International Law, Vol. 8, No. 3, pp. 478-507.

101 Korkor, Francis O. (2001): The Surveyor and the Boundary: A Spatial Odyssey: 42nd Australian Surveyors Congress.

102 Özcan, Mesut (2002): "Border Concept and Turkey-Iraq Border," Turkish Review of Middle East Studies, no.13, pp.41-85.

103 Caflisch, Lucius (2006): "A Typology pf Borders," International Symposium on Land and River Boundary Demarcation and Maintenance in Support of Borderland Development Bangkok, 7-9 November 2006.

Geographics and Boundaries

- Administration of the boundary.

Academicians define allocation as the initial understanding between states as to their territorial claims. Lines may be crudely drawn on maps, but no accurate description or field survey has been attempted. Allocation or historical precedent involves the process of identifying the cultural characteristics of the people in the area and considering the previous attempts to establish a border. This phase is the cause of the many border conflicts in South Sudan and Sudan today because most of the borders of former Anglo-Egyptian Sudan Condominium lack these precedents. This stage usually is the responsibility of a Border Demarcation commission, mediating diplomats, soldiers, and heads of state.

In Sudan, Uganda and Kenya, the British colonizers agreed very crudely to create three countries without considering their inhabitants. Since this was the first stage of artificial boundary creation in the region, allocation involved the use of the available maps. If they were not available, they created their own maps. Today, the politicians from S. Sudan and Sudan need the support of various teams of advisors such as lawyers, historians, economists, influential ethnic leadership, technical experts in cartography, geography, geodesy, computer science etc.

Delimitation refers to the description of the alignment of a border in a treaty or other written document and/or by means of a line marked on a map. Academics define boundary delimitation as: "The establishment and ratification of the treaties that deal with the subject or boundary". Delimitation is essentially a political process. It is the signing and ratification of treaties on border issues. Negotiators from both sides determine the boundary lines based on the existing documentation on paper. They then define the boundary in detail. Delimitation is the critical phase of boundary making. Most of the time, it is done by a joint commission. When South Sudan became independent the boundary commissions of both countries appointed their commissioners. They were conducting their rough surveys at the time of writing this book.

The British established via their Royal Engineers, the delimited borders of their colonies. Today technological advances have simplified the process. Satellite imagery gives the latest and most accurate information about the landscape. GPS is a simple and speedy method of positioning to within an accuracy of two meters or less if done with decent equipment. It has truly revolutionized the process. Its prime use is in the location of demarcation sites after delimitation and producing a set of boundary coordinates to be used for treaty purposes. It clearly enables interested parties to test the accuracy of past boundaries where these were delimited by coordinates in a treaty and marked out on the ground in accordance with those coordinates.

The third phase of demarcation involves interpreting the intentions of the delimiters on the ground. This phase is technical or mechanical involving erecting monuments and signposts, cairns of stones, concrete pillars etc. Demarcation experts try to interpret on the terrain the intentions of the delimiters. There are difficulties of interpretation when finding the rivers, lakes, mountains or other landmarks that served as the base for the delimitation. In the demarcation process, markers are erected that define the lines of the boundary and involves records such as maps, sketches, photographs, etc.

The last phase is characterization or maintenance. In it, new marks are erected to satisfy the necessities of the population growth along the borders. This is for management and administration of boundaries and is a continuous process. The major problem at this stage can be for large states with long boundaries to manage and administer their borders due to the very high cost. Boundary marks are categorized as primary and secondary phases. The secondary marks are placed during the characterization phase.

International boundary disputes are generally of three kinds: territorial, positional, and functional. Territorial disputes occur when countries contest for large tracts of land. Positional disputes are disputes that usually follow boundary allocation. They usually happen before delimitation but can also occur after. Functional disputes arise in relation to the everyday management and operation of boundaries.

Geographics and Boundaries

Borders and Consequences

No one can have a Jieng nation without first defining Jieng, or Anyuak nation without first defining Anyuak. Likewise, you cannot have a South Sudan anything, without first defining South Sudan. Scholars have described borders as imaginary lines that are rarely demarcated on the ground, demonstrating their nature as artificially constructed and merely apolitical invention[104]. Boundary experts characterized some borders in Africa as "Borders of an arbitrary and artificial nature, delineated by exogenous colonial powers with little knowledge of the local communities, dividing pre-existing and homogeneous ethnic groups and thereby stirring up frustrations and conflicts". [105]

From 1899 to the present day, boundary challenges and demarcation connected consequences in the South Sudan region are the subjects of intense debate between governments, their boundary committees, advisors, experts and the demarcation team. The main ones include the Panthou, Hafra El Nahas, Kafia Kingi, Kaka, Rodam, Abiemnhom, and Kurmuk areas. So far, however, political processes and diplomatic negotiations are ongoing only in the Abyiei area caused by the 1956 border problems, and regarding the people of the Ngok clans due to 1905 and 1956 border problems. Their identity remains under threat politically and historically.

At the beginning of the twentieth century, the Anglo-Egyptian Sudan Condominium Administration found that a group of Arop Biong of Ngok Dinka clans had a good relationship with some of their Arab neighbours. However, only the Humr, as opposed to the Mahdist Humr, had a good relationship with them and they were being displaced by Ali Jula of the Mahdist group. He was responsible for raids against the Ngok and Twic Dinka, and of extortion in claiming to collect cattle taxes on behalf of the government. The administration of Bahr El Ghazal Province found that the Dinka living around the Kiir River were largely inaccessible to them because of the *sudd* (barriers of floating vegetation)

---

104 Loisel (2004: 4) argues that in 1990 almost 87% of African borders were inherited from colonial era
105 Loisel (2004: 4) etc.

on the river. There were reports claiming that the Kiir River (they called Bahr el-Arab) was the provincial boundary between Kordofan and Bahr el-Ghazal Province. This was without prior study regarding the claim to verify the exact location as to where the Kiir River was as the Dinka used the name Kiir and the Baggara used the name Jurf[106]. The whereabouts and taxonomy of these waterways were not known for some years until the transfer of the Dinka to Kordofan.

The trace map folder for map 65-K of the Abyei area in the Sudan National Survey Authority in Khartoum shows that the 1912 copy of the map bore warning remarks added later: "During the course of December 1918 we shifted the known position of the Jurf/Kiir River, which was easily identified as further north and east of its position on earlier maps. We also changed the name of the Ngol from the Bahr el Homr' to the Ragaba Ez–Zarga".

It was decided to transfer the Ngok and part of the Twic Dinka from the administration of Bahr al-Ghazal Province to Kordofan. This was due to Dinka complaints so that they would not be placed under the same Governor as the Arabs of whose conduct they distrusted.

Various readjustments to the province's boundary were made between 1912 and 1931, leaving only the Ngok in Kordofan. Prior to Sudan's independence, the rural administration throughout the Sudan was reformed with the creation of Rural Councils. The Misseriya were detached from the Nahud District and made part of a Rural Council with its headquarters at Rigl el-Fula (now Fula). At the beginning the Ngok Jieng clans were not included in this council but were eventually admitted following negotiations between the two tribal leaders, the *nazir umum* of the Misseriya: Babu Nimr, and the paramount chief of the Ngok: Deng Majok in 1953[107]. Around the same time the Condominium Government offered Deng Majok the option of being

---

106 B. Mahon, "Extract from a report by Mahon Pasha, on country from El Obeid, via Kadugh [sic] and Shibun, to Sultan Rob's country on the Bahr El Homr, about 2 days from Lake Ambady", in "Sudan Intelligence Report" ['SIR'] 92 (March 1902), App. F, pp. 19–20;

107 Michael and Anne Tibbs, *A Sudan Sunset* (Hobbs the Printers, Totton, 1999), p. 167. In the hierarchy of Native Administration, the nazir umum among nomad Arabs was the equivalent of paramount chief among the African tribes of the South.

Geographics and Boundaries

reincorporated into Bahr al-Ghazal Province. His rejection of that option was opposed by many chiefs and sub-chiefs. That split the clans of the Ngok Jieng Padang ethnic group. The administration of Ngok and Humr use of the same territory must be understood in the context of the overall administration of inter-clannish or tribal boundaries during the rule of the Condominium Government.

This was the type of cheating that caught the attention of international bodies. They took a second look at treaties negotiated and signed by the Ngok clan chief and the Arab clan chief. They found these treaties to be unequal and avoidable as they weakened the Ngok clans of Padang Dinka in Abyiei and cheated them. It is challenging the identity of the divided Padang society today and will do so in the future.

International lawyers have rejected any remedy for the breach of treaties entered into with chiefs or kings. International Law experts have stated that colonial treaties and boundaries were too challenging, intimidating and subjected indigenous clans or tribes to coercion. The treaties concluded with and by traditional clan chiefs or clan kings on the Sudanese common border fell within the category of 'unequal' treaties. They were defective in many respects. There is strong support in neighbouring countries and in African Union states to invalidate unequal treaties. Experts said: "Insofar as unequal treaties of boundaries are one of the forms of neo-colonialism, the complete and final abolition of the latter envisaged by the Declaration adopted by the United Nations General Assembly on December 15, 1960 must likewise include the repeal of all unequal treaties and a ban on the conclusion of such treaties in the future."[108]

They were borders of imaginary lines that were demarcated on the ground, demonstrating their nature as an artificial, political invention. An example is the previously mentioned secret bill passed in 1980 that moved borders deep inside South Sudanese lands and cut the Hafra el Nahas, Kafia Kingi, Panthou, Rodam and Abiemnhom away from the south.

---
108 Umozurike, U.O., "Unequal in the eyes of the law" Africa now, no. 47, (March 1985), page 33.

Other borders were introduced during colonialization and were created without the knowledge, consent and consultation of the indigenous people of South Sudan and are considered arbitrary[109] and artificial. They were delineated by exogenous colonial powers with little knowledge of the local communities, dividing pre-existing and homogeneous ethnic groups thereby creating frustration and conflicts[110].

There have been many arguments concerning the arbitrary nature of South Sudan's boundaries. The dissection of the Padang Jieng groups and Ngok clans, the oil-rich areas of Abyiei, Panthou (Heglig) and Kharasana. The ethnic clan wars of the Panthou (*Heglig* in Arabic), Kharasana, Hafra el Nahas, Kaka and Kafia Kingi, Malakal, Ruweng, Renk, Gogrial, Wau, Tonj resulting from those boundaries is a major cause for instability. The mismatch between states and nationalities is responsible for the instability, inter-clan conflict, and so on.

The borders were drawn initially according to the geopolitical, economic and administrative interests of the colonial powers and later for Arab territorial and economic interests. The most cited dispute example is that of the division of the Ngok clans of the Padang Jieng. The British colonial treaties of 1899 and the early 1920s redrew the border in favour of Egypt/Sudan, in exchange for British Suez Canal rights. Egyptian water and fishing rights flowing from White Nile River and Blue Nile River towards Egypt were 'bundled' in. South Sudan's borders are artificial everywhere. However, even when boundaries are arbitrary, they have also advantages, because they are assets for consolidation and bargaining.

The writer must make himself clear that South Sudan should also respect and accept the status quo of some South Sudan colonial boundaries despite their arbitrariness because it will be extremely costly reverse them. They should manage to share a strong cultural identity, management and sustainable economic and social integration on

---

109 Atzili, Boaz (2004): Good Fences Can Make Bad Neighbours: State Weakness, Border Fixity, and the War in Congo. A Paper prepared for delivery at the International Studies Association conference in Montreal, Canada, March 17-20, 2004.

110 Loisel, Sébastien (2004): The European Union and African Border Conflicts: Assessing the Impact of Development Cooperation. UACES Student Forum Regional Conference, Cambridge, May 7th, 2004

Geographics and Boundaries

these borders. The African Union acknowledged the imperfections of the national boundaries of many African countries and decided to accept the inviolability of the same in its 1964[111] resolution. "Many resolutions adopted by the OAU continually strengthen the territorial foundation of the African States and their respective frontiers. All the member States are committed to respecting the frontiers existing at the time of their independence[112]".

Territorial disputes, as well as historical and cultural identity issues, were the causes for war of Panthou-Heglig. Artificial borders with physical characteristics and ethnic characteristics are the causes for constant disputes.

They have manifested themselves in conflicts such as those between the Shilluk and Ngok Lual Yak over Malakal ownership, the Padang Jieng and Maban of Ruweng and Renk, the Aguok and Apuk, the Waw and Jurchol-Luo, and the Apuk and Jurchol-Luo all over a strip of land around Gogrial State and Wau State. In a brief war, the Muok fought the Thony in 2015 over Majak Kot Island, their common border. It spread into the common borders when the Apuk and Yar Ayiei were involved soon after over grassing, water sources, common borders, and social issues. Over a brief period, the Muok and Thony, Gok and Bongo of Bantu stock, the Jurbel and Agar, and the Jurbel and Gok had fought a boundary war with one another over the rightful ownership of a small strip of lands in a triangle between their common borders.

Demarcations

Though historical, cultural and archaeological evidence indicates the very long economic, historical, religious and political connections between the Sudans, their most visible connections in the contem-

---

111 Atzili, Boaz (2004): Good Fences Can Make Bad Neighbours: State Weakness, Border Fixity, and the War in Congo. A Paper prepared for delivery at the International Studies Association conference in Montreal, Canada, March 17-20, 2004.

112 Wembou, Michel-Cyr D. (1994): "The OAU and International Law." In: The Organization of African Unity after Thirty Years, (ed.) Yassin El-Ayouty, London: Praeger.

porary period began in the 15th century AD. Later, in the early 1870s, the Turks and Egyptians occupied and controlled the region. Though the British took control of Egypt and its colony Sudan in 1882, it was not until 1902 they were able to delimit Sudan's border with Ethiopia. For the British authorities in Sudan demarcating this border, even their political control in Sudan itself was in a great danger due to the rebellion led by Khalifa, the successor of Mahdi. The British sent Captain Harrington to the Emperor of Ethiopia, Menelik II to convince him to recognise British and Egyptian territorial rights throughout the regions of the White Nile, including Kordofan and Dar Sennaar[113].

It was evident that the slave-raiding chiefs gave some trouble as well. The whole frontier was perambulated from the Setit River in the north to the junction of the Pibor and Akobo Rivers in the south. The physical features marking it were pointed out and a certain number of artificial marks erected where more detail was required. The tentative frontier could only be represented by a blue chalk line drawn on the map without any very definite topographical or ethnographical meaning. The exploration teams were "to make as good a map and to collect as much information as they could regarding tribal boundaries and local conditions as circumstances permitted and to select physical features which might constitute recognizable landmarks for a frontier approximating to the blue line and to tribal limits. It is interesting to note that without proper study and in the absence of representatives, the British team arbitrarily decided to give the areas to Sudan. The only criterion used to make this decision was the tribal fighting in the area. The outlying communities were living in fear due to the conflicts.

British Engineer, Captain Charles said that: "I decided, therefore, to recommend that most of the detached hills should be included in Sudan as this would correspond fairly well with the position of the blue line[114]."

---

113 The New York Times (7 March 1897): Britain's aim in Abyssinia."
114 In the following years, some of the communities resisted the British's attempt to put them in Sudan. One of the leaders of the resistance was Ibrahim Wad Mahmud. Then, the British sent an army to crush the resistance and hanged Ibrahim Wad Mahmud in Khartoum (See Gwynn 1937: 154).

The fact that British Engineers single-handedly "delimited" the Ethiopia-Sudan border without consultation has created border disputes between the two for many decades. It is the cause of the on-and-off tensions between Sudan and Ethiopia today. In fact, it was quite evident that respect for the frontier could only be enforced by adequate policing, and this was highly improbable considering the financial position of the Sudan Government, the valueless character of most of the frontier region, and the terrible depopulation of the country as a consequence of the Khalif 's regime and Abyssinian raiding[115]. However, the delimitation of the frontier along Kenya-Ethiopia border ended simply by showing the local clans or tribes in the frontier that the British Government were prepared to recognize them.

After hosting successful mediation talks between the South Sudanese rebels and the Sudanese government, Ethiopia started boundary demarcation negotiations with Sudan. They exchanged notes regarding their boundary issue but did not make any progress to settle the disputed boundaries or agree on arrangements to stop banditry and establish peaceful coexistence among the pastoral people located there.[116] The 1972 Ethiopia and Sudan peace talks stopped in the middle without a viable long-term solution and did not define where the boundary should run regarding contested sections.

South Sudan and Sudan Need Good Relations

Boundaries that are clearly defined and well-managed are very important for good international relationships, cultural, national and local security, competent local administration, and for using resources efficiently.

---

115 As testified by Mburu (2003:20) "Addis Ababa renounced Britain's attempt to rectify this border through a survey by Major Charles Gwynn (Royal Engineers) in August 1908 for excluding Ethiopian surveyors."

116 Mburu, Nene (22 March 2003): "Delimitation of the Elastic Ilemi Triangle: Pastoral conflicts and official Indifference in the Horn of Africa." African Studies Quarterly, vol.7.

APUK : A STATE IN WAITING

Therefore, the failure to resolve these issues may prevent South Sudan, Sudan and other neighbouring countries from normalizing relationships and dealing with pressing clan, nationality, social and economic disputes. It is important that any territorial differences be resolved on a mutually acceptable basis in harmony with the standards of international law and practice. The delimitation of the boundaries between South Sudan and Sudan was dictated mainly by the colonial powers being apprehensive of the expansive potentialities of post-Abyiei South Sudan.

In the 1905 treaty signed by the traditional chief of the Dinka Ngok clans of Abyiei and the chief of the Misseriya Arabs of Southern Kordofan, Abyiei was deemed a separate entity and part of the Twic clans in Bahr El Ghazal Region while the Misseriya Arabs were under the administration of Southern Kordofan. Southern Kordofan refers to the geographical area that is defined by Article 2 (1) in the Protocol of the Resolution of Conflict in the Blue Nile and Southern Kordofan and Article 182 in the National Interim Constitution. Abyei has been at the crux of a recent ruling made by the Permanent Court of Arbitration at The Hague in mid-July 2009 about the demarcation of the North-South border. The town lies at a cultural and political fault line that divides Sudan into two distinct ethnic, religious and political entities.

Abyei has long been the location of violent clashes between the inhabitants. In the worst and most damaging incidence since the CPA in May 2008, the town was attacked, scorched and virtually destroyed by armed groups loyal to the North. It left tens of thousands of people displaced and hundreds killed. The demarcation of the town's borders was also a key cause of the second civil war in the early 1980s. Thusly, Abyei became a proxy of the war between North and South. Importantly, the region has potentially vast oil reserves.

The ruling entailed moving the eastern border to the west, thereby decreasing the size of the town while enlarging the area controlled by the North by more than 10,000 square kilometres. This notably includes the rich Heglig oil field. The decision was a major test for the implementation of the CPA, as part of which an agreement called the Abyei Protocol stipulates that the 2011 referendum should allow Abyei inhabitants to choose between the North and South should the GoSS decide to secede and regulates the distribution of oil revenues.

On May 15, 1902 Ethiopia signed a treaty with the British over its border with Sudan. This treaty was territorially advantageous to the British. It gave Gambella to the British and guaranteed their hydro interests at Lake Tana.

The boundary delimitations made with the colonialists had the following challenges:

Firstly, delimitation on a map was not always followed by demarcation on the ground. The long boundary with Sudan was only partially demarcated.

Secondly, the absence of competent administration in the frontier regions made the boundary delimitation little more than a cartographical exercise. The South Sudan boundaries were constantly violated by cross-border raids and incursions. In fact, this was the way of frontier peoples nullifying boundary agreements which were concluded without taking cognizance of their needs for seasonal movements of their flocks, such as the nomadic Arabs of Rezigat, Bagara, and Misseriya, and for ethnic unity in common borderlands.

The need for good relations with a neighbour outweighed the particular claims of one of the parties. However, in principle, boundary demarcation should be transparent and ratified according to the legal procedures of both countries.

Since border disputes are one of the major causes for conflicts among countries. The major factors that should be considered in any boundary are:

- Unilateral transparency.
- Official joint commissions should be established to facilitate demarcations.
- The local population should be consulted.
- Visa requirements should be simplified to facilitate border crossing procedures.

- Consulates should be opened in border cities.
- Border guards should be trained in border and visa procedures. Trained to stop corruption amongst them and customs authorities and to prevent harassment of travellers. Map archives should be open.
- Regional governors along the border should be granted a relatively free hand to deal with the social concerns of local populations in the disputed areas.
- NGOs should be allowed to engage in dispute mediation along the border.
- Ethnic minorities in border areas should be protected.
- Boundaries should be ratified according to the country's legal procedure.

Apuk Sections

The Wanhalel River lies on the common border between the Thony Dinka clans on the eastern bank and the Yar Dinka clan on the western bank together with the Apuk. It is a bona fide and fiat border. A bona fide border is a physical boundary such as river banks, lakes, and shorelines. They exist in the absence of delineating activity. The Wanhalel River exists independently of all human cognitive acts. Other boundaries are natural or geometric boundaries existing without human involvement. On the other hand, the boundaries between the Nyang and the Apuk clans at the Maluach and Machuet divisions in the northern frontiers are both artificial and bona fide borders marked by the Pagol Rivers and boundaries marked by a monument spear buried beneath the ground. The boundaries between the Luanykoth and the Apuk of Aliai and the Maluil divisions in the eastern frontiers are bona fide boundaries marked by rivers more than five miles from Thiet centre and by physical characteristics. The Apuk-Luanykoth sub-clans are on the eastern boundary. Artificial borders between neighbours and the Apuk on the north, east, south and west are borders that depend on both physical characteristics and

Geographics and Boundaries

ethnic characteristics.

Wanhalel is a shared county composed of the Malong in the west and the Tarweng in the south. They are combined with the Dinka Yar Ayiei to form Wanhalel County along the western bank of the Wanhalel River.

Tarweng borders the Wanhalel River on the west bank, the Yar Ayiei Dinka clan to the south and the Thony Dinka clan across the eastern bank to the extreme south, extending towards swampy land to the southeast. Malony covers a very long common border with the Yar Ayiei from the southwest to the west and borders with the Muok Dink clans to the west where it borders the Jurchol-Luo of Wau State.

Chuei Ajai was the first colonial military post and administration headquarters established 1903. The name "Jur River District" emerged later when administration was transferred from Chuei Ajai to its current location and named as "Tonj, to be known as Jur River District Tonj"[117] because it is located at the river bank of Tonj River. The area around the river is Toch or swampy up to Wanhalel River to Toch Apuk and beyond.

The Aliai, Manging and Angol sections of sub-clans were brought together to be one Apuk county in the capital at Thiet. They share artificial boundaries with the population occupying a geographical area bordering the Kuach of Kerik centre to the northeast and the Luachkoth of Ananatak centre to the east, and far to the extreme eastern swampland at Akarap and Mading Apuk Sudd land.

Machuet and Maluach are the two divisions of the Apuk inhabiting the northwest and north, with similar boundaries and borders as described above. They have been established to be Apuk County at

---

117 Tonj is defined in many ways. There are those who believed Tonj means "Thony", but newcomers did not know how to write 'Thony" and only wrote "Tonj". Other people say that it is "Toch", but newcomers wrote "Tonj". Tonj Town is located between Mouk to the north, Thony to the east and Bongo to the extreme south. But Chuei Ajai which was first established, is the border between Jurchol to the west, Apuk to the north and east and Mouk to the south. It was the place where many Dinka Rek clan leaders including Chief Malek Agei and Subchief Ayuel Bak were brutally murdered in cold blood by the Anglo-Egyptian Sudan government

the capital of Jak centre. It is composed of the Kongdeer subsection, the Maluach subsection and the Agurping subsection. These are the earliest or oldest 'Motherlands' of the Machuet of Apuk Bol, Apuk Bek Amuuk and Apuk Aguet Lokbaithok, following the arrival of Rum, the founder of the Parum clan. Its population occupies a large area.

Apuk county at the Jak centre of holy shrines has its borders with Malony in the west, Jurchol-Luo of Wau State in the northwest, the Nyang (Kuanythii) and Pagol Rivers in the north, the Aliai section in the east and southeast and Manging in the extreme south. These are large territories with vast green forests near the Maluach village of Machuet on the border with the Jurchol-Luo ethnic groups of Wau State and the Dinka Nyang clans of Paramount Chief Akoch Majok. The Apuk are believed to have expanded from Machuet widely to Aliai, Malony, Manging, Tarweng, and Angol and to the Sudd wetland now in Akarap and Mading territory covering Madol Alian Apuk.

Social and Economic Development

The Apuk homeland houses the Dinka Rek clan. It is part of the flood region of South Sudan and receives about 800 to 900mm of rainfall per annum. There are rich, fertile soils that give high yields of sorghum, groundnuts, short season maize and a variety of other crops adapted to the semi-arid conditions. The area also supports one of the highest concentrations of cattle of any area in South Sudan. However, in recent years rains have been erratic leading to a reduction in the size of the land area under cultivation. This has raised concerns, especially over the welfare of the numerous internally displaced people from the Gogrial parts of Bahr El Ghazal Region of Western Wau. These people, despite owning livestock, have limited access to grain when their crop yields are inadequate, and other's surpluses are small.

Development of Trading Activities

Trade developed between the Apuk clans, other Dinka Rek clans, Bantustan ethnic groups, the Jurchol–Luo of Nilotic stock, and Arab merchants over the centuries. Arab caravans carried grains, ointments, charms, jewels, necklaces, earrings, costume jewellery, ornaments, bits and knick-knacks etc. through the White Nile River to the Machar Rek River. They returned to Aswan with ivory, hides, and arrowheads for shipment downriver.

Arab merchants also valued slaves captured from the Nilotic people. Arab military expeditions penetrated the Apuk clans sporadically during Bol Mel's time in the earliest dynasty era and even predated the offspring descendants of the Malek Rum periods. Yet there was no attempt to establish a permanent presence in the Apuk clan homeland until the Middle Rules between 1800 and 1900 AD. This was when the British Government constructed a network of forts along the Nile tributaries and then railways far south into South Sudan. These guarded the flow of gold, ivory, timber, animals and other valuable items from sources in all over the Bahr El Ghazal region covering the Apuk clans in the savannah valley region of southern Tonj State.

Market Centres

Trade flourished inside the Thiet market centres of the Apuk clans in. Local and external trade activities today are on the increase. Thiet and Tonj towns are the predominant ones. The locally traded items, among others, include pharmaceutical drugs, sorghums, groundnuts, fish, cattle and livestock. The Thiet trading centre of the has good linkages with the Wau, Warrap and Rumbek trading centres. Community members walk in their livestock and commodities for sale and exchange for assorted goods (clothes, sugar, bicycles, footwear, etc.). Goods are also obtained from Uganda via Equatoria, and Kenya through the Rumbek market centres. Trading activities are usually conducted via a multi-currency basis used according to the location of each. There are several main currencies used. The US Dollar is accepted everywhere. South Sudanese pounds are accepted in the market centres in Apuk, and Ugandan and Kenyan Shillings are also accepted.

Social and Economic Development

Security and Insecurity

Historically, the relative stability in the Apuk homeland and in Thiet Town[118] made it a haven for the SPLA Headquarters established in Mayom and Yinh Kuel. SPLA soldiers, their family members, and internally displaced persons from the Bahr El Ghazal Region and Wau town conducted job-market activities there. Inter and intra-clan fighting, military and Gelweng militia security situations improved as a result of the Comprehensive Peace Agreement (CPA) signed on January 9, 2005 between SPLA/M as the de facto Government of South Sudan and the National Congress Party (NCP) of the Government of Sudan.

The insecurity which emerged on December 15, 2013 did not affect Apuk in any way. The IGAD mediated and negotiated peace was signed in August 2015, by the SPLM-In-Government and the SPLM-In-Opposition. No inter-clan clashes have been reported between the different neighbouring communities' militia groups during the time of writing.

However, there have been reports of insecurity caused by the Jurchol-Luo ethnic group of Wau state and fighting between the Dinka Rek clans of Apuk, the Yar, Muok, Nyang, Abuok, and Abiem of Tonj State, as well as inter-clan fighting between Dinka Abiem clan of Tonj State and the Dinka Apuk Giir of Gogrial State. There was also inter-clan fighting between the Dinka Apuk Giir and the Dinka Waw, Kuach-Agor and Aguok clans of Gogrial State. Incidents have been reported regarding cattle rustling between the Dinka Akok, Jalwau, Apuk, Thony, Yar and Muok clans, and the sub-clans of Tonj State and the Dinka Gok clans of Gok State. Fortunately, this did not impact negatively on the job situation or the numerous trading development and economic activities to date.

Apuk has long been considered one of the most underdeveloped regions in the world. Poor accessibility and underinvestment have

---

118 Thiet was one of the first towns to be captured by the SPLM / A in the current civil war. It has been under uninterrupted SPLM / A control since 1983.

resulted in a scarcity of the most basic services. The area's resource potential has nevertheless attracted outside interest since colonial times.

Cattle, goat, and sheep herding has long been an important source of livelihood. The regulation of its distribution was attempted during the Anglo-Egyptian Condominium (1899–1956). Since then, livestock has increasingly made its way to the urban markets that extend beyond the local economies. In recent years, the Apuk has had some of the largest herd populations of any region in South Sudan.

A UNICEF undertaking in Thiet confirms the extent of the livestock markets from 1995 to 1999. In times of civil war between Thiet (which is mainly inhabited by the Dinka and lies on the shortest route to Juba) and the town of Wau. Apuk herders have found an alternative route to the capital cutting westwards at the deviation in Jurchol–Kuanythii (Nyang Akoch). Cattle rustling arrived in Apuk as a new phenomenon which cannot be completely understood without attention to this growing trade, its transformation and the Jur River route system, which in recent decades has been shrinking. This is forcing some people to move with their cattle further westwards and northwards, putting pressure on the Jurchol population and herders.

Access to water has been an issue of major concern in Apuk for at least a century. Before Sudan's independence, the construction of a Machar Achol River canal to the Tonj River passing through Wanhalel River was a major focus. The Tonj River originates from the Ezo River in the Congo. It runs through the Nadiangere River in Tambura State and branches to the Jur River. Another canal branched to the Tonj and Wanhalel rivers respectively.

The plan was to widen the Machar Achol River for transport use from the area of the Machar Achol Riverport. It would be reconnected downstream from the Wanhalel River to the Tonj River, passing near Thiet, at the likely expense of the people living in the Sudd swamps of Wanhalel River. Routes from Jur River in Wau and other possible routes have been assessed over the last century.

They were eventually abandoned in 1956 due to its political and economic benefits imbalance. But these should have been under discussion in the post-independence years of South Sudan as critical works.

In fact, this hesitation seems due to the lack of regulation in the oil business. After the South's independence, and despite resistance from the French, the Government decided that the area was too vast to be granted to only one firm and acknowledged only one-third of Total Oil's original concession. They began inviting other investors to bid on the rest. This was a significant change in the direction South Sudan's commercial relations.

In an area like Apuk, so inaccessible due to its poor road system, exploration would be prohibitively expensive due to depressed oil prices. So, while the insurgency of Riek Machar certainly played a role, the main obstacles faced by the extractive industry were more of the economic, legal, and logistical types. They remain unresolved even though the government signed peace agreements with the rebels in August 2015.

Although the oil exploration project struggles to take off, important regional investments are expected for the improvement of the road system between the states of Gok, Tonj and up to Gogrial and Twic bordering Sudan to the extreme north. Part of the plan includes road construction to connect Rumbek, Chueibet, Thiet, Jak, Pagol River, Wau, Warrap and Kuajok via Luonyaker in Gogrial East to an alternate highway. Apuk is considered rich in resources, particularly in the areas along the border.

What to Do?

What the Apuk officially want and clearly desire, is a strong and transparent administration to strengthen economic development, ethnic security, social harmony and collaboration with local governments and neighbouring states. There is also a need to create an Apuk administration with a harmonious decentralization policy. This will generate new opportunities to strengthen the capability of the Apuk authority leadership and its entire population to deal with threats to its stability, peace, social harmony and security.

An Apuk administration has four official objectives:

- Strengthening ethnic security, peace and social harmony in the territory.
- Preventing and responding to manmade and natural disasters.
- Improving collaborative efforts between the ethnic group rivalries, local governments, civic organizations, and national and state governments in order to stem inter-tribal terrorization.
- Sustaining enduring efforts to attract unity and peace with various tribal groups, with a fundamental focus on preventing tribal conflicts.

Apart from these objectives and other official pronouncements, we suggest that the creation of an Apuk State and the attainment of progressions in harmony will go beyond tribal security concerns by addressing non-tribal security issues such as good governance, charity support and economic development. Apuk is basically a socio-economic development state. This is a central issue of concern for those supporting the idea of a harmonious decentralization of Tonj State.

Goals

The main goal is to promote entrepreneurship within Apuk clans by encouraging youth and the general public to embrace business and innovation as a means to wealth creation and empowerment. The state would bring together local, regional and international investors with a view to showcasing the trade and investment opportunities there as well as allowing for an exchange of innovative ideas that will ultimately lead to increased investments.

The People

The people of the Apuk clans shall continue the drive for a distinctive identity. Apuk is a common unifying demography

Social and Economic Development

within a definite geographical area with a population estimated at over 50,000 people in southwestern Dinka Rek inhabiting southern Tonj State. The Apuk clans' border Yar and Thony to the extreme south, Luachkoth to the east of the Rek sub-clans further to the extreme east of Mading swampland, bordering the Kuach and the Nyang-Rek sub-clans to the northeast and far north, and bordering the Jurchol-Luo of Nilotic stock to the extreme west. The people of Apuk may follow a similar run taken by Gok and Twic States to see an Apuk state established with the idea of bringing services closer to the community so that they are not left out in the development of the country.

Reviving cultural identity, rudimental aspects and appreciation of traditional values began with Republican Order Number 36/2015 under which the states of South Sudan were created. Foreign interference has damaged the cultural identity of the Apuk and overshadowed its historical identity, beliefs, norms, customary principles and values. Outside interference has rendered the Apuk identity and its value systems irrelevant. It is not acceptable for the sons and daughters of heroic generations to allow their valued identity to be compromised. Apuk will continue to stand proud. Apuk values and identity are precious and they deserve to be upheld and not eroded away. The eyes of succeeding generations exposed and influenced by new cultures search for new identity around the world, at the expense of our precious Apuk identity.

Thirteen representatives in the National Legislative Assembly of the Republic of South Sudan from the Apuk, Thony, Muok, Yar and Bongo ethnic groups met on October 11, 2015, at my residence in Juba, the capital of South Sudan. They discussed the future in relation to the creation of the 28 states that increased to 32 states and revised the counties incorporated within. I chaired the meeting and discussed the agenda. The payams were proposed to be upgraded into Apuk counties and that information was given to out to circulate.

Proposed Apuk Counties

TONJ STATE Division of Apuk tribes into three Counties as below:			
County	CAPITAL	Payam	Geographical regions
Apuk County at JAK	JAK	Kongdeer Maluach Agurpiny Padwer	Kongdeer, Agurpiny, and Maluach sections of Machuet Division
Apuk County at THIET	THIET	Thiet, Panakdit Ngapanet Angol	Aremrap and Atokthou, sections of Aliai Division. Angol and Manging sections of Maluil Divisions
Wanhalel County SHARED by border clans: (Yar Ayiei plus Tarweng and Malony)	WANHALEL	Wanh Alel Pawel	Tarweng and Malony sections of Maluil Division

Funding Misallocations

Indeed, with the signing of Comprehensive Peace Agreement, tribal security remained fractured in Apuk, because inter-tribal fighting had not ceased. There is major insecurity caused by inter-clan and inter-tribal fighting. Even more is caused by cattle rustling across borders. The Apuk lacked strong institutional foundations and faced a set of interrelated challenges which included the weak rule of law and insecurity arising out of weaknesses within the government and the proliferation of arms. There have been very weak institutions such as the police and the judiciary. There are so many clan crimes that are not seen or heard in court. In some areas, the government invested in solutions. In Apuk the government left it broken.

How many children will be denied their basic education? How many children and pregnant women will be denied primary health care service and safe drinking water access due to poverty?

This will remain unknown for as long as their stories remain private. It has attracted commentary, including apportioning blame or responsibility on certain individuals or offices. Others think that it is the duty of parents or the community to support them. To others, there is a social contract between communities and the government that must be formed to address these needs.

Locking out bright students from quality education and locking out pregnant women from quality health care service is simply wrong. This is the case of citizens whose chances to access basic social services are fast dwindling. Why should poor families miss out on these services when funds have been allocated? The colossal allocations to the rural development projects are meant to support the vulnerable. Yet the existence of needy families threatens to devolve into poverty for all.

The allocations to rural development projects for this fiscal year alone are quite substantial per quarter according to information from the fund's sources. Members of Parliament ought to equitably allocate the resources from the project's kitty or pooled money in line with its goal, which is to provide leadership and policy direction regarding the optimal utilization of devolved funds for equitable development and poverty reduction at the community level.

Questions must be asked: Why do children have no school despite the rural development project allocations? What are the priorities of the development projects? Why are the police and prisons operating under trees and perpetrators arrested are still chained to trees in the sub-counties of Wanhalel and Jak when development project money is available? Is education prioritized as a development goal? Do the leaders know that with the funds, they have the power to eradicate poverty in their regions and that lack of conscientious allocation threatens to devolve into poverty? If they are, how do they allocate these funds? What are the parameters of need analysis? Is the list of allocations published?

To achieve more with the development project budgets, a greater sense of responsibility, justice, and transparency should be used in allocating funds. MPs should use the resources fairly and equitably to benefit all without dirty politics, corruption, and favouritism.

The people knew that there were some elements of corruption involved in the projects. The people who were handling them were not straightforward. Many people see a project as a cheap and manageable political marketplace. Corruption and patronage are the norm.

However, it is observable that those twin evils are distortions of the development project management system. Since Thiet was captured on the 22nd October 1984 by the Movement, the leadership failed in transforming the rural programme of Apuk into one that could be articulated into basic social service delivery. People have leaders who have no vision. That is why we have these frustrations today. Tribal fighting in the north, fighting in the east, and fighting everywhere in the south. The promises that development budgets were going to eradicate poverty in rural areas are not there for the Apuk. The votes only count for us during election time, but life does not matter in the eyes of the government. The real problem for us is to create a state where life matters.

The fund should be used to support projects under the auspices of the national government. This means more money for schools and security-related projects such as police stations, police posts, prison stations, and bursaries for bright and war orphaned students who are in need. Rural development project committees should have a sub-county administrator, two men, two women, one disabled person, two representatives of the constituency office, an officer from the Development Board and one member co-opted by the board. MPs who control the pooled money should play the role of spectators. The Constituency Oversight Committee should supervise all projects to avoid corrupt practices.

Developmental Emergencies

Lack of an adequate education system in the area is considered to be a developmental emergency. The education authorities, teachers, parents, and society share the blame for the mass failure regarding enrolment. Statistically, it is not possible right now to have accurate numbers of functioning schools and enrolled children recorded properly.

Such dilemmas point to a serious breakdown in the systems that determine enrolment performance. That creates a chance for the enrolled few to proceed to the next level of education while condemning the masses to scramble for the few slots in other levels offering certificate courses. Those who were unable to secure a school for enrolment were consigned to rot and waste.

Education outcomes are the sum total of the aptitude of the children and the influence of their educational environment. The quality of the environment should ideally harvest schoolchildren who have basic skills that can be yoked for the socioeconomic transformation of Apuk.

The education system needs major consideration and overhaul to give schoolgoing children hope and prepare them for a future of work and entrepreneurship. The current education development program falls far short in providing this much needed link between education and the demand for skills necessary support productive economic activities.

The administration and other education stakeholders must diagnose the causes of the weaknesses in the system and find solutions to improve education outcomes. They need to assure children that going to school is not a waste of time but lays a foundation for their prosperity.

The future of the economy depends on an efficient and competent transport system that facilitates movement of goods and services, and an education system that produces human resources with the right skills for development. Transport and education are two sectors popularly known for complementing each other as the lack of an effective system of education and effective transport will severely affect economic growth and social transformation.

Meaningful Partnerships

The state should create a platform that will celebrate entrepreneurs, create meaningful connections, build cross-state bridges and spark much needed conversations aimed at generating sustainable investments and partnerships with youth and the entire country.

As the leadership of the state, we realize that economic growth must be driven by focused public and private sector investments and our comparative advantage in natural resources.

In this regard, we intend to leverage on our rich agricultural base to build a robust economy hinged on value addition through agri-processing, branding and marketing to foster employment and create wealth.

Other areas with rich investment opportunities are health care (private practice), value addition to soap processing, technical education, and manufacturing, generation of solar energy, hospitality, and real estate.

The necessary enablers are already in place, including a policy that targets domestic and foreign direct investment. This policy seeks to protect the rights and interests of investors and guide initiatives that will make the Apuk State an attractive investment destination.

The high population in the state is a source of abundant skilled labour and a ready market for goods and services. The state also enjoys ample security and a peaceful community with an entrepreneurial spirit.

Social and Economic Development

The installation of over 200 solar-powered streetlights in the capital of Jak Apuk County, capital of Thiet County and Wanhalel capital in Apuk state will spur the rise of a 24/7 economy. The project will be replicated in 7 other market centres across the state.

Infrastructure

An Apuk State Government would invest heavily in infrastructure development, especially in the areas of roads, ICT, healthcare and water reticulation.

Upgrading of the key lifeline road in Gok, Thony, and the bridge over the Wanhalel River, to Thiet, Jak, Pagol and Lurchuk connecting to the main Wau and Warrap road and to cross through to the Abiem clan of Pankot up to Luonyaker and Wau road. This road is important for Apuk and is a key factor in a cumulatively estimated 500 kilometres of government class C roads to be built or upgraded in central the Bahr EL Ghazal region under South Sudan projects initiatives.

From 2007 to 2012, millions of dollars were initially invested in this road as an economic corridor designed to connect the Rumbek and Tonj highway roads to Chueibet of Gok state, through the Manyang-ngok sub-county of Thony and the Thiet-Jak sub-counties of Apuk, linking the Pagol sub-county together with the main Wau-Warrap highway road. It also links some payams and counties to major states and acts as feeders for major highways in and out of the Apuk.

It became evident phantom companies contracting roadworks siphoned millions of dollars given to them by the political leadership in huge patronage deals. The politicians are corrupt, and they fortify networks aimed at self-enrichment and brutal repression of dissent.

In health care services, the state Government must elevate the Thiet hospital into a referral facility, invest in a major infrastructure upgrade, install modern diagnostic equipment and empower additional health workers. It must initiate and sign loan agreements with the banking institutions around the world and pave the way for the establishment of a modern Child and Maternal treatment centre in Apuk.

With our proximity to the niche tourism venues of the Titadol Games Reserve and Machar Acol National Park and with our strategic location as the Central Bahr El Ghazal regional economic hub, we are undoubtedly a quality investment destination.

The Creation of an Apuk State is the Best Option

The region between Jak and Pagol, which lies on the oil-rich Warrap basin, has long been in the crosshairs. The commodity trade route from Thiet through Jak via Kothngoro in Jurchol-Luo was initially constructed during the war. The section from Thiet Airstrip and Kuanythii to Wau Town is the object of competition in the demarcation of the new counties. Livestock, cereal and peanut crops from Thiet transit through the Jak towns that were the main strategic bases for the liberation movements and the site of refugee camps during 21 years of civil war. They are often sold in Wau in the Bahr El Ghazal region.

The people have a historical obligation to identify themselves with the symbolic identity of Apuk. It has resources and territory similar to The Twic, Gok, and Luanyjang nations, and that of the Apuk Toch (also called Apuk Giir Kir).

Countries such as the Philippines, Cambodia, and Macedonia have adopted a decentralized system of governance as a way of reducing opportunities for corruption and devolved decision-making power. This has enhanced services delivery to local communities and organizations. There is light at the end of the tunnel in the Kenya devolution system. Good governance and democracy is the laboratory where integrity and transparency can be ripened. In line with the governance principles enshrined in the constitution, we have also done well in securing basic welfare and democratic rights equity, non-discrimination, public participation integrity.

The creation of an Apuk State, as many wish, is the best option. Apuk has been under constant siege on economic and political fronts

Social and Economic Development

for so long and is hated by the surrounding communities for their numbers and visionaries. The Apuk people noted the antagonism displayed regarding the most basic socio-economic benefits, development benefits in certain quarters against individuals. There is constant intimidation, dissemination of hatred, and violence against individuals based on their ethnic identity and political views. They continuously resort to hateful remarks and provoke hostilities. The people of Apuk deplore the particularly vulgar remarks recently directed, not for the first time, against them. We must be vigilant in pursuit of a long-term goal to achieve the creation of the Apuk State and progressive attainments in the future.

Investment

The fact that several investors have already plugged into the existing opportunities in Thiet centre goes to show that there exists an ideal investment climate.

The people of Apuk must assure all investors and development partners that the community innovations have put in place requisite measures to safeguard investments and to avail incentives.

The challenge to investors across the board is to take full advantage of this state by committing to take up viable investments derived from local resources that will trigger linkages to all sectors of the economy. All parties must be committed to offering full support in the firm belief that only through value addition, trade and investments will we all achieve our goal of transforming Apuk into a middle-class based economy.

The main goal is to promote entrepreneurship in Apuk by encouraging its citizens to embrace business and innovation as a means to wealth and empowerment creation. An Apuk state would bring together local, regional and international investors with a view to showcasing the trade and investment opportunities as well as allowing for an exchange of innovative ideas that will ultimately lead to increased investments.

The Dynasty Founded by Rum

As we know from earlier in the book, Rum is the ancestor father and founder of the Parum clan and is commonly known as Rum Wenkook, or Rum, son of the cave.

Oral tradition gives a picture of Rum as a spirit subsidiary to Nhialic, sometimes known as a Supreme Deity, the Divine High Priest Chief sent down to earth by the Creator Nhialic and the ancestry spirits. Rum is the sky god of rain and fertility, empowered by Nhialic and sometimes alleged to be a son from or even a different form of Nhialic, akin to spirit, with greater power and commanding wide-ranging acceptance by the Apuk of Dinka Rek Muonyjang. The Rum myth may ultimately be close to a fused folktale regarding the relationship between Deng Mayual and Nhialic. Deng Mayual or Deng Kur meaning great rain is the offspring of a union of Garang, son of Nhialic, the sky, and Abuk, daughter of Apiny, the earth.

Rum is the divine spirit that had fallen into the cave of the sausage tree, *rual* or *rual mangok* from the sky portrayed by the folktale as follows:

Rum was begotten from the cave of the sausage tree. His first son was Atany, the second son Wol, Rum Wenkook, Aleek and the other child evaporated into the air back to the sky to join the Nhialic God, the Creator. The structural dynasty of Rum is summarized as follows[119]:

---

119 Interview with elders and living family members descended from Rum and practicing the Parum clan culture.

The Dynasty Founded by Rum

Descendants of Rum and Aleek
Atany is the son of Rum.
Rum is the son of Atany Rum.
Atany is the son of Rum Atany Rum.
Rum is the son of Atany Rum Atany Rum Rual.
Jiel is the son of Rum Rual Ngoth Rum Wol Jiel Ateny.
Rual is the son of Ateny Jiel Rum Jiel Atany Ngoth Rum Rual.
Malek is the son of Rum Agei Rum Atany Kur Ngoth Jiel Rum Agei.
Malek is the son of Ngoth Rum Agei Wol Atany Rum Wol Rum Ateny.
Ngoth is the son of Malek Rual Rum Ngoth Ateny Wol Jok Malek Jiel Malek.
Agei is the son of Malek Rum Manyiel Rum Atany Malek Rum Wol Agei Malek.
Malek is the son of Agei Rum Malek Jiel Agei Atany Akook Rum Agei Malek Agei.

This lineage has continued unbroken to the present day

This is a simple structure for the first formation of the Parum clan family to the dynasty era. It engulfed regional society on an unexpectedly large scale and was coupled with spiritual and military leadership in a growing spectrum.

Malek Rum Wol Rum and Agei Malek Rum followed from the union of Amel and Achol Gong. Rum was the only son resulting from the union of Wol Rum and Amel, but the second wife Achol Gong begat Ngoth Wol Rum, Agei Wol Rum in the union with Wol Rum.

As the power of Malek Rum Wol Rum (and later their son, Agei) grew, so did his Parum spiritual clan and the size of the Apuk nation. Rum was a spiritual master and leader of the Apuk clans. A day would not pass by without Rum Wol showing the high regard he had for the protection of human life. He placed himself in a prominent spot to clearly give orders and always ran the risk of death. Once he ordered his warriors to prove their loyalty by marching to a faraway temple. They honoured him so much that they obeyed.

Rum Wol Rum married Athiech Mathiang and gave birth to Agei Rum, Malek Rum Sr, and Malek Rum Jr, and Ajok Rum. He hoped that an heir would someday carry the fight against the predators. However, Malek Rum Sr., who led the chiefdom, died from injuries sustained in battle and was survived by Agei, Manyiel, Wol and Ajok Malek Rum respectively.

Agei took the throne and kept as many as 5 wives. On one occasion he came back unexpectedly early from a journey and had 145 young men and skilful warriors put to death on a suspicion of wrongdoing.

The only people he felt generous toward were the Jurchol-Luo ethnic groups and the Nyang and Kuach clans since at this stage they could not be a threat to his chiefdom. In the 1900s he allowed small groups of immigrant clans to build settlements at the Maluach, Agurpiny, Malony, Aliai and Maluil sections. These were made up of various renegade and weak clan members. The settlements were too far away to receive help from the Jur River District Colony base in Tonj, so it only existed at his pleasure. The settlers did whatever they could to stay on the Parum dynasty's good side.

Malek didn't fear the single-shot rifles used by Arab slave hunters and Government platoons. In the time it took a soldier to reload his gun, he reasoned, a young clan warrior could confront and slaughter him with a spear. Still, the immigrants were useful in finishing off his enemies, so Malek used the diviners and supporters as mercenaries, and gave them the blessing of clan spirits and promoted inter-marriage with existing clans. Most of what we now know about Malek, in fact, comes from the accounts of his father Malek Agei, elderly uncle Aguelet Agei-Thii, aunt Angau Aguelet and a second Agei Aguelet from who we learned to know more about two principles in one body: dual control of war and high priest chief leadership.

I mention these descendent groups to show that Rum Ateny was a great priest chief of the powerful Parum clan divinity whose offspring unite two things or two dogmas in their bodies. These are visibly

The Dynasty Founded by Rum

superior descendants, more so than most of their clans through the Parum clan divinities. His offspring represent the model of religious leadership and he was the pre-eminent Deity in the clans. He and his descendants inspired the Apuk clans, and as the Rum, would lead his supporters against all invaders. The truly great spiritualists are like the hereditary masters of the fishing spear whose clan's religious convictions are thought to have much more power than those of other clans.

The distinct power of clan divinities who are deities or high priests in a dynasty emanates from their proficiencies. Another is that spiritualists or spear masters are ambassadors on earth of spirituality or divinity. Powerful clans like the Parum, Pagong and Pabuor do not have ordinary diviners. They are placed among a priestly association of clans in Apuk, where they are able to display powers denied to an ordinary priest through instinctive inspiration. The normal diviners appear low when compared to the powerful priests of divine clans and their ability to help or injure others via the almighty divinities.

Great reputation came to the masters of the fishing spear of the Parum clan quickly. This was also accepted by those with whom priests made sacrifices of beasts offered through prayer to divinities and to the clan divinities of those most concerned in the event, and to other clan spirits or other powers directed through the diviners.

Diviners vary in reputation. Quite often the diviners ask for a sacrifice or dedication of an animal or beast offered for invoking a treatment. The diviner might sacrifice the beast or animal himself, or he might leave it to the headman of the clan family in the homestead, or somebody requested by him to oversee the event. A master of the fishing spear might be requested to undertake the instructions of a diviner on behalf of the suffering clan family or member of the family. He would then add his own prayers, to the divinity and his clan divinity to those of the diviner and the people. The suffering clan families pray to the divinity and to the clan divinities of those lineage members most concerned in the situation, and to such other powers described by the diviner including clan spirits, *jak*, *atiip*, *machardit*, or *cholwich*.

APUK : A STATE IN WAITING

The clans believed that there exist diviners of inferior temperaments and no great importance, whom clans accused of practising dishonesty, witchcraft, or even black magic. For example, Machardit kills. Machardit hides when it is offered cows. Machardit kills when it is not well served. Machardit rejects any cows offered to it for saving a life. Or, Machardit is very bad *jok* in the house.

Intermediate diviners are proper and of good reputation as clansmen whom the clans compare to creators. People try to distinguish between the poor categories of diviners, who change into doctors with magic roots, or magicians. The *tiet* changes into a symbol of a fairly diverse category, the *ran Nhialic* clansman of divinity, or *aciek* 'Nhialic-God', which people then refer to as the "prophet or master of the fishing spear" albeit in the lowest level of regard.

Clans know that the masters of the fishing spear in the Apuk are of the Parum, Pagong and Pabuor clan and are commonly acknowledged as true deities. Other spiritualists were understood, to be proficient at falsehoods, wrongdoing, or black magic.

There had been only four descended deities whose names are commonly known. One is Bol Mel or Bol Chiirial, the second is Rum or Rum Wenkook, the third is Atany or Ateny Wun Dior (Atany Wundior) and the fourth is Jiel. The Padior or Dedior or Wundior clan founded by Atany Wundior and the Pakuin clan founded by Akuien, constitute parts of the Parum clan with a single identity symbol or emblem of the *rual* (sausage tree) that ties them together. Ateny Wundior is said to be the first son of Rum.

All Parum descendants are linked to the past and each other by worshipping a single clan divinity symbol of identity. These deity descendants turned priests or prophets exerted enormous influence. The clan divinity powers became fully realized after the Rum who was kidnapped was returned. Afterwards, the clan and associated clans alike conferred deity status on Parum priests and gave faithful devotion to their commands. Parum spread clan divinity was institutionalized through symbols or emblems of descent groups like the Jok family in the Luanykoth homestead, the Madhieu family in the Jalwau homestead, the Makom family in Thiik homestead, and in so many other Padior or Dedior of Wundior and Akuien of Parum clan sects all over the region.

The Parum clan was so great that they spread their divinities and exercised influence as far east, west and north as the Rek Apuk clans in Apuk Padoch, up to Apuk Toch (Apuk Giir) of the Northern Rek Jieng Clans. This influence even spread to their priests to persuade those who had raided herds to return them to their rightful owners before *yath, jak,* or *jok* would strike back at them for punishment for crime clans for stealing the cows of *yath* from different clans and sub-clans.

Malek

Most of what we now know about Malek, in fact, comes from the accounts of Malek Agei, elderly uncle Aguelet Agei-Thii, aunt Angau Aguelet and a second Agei Aguelet from who we learned to know more about two principles in one body: dual control of war and high priest chief leadership. Malek used the diviners and supporters as mercenaries and gave them the blessing of clan spirits and promoted inter-marriage with existing clans.

The dynastic court of Malek's order regarding criminally run clans was known of very quickly. Any poor diviner or an ordinary master of the fishing spear could not think to have any influence whatsoever. He sent envoys to as far as the Nyang clans in the north, the Kuach clans in the northeast, the Luanykoth clans in the east, the Thony clans across Wanhalel River in the south and the Rek Jieng (Dinka) and Jurchol-Luo. Those from the more remote parts of the country visited Malek's court, with many more settling within the Machuet homestead where it operated.

The newly established government of Anglo-Egyptian Sudan's representative met Malek when he paid his first visit to the Apuk. The clans and sub-clans of the Apuk maintain that Malek wanted only peace between them and with the new government. However, he was misrepresented because some people took false reports to the government and other war leaders rejected his advice by defying the authorities.

Whichever might have been true explanation, Malek and his people did eventually defy the government as well, who dispatched a platoon of troops to deal with the situation.

Malek said that his father, Rum, father of greater Wundior Deity, *ee yin Nhialic* Atany Wundior, the creator, and ancestry spirits, would change bullets into rain. The great rain or water of Deng Mayual, Deng Kur or Deng Piol. When the bullets shot at them were heard with sounds like thunderstorms coming with great rainfall, they concluded that the divination was accomplished. Then, both the diviners and supporters of Malek, looked around and saw that their fighters were not panicking and had no injuries. They were encouraged enough to charge the government troops, killing some, stabbing others. However, many clansmen lost their lives in that battle. From 1903 to 1908, Malek's reign did not go smoothly during the conflicts. Malek was injured and survived for a short time. His son, Agei, was immediately ordered to return from the frontlines of Bur Apuuk and Akon Ageu. There he was to ascend to chieftaincy throne since his father's wounds would not allow him to lead another battle effectively.

The name of Malek, son of descendants of Rum the founder of the dynasty, is held in the highest regard by the southwestern Rek clans in the Apuk homeland today. Agei and the government decided to work together for reconciliation and to pardon and forgive the past.

When Agei came to the throne, the modern administration era began. From 1910 onwards, Agei Malek Rum Wol Rum consolidated the chiefdom and his own authority in Apuk. He began to gather followers from among the prominent community leaders from various clans and sub-clans. He found high priest chiefs with good reputations and clan youth leaders. However, the Anglo-Egyptian government also entrenched itself with modern political tools. As an offspring from the dynasty era, Agei maintained the position of the descended fathers partly to live at peace with their neighbours, the Rek Muonyjang, and partly to prepare for disaster from traditional adversaries and those who would not live at peace with the chiefdom of Apuk.

The Dynasty Founded by Rum

Recent Historical Lineage

Wol Rum married Amel Akoon Angich of the Pabol clan. They had only one boy child called Rum Wol Rum in their union. Since Rum Wol, was the only boy child, known as *juol*, in the family of the high priest chief and war commander, for insurance he took a second wife called Achol Gong. She gave birth to two boys: Ngoth Wol Rum and Agei Wol Rum.

Many offspring of Achol Gong are inhabitants of Ju village in the triangle between Wanhalel River and Tarweng section to the west, Manging section and Angol section to the northwest and Wun-ngap village and Toch Apuk wetland to the east.

Rum, the first son and only juol from first wife Amel Akoon Angich, married Athiech Mathiang of the Padolmuot clan. They gave birth to three boys:
1 Agei Rum Wol Rum
2 Malek-Dit Rum Wol Rum; (Malekdit or Malek Senior)
3 Malek-Thii Rum Wol Rum (Malekthii or Malek Junior)
4 Ajok Rum Wol Rum

Malek-Dit Rum Wol Rum married as his first wife Angau Anei Akol Kuot from the Pakot Clan. Today's name for Angou or Angau is Aluat. She acquired a new nickname after marriage: Angan Apiok or Angau of the ivory or elephant tusks, because she was exchanged or married off with elephant tusks. Just like Aleek Jiel was exchanged or married off to Rum Wenkook with grass water known as "*awar*" in Apuk language which was given to Jiel as dawry for Aleek. This was paid by Malek Dit Rum Wol Rum to Anei Akol Kuot, father of Aluat. Children in the union of Angou and Malek Rum are as follows:
1 Agei Malek Rum
2 Wol Malek Rum
3 Manyiel Malek Rum
4 Ajok Malek Rum

Agei Malek Rum married five wives as follows:
1 Athulueth Deng Thou
2 Ajok Mathiang,
3 Athieng Mayom
4 Adut Malek Yor
5 Ayak Kuac

Athulueth Deng Thou is from the Padiangbaar Clan and first wife. She gave birth to one son and two daughters as follows:
1 Aguelet Agei Malek Rum Wol Rum (son)
2 Amel Agei Malek Rum Wol Rum
3 Awien Agei Malek Rum Wol Rum

Aguelet Agei Malek married Adut Ngor Bak Matik, known as Adut deMalek. Their children are as follows:
1 Agei Dit Aguelet Agei Malek Rum
2 Agei Aguelet Agei Malek Rum
3 Atany Aguelet Agei Malek Rum
4 Angou Aguelet Agei Malek Rum

Agei Dit Aguelet Agei married Abuk Anyar Wol and their children are:
1 Malek Agei Aguelet Agei Malek Rum
2 Aguelet Agei Aguelet Agei Malek Rum
3 Athulueth Agei Aguelet Agei Malek Rum
4 Kuom Agei Aguelet Agei Malek Rum
5 Adut Agei Aguelet Agei Malek Rum
6 Awien Agei Aguelet Agei Malek Rum
7 Adut Agei Aguelet Agei Malek Rum
8 Deng Agei Aguelet Agei Malek Rum
9 Ateny Agei Aguelet Agei Malek Rum

The Dynasty Founded by Rum

Agei Aguelet married Achol Bol from Lou Ariik and gave birth to the following children:
1. Wol Agei Aguelet Agei Malek Rum
2. Amel Agei Aguelet Agei Malek Rum
3. Athuech Agei Aguelet Agei Malek Rum
4. Athulueth Agei Aguelet Agei Malek Rum
5. Aguelet Agei Aguelet Agei Malek Rum

Malek Agei Aguelet Agei is the father of the writer. Malek married Ajok Mabuoch Jang of the Patiir clan as the first wife and their children are as follows:
1. Deng Malek Agei,
2. Agei Malek Agei,
3. Athulueth Malek Agei,
4. Madhel Malek Agei (myself)
5. Mador Malek Agei

Malek married Yikor Kok Akeen of the Pabuor clan as the second wife after Ajok Mabuoch and had the following children:
1. Agei Malek Agei
2. Madut Malek Agei
3. Angau Malek Agei,
4. Madhel Malek Agei,
5. Achol Malek Agei,
6. Aguelet Malek Agei,
7. Ajak Malek Agei

Malek Agei Aguelet Agei Malek Rum married Nyibol Agurwel of the Pabuor clan as the third wife and their children are:
1. Yom Malek Agei Aguelet Agei Malek Rum
2. Adut Malek Agei Aguelet Agei Malek Rum
3. Abuk Malek Agei Aguelet Agei Malek Rum
4. Awien Malek Agei Aguelet Agei Malek Rum
5. Deng Malek Agei Aguelet Agei Malek Rum
6. Wol Malek Agei Aguelet Agei Malek Rum

Ajok Mathiang was the second wife of Agei Malek Rum and their children are:
1 Malek Agei Malek Rum
2 Malek Agei Malek Rum
3 Deng Agei Malek Rum

Malek Agei Malek Rum got in love to Arek Dor of Padiangbar clan while he was young, but his senior half-brother Aguelet Agei Malek Rum approved his marriage with Arek Dor. Malek Agei Malek Rum and his first wife Arek Dor gave birth to the following children:
1 Agei Malek Agei Malek Rum (only Son)
2 Angou Malek Agei Malek Rum
3 Bob Malek Agei Malek Rum
4 Arual Malek Agei Malek Rum

The issue important for the reader to know is that Aguelet Agei was juol and first son of Chief Agei but was approved for his young half brother Malek Agei to marry Arek, though the culture does not allow it. Malek got married to Rek Dor as agreed and they gave birth to Agei as the first son and juol like Aguelet, half-brother of Malek. It was said that Aguelet loved Agei very much. Because of this love, Aguelet appointed Agei Malek to the throne when Malek was brutally murdered with Sub-chief Ayuel in Chuei- Ajai by the Aglo-Egyptian Sudan Government. Agei did not forget this and as Paramount Chief, he dispatched a delegation to Pachien to bring back Agei Aguelet Agei when he heard the death of senior uncle Aguelet Agei whom he also loved. Agei Aguelet returned and created Malou Cattle Camp for both Agei Aguelet Agei and Agei Malek Agei. Malou Camp is where these great leaders have been buried and it is known the holy place, overlooking Ahoom Lake covering wide area known Tonch Ageeth (Ahoom Lakes of wetland for two Agei's or for Agei Aguelet and Agei Malek respectively).

The Dynasty Founded by Rum

Malek Agei Malek Rum married again. This time to the second wife Ajak Ayom. Their children are:
1. Mathok Malek Agei Malek Rum
2. Awien Malek Agei Malek Rum
3. Kur Malek Agei Malek Rum
4. Athiech Malek Agei Malek Rum
5. Bob Malek Agei Malek Rum
6. Agei Malek Agei Malek Rum

Malek Agei Malek Rum, a child of the Ajok Mathiang, succeeded his father Agei Malek Rum when he died from sustained wounds in the battle of Thou Gai. His only son from his first wife, Aguelet Agei Malek Rum was also in the battle. Aguelet, who was a brave fighter, requested that his half-brother Malek Agei take the throne because he wanted to avenge his father after healing. However, Paramount Chief Malek Agei was then arrested with his Deputy, sub-chief Ayuel Baak and killed by the Anglo-Egyptian government in Chuei Ajai. His son Agei Malek Agei took the throne of chieftaincy between 1920 and 1930.

Athieng Mayom gave birth to:
1. Adiar Agei Malek Rum
2. Ngoth Agei Malek Rum
3. Jiel Agei Malek Rum
4. Angau Agei, Malek Rum
5. Abak Agei Malek Rum

She is the third wife of Agei Malek Rum and was from the Pagong Clan of Muok of Rek Dinka clans.

Jiel Agei went to the house of Abak Agei after she was married to a clansman in the Lou Ariik sub-clans in northern Tonj State. Jiel Agei settled down there in Lou Riik where his family had expanded rapidly alongside the children of his sister. He did so in order to help her regarding domestic issues.

It has been said that Ngoth Rum settled in the Nyang sub-clans around the 17th century AD. Jok Malek settled in Luachkoth sub-clans and clans before that period. It is important for the coming generations to learn more about these strong personalities, their success in life and why they continue to be great people far away from the immediate family of Rum Atany's ancestors.

Agei also married Adut Malek Yor from Nyang Akoc clans as the fourth wife, and gave birth to one son Akook Agei. When Akook Agei got married to Anon Kuach Mador from Padiangbaar Clan, they gave birth to Agei, Madut, Akook, Ajok, Adut, Agum and Awien Akook Agei.

The fourth wife of Chief Agei Malek Rum was Adut Malek Yor from Nyang clans in Kuanythii Section of Fishing Eagle of cultural identity in Dinka Rek. They gave birth to one child boy only and named as: Akook Agei Malek Rum.

Family members decided to marry a wife for Akook Agei Malek Rum to have children as soon as possible to fill the gap previously attached into the marriage of his mother Adut Malek, thoughtfully planned mainly to poster a long traditional relationship cordially prevailing between two communities of Apuk Agei Malek Rum and Nyang Majok Akoc Majok, bordering each other in the north.

Akook Agei Malek Rum got married to Anon Kuach Mador from Padiangbaar Clan as planned and begotten the following children:
1   Agei Akook Agei Malek Rum
2   Madut Akook Agei Malek Rum
3   Akook Akook Agei Malek Rum
4   Ajok Akook Agei Malek Rum
5   Adut Akook Agei Malek Rum
6   Agum Akook Agei Malek Rum
7   Awien Akook Agei Malek Rum

The fifth wife of Chief Agei Malek Rum was Ayak Kuach. They gave birth to the following children:
1   Deng Agei Malek Rum
2   Dhel Agei Malek Rum
3   Kok Agei Malek Rum

The Dynasty Founded by Rum

The fifth wife of Agei Malek was Ayak Kuac and her children are Deng, Dhel and Kok Agei Malek Rum respective.

Summary

Aguelet Agei Malek, the first son, was nicknamed Aguelet Matiat, a name he acquired in battle for his bravery. Aguelet Matiat married Adut Ngor De Malek from the Patiop clan. Athulueth Deng of the Padiangbaar clan was the first wife and gave birth to her first-born son Aguelet, as the only son with Agei Malek.

The second wife Ajok Mathiang gave birth to son Malek who became the second son in the family of Agei Malek. However, Malek felt in love with Arek Dor from the Padiangbaar clan. Aguelet approved the marriage of Arek to Malek although this is not traditionally acceptable. Aguelet, however, was a military tactician who carefully watched out for his family.

Below is the list of Paramount Chiefs for the most recent chiefdom dynasty of the Apuk clans.
1 Malek Rum traditional leader with dual control of High Priest Chief and war leadership, 1880s
2 Agei Malek, Modern Paramount Chief with dual control, 1900s
3 Malek Agei, Paramount Chief, 1930s to 1940s
4 Agei Malek, Paramount Chief, 1940s to 1950s
5 Mathok Malek, Paramount Chief, 1950s to 1960
6 Malek Mathok, Paramount Chief, 1960 to December 9, 2006
7 Kur Malek, Paramount Chief, 2007 to date.

Rum

Rum the clan god controls the dynasty as a clan deity in the southwestern Apuk, this is important to the Rek clans of high priests, the Parum Wundior. The name 'Rum' is repeatedly used by members of the Parum clan for naming children partly to keep line continuity and

partly as a lineage guide to the children named after him.
His offspring mobilized forces from the sub-clans for expeditions. They succeeded in establishing a dynasty with powerful spiritual clan descendants built on long traditions and via various clan cross marriages and cultural exchanges. They managed to articulate a vision that acknowledges the commonalities of history. Their descendants had greater control with military and high priest leadership roles combined. Also introduced were strong social practices primarily at the Wunriir habitats across Maluach, then in Machuet of the present day Apuk. Cattle herders were orientated on warfare at camps established at Akuwei, Paduer, Jak, Manyiel, Malou. Pankiir, Tarweng, Git, Angui, Panhial and several other locations.

Recap

Rum fought against Lwalla attacks at the Wunriir villages in the Maluach habitation, and Machuet homesteads. Bol Mel later addressed these as "Apuk Lith, Apuk land and Apuk Juwiir".

Predators kidnapped and kept Rum for more than two months in captivity as I have stated previously but returned him back safely. Rum then organized his forces. He conquered the predators and their bases. These were held for his descendants.

Rum waged war against the nomadic adversaries who invaded the Apuk clans in the southwestern Dinka Apuk regions. The war between rival Pabuor, Padiangbaar and Patiir sub-clans was also likely quite real.

The nomadic Lualla of the Bantustan ethnic group conquered much of ancient Apuk through to the Toch wetland and Chiir villages in Maluach areas. However, they in turn overthrown by Rum and his descendants.

The dynasty of the Ateny deity, the Rum deity and the high priest offspring united clans and sub-clans of the Apuk clan. Control from Wunriir the oldest capital was established in Machuet. Trade with the Jurchol-Luo and bordering sub-clans and clans was thereby opened.

The Dynasty Founded by Rum

The dynasty of Akook Rum, and lower diviners maintained the alliance of the united chiefdom following a period of intense war for the control and total hegemony.

The dynasty of Malek built the alliance of the old chieftaincy to be strong. His ambition as high priest and war leader were to have it all. He modernized his forces and they earned him victories that elevated him to the chiefdom of the Apuk clans. He conquered many regions, then annexed and assimilated them into the Apuk nation-state. Malek opened the trade for ivory, weapons, jewellery and other valuable materials. For this reason, Malek was able to marry his wife, Aluat, commonly known as Angou with ivory issued to her family as dowry. These included smelted iron and the acquisition of blacksmithing skills from the Jurchol-Luo of the Nilotic ethnic group bordering to the west.

The dynasty of Wol Malek saw the beginnings of expansion beyond Akon-Agiu in the north, and areas in the northeast of the Apuk. The rivalry of Thony versus the Apuk, Luachkoth versus the Apuk, and Yar versus the Apuk, all intensified at the grazing lands, and the wetlands or swampy streams of vast Sudd land where the cattle owners drive their cows during dry seasons. The Wunreel cattle camps dividing adversaries in the middle wetland became the dominant centre of war every grazing season. Wol continued with the unity of Apuk subclans and pragmatic controls established by Malek the conqueror and reinforced territorial assertions.

The dynasty of Rum Wol established cattle camps that even today are under the control of the Apuk at Toch. The Madol River branch from the Wanhalel River became sacred and was managed by Wol Rum, then inherited by his descendants Akuien, Lueth, Kur, Rual, Wol and later offspring possessing spirituality within the Pakuin, Padior, or Wundior clans, collectively known as the Parum clan.

From the 1870's to 1890's, Malek Rum expanded the Apuk clan dynasty to bring new territories under control. The Apuk was dominant, and its sub-clan and clan alliances were built while adversaries were conquered. This was eroded and ended with successive invasions by the Arab slave traders, the Turkish regime, and later when Anglo-Egyptian government policies were launched.

During the latter days of the century, there was a war against these same government policies. This happened even though they recognized clan traditions, courts, chiefs and clan chieftaincy. It became known as the "Indirect Rule Policy" that cemented the traditional dynasty over all the clans and sub clan's homelands. The head of clan Parum, Agei Malek Rum, was recognized as the first traditional chief of the Dinka Apuk state in 1903[120]. From 1910 to 1930 Chief Agei modernized the region and created an Apuk chieftaincy in dynastic fashion. He operated a traditional system parallel with what was introduced by the government. He became the government agent for the new colonial administration for tax collection. Chief Agei Malek Rum was then confirmed for the chiefdom throne. His borders were expanded, secured, demarcated, recognized, and he was legitimized as the traditional chief of the clans and sub-clans of Apuk. He legalized its borders which were added to the map of the Local Traditional Administration of the government in Sudan.

The Capital District for the Dinka Rek clan was first established at Chuei Ajai in 1903 and relocated in Tonj as the Jur River District in southwestern Rek Jieng, covering Dinka Thony up to Abyei. But Abyei pulled out in 1905 and joined the Kordofan District with the Arab tribes to the north. Malek introduced horses captured from Arab slave traders for transport. Agei Malek Rum began using them also for the transport of his family and himself between Tonj town and his village in Jak in the Machuet Apuk region.

In the ensuing months, the Turko-Egyptian, Anglo-Egyptian and Arab soldiers escalated raids on the chiefdom, inflicted severe gunshot wounds on Chief Agei, his son Aguelet, and people from the Kongdeer, Agurping, Malony, Maluil and Aliai clans and sub-clans loyally fought alongside their leader.

---

120 Tonj District of Rek Jieng was reportedly established in 1903, where all tradition chiefs of Dinka Rek clans were asked to show themselves up by order to the Commissioner of Government controlling in Tonj. It was first stationed in Chuei Ajai before transferring to Tonj town near the River passing through Tonj to Wanhalel. This River originated from Ezo to Wanhalel and connects all the way to Machar Rek River, opening water streams to tributaries leading to the White Nile River tributaries to the main Nile River.

The Dynasty Founded by Rum

He retreated eastwards to Thon-Gai, where Government patrols pursued him and eventually killed him in the battle. He was later regaled by the gathered elders with ancient tales of the killings and growing numbers of martyred sons in that great house of dynastic chiefdom.

It was reported that the British Administration initiated the National Conference for the Traditional Chieftaincy Courts and Customary Laws around 1927, with the aim to formulate customary laws. The Chiefdom of Apuk hosted this Conference in Wanhalel and adopted these laws, popularly addressed as 'Wanhalel Dinka Customary Law'.

Thiet was established as the traditional administration capital. It was addressed as The Thiet Rural Council of the Tonj District. The Jieng written language, letters, and records began to appear in Apuk in the 1920s as well. Christian missionaries took the lead in this when the Catholic Church founded the Catechetical School of Mayom Mission in Apuk.

Years of horrifying reports on devastation by conquerors and adversaries followed, detailing intense fighting, systematic targeting of women, ethnic cleansing of indigenous populations and extrajudicial killings. This was a period where countermeasures to respond to the atrocities were launched.

History puts the size of the raiding Turkish forces as high as thousands. Most were on horseback. Others were identified as known Anglo-Turk, Turko-Egyptian, Anglo-Egyptian or Condominium assailants. Warriors of the Dinka Apuk united behind their successive chieftaincies and overcome the history of decades of hostility and the memory of the atrocities of the near past.

Following one clash, warriors from several sub-clans captured the following weapons and equipment: one sword, thirty horses, sixty knives, fifteen axes, and eight firearms.

Utilizing the growing population of the Apuk clans before he was killed, Chief Agei mobilized the chiefdom to remain united and to emerge as a more powerful, dominant regional power. He worked via established traditions, ethnic clans, intermarriage and cultural exchange to articulate a new vision that acknowledged the commonalities of history, however painful it has sometimes been and the strong linkages that exist today between all the peoples.

When Chief Agei received the British title of 'Traditional Chief' he articulated a new vision that acknowledged history and its commonalities that traced back to the beginning of the first dynasty. He re-educated the clans as to how predators from Bantustan ethnic groups were defeated and swept out for good. The strong linkages that exist today between all the peoples of what are now governmental units of the Apuk in the Capital of Jak for the Kongdeer, Maluach and the Agurpiny clans and sub-clans, the Apuk in the Capital Thiet for Aliai, the Manging and Angol clans, and the Apuk Wanhalel in the Capital Wanhalel, will remain even when and if the three regions constitute an executive state proper.

1920s: Malek Agei Malek Rum on the Throne

Malek arose to the chieftaincy throne in the late 1920s after his father Agei had died from wounds sustained in battle. As previously mentioned, this happened because the eldest son Aguelet Agei Malek Rum wanted to personally take revenge for the killing of his father and declined the throne. He ordered his younger step-brother Malek Agei assume the title.

Aguelet is said to have stated:

"A throne on which I will never rule because I have no secured power with which to govern is useless. What is the gap between a 'chiefdom' and a 'visionary chief'? What is the difference between aggression and killing cruelly?"[121]

"I speak of warriors that must fight a suicidal war because they have no effective weapons!"

---

121 Father Malek Agei who spoke to me narrated some works done by his grandfather Aguelet. He also showed me traditional weapons belonging to brave Aguelet.

The Dynasty Founded by Rum

"I cannot allow these dangerous foreign invaders who do not care for the lives of our people to take over our chiefdom. We have defeated many enemies. We shall emerge and overcome these aggressors".

"In these darkest moments, the uncountable indignities heaped upon us produce in me anger, defiance, and a desire to fight the those who killed my father and so many others. I am here to die fighting in the defence of my people. I will fight in the lead of our gallant young warriors whose abilities and intelligence will wipe out the government patrols and Arab militants."

Malek Agei Malek as chief, inherited the existing wars. As well, forceful conscription of young people to be taken to the European army was launched in the region. The people of Apuk declared war against these alien forces and their alliance.

Chief Malek and his brother Aguelet railed against the government, whom they believed had deliberately weakened the chiefdom by moving populations and borders at will.

Aguelet urged his warriors to strongly resist the abduction of young people being sent to train to fight in the European Wars. The recruitment was extremely ruthless in the chiefdom and provided the shock that led to the instinctive response that Apuk natives are the people who have always been here, sharing the one blood that we have today.

He stated:

"We are going to fight this new wave of conquerors conscripting our young people. The unfair treatment they are receiving must be addressed and we need to reverse it."

Aguelet's bravery made him so vehement that he fought extremely fiercely against the new wave of invading forces of European occupation. These skirmishes encompassed all the three main frontiers. He received many injuries and survived in the fighting that resulted in the capture of his half-brother Paramount Chief Malek and his Deputy Ayuel Baak. They were taken to Chuei-Ajai. Later they were driven to Manyang-Ngok across the Wanhalel River in the east and were murdered. Other traditional leaders were driven to Manyang-Ngok across the Wanhalel River in the east and were murdered. The bodies were never located.

Aguelet summoned family members within the community and declared Agei, the young son of the deceased Malek Agei successor to the chieftaincy throne. Agei then took over and declared war against the new government policy of intimidation, division of the minority clans, sub-clans, and lower diviners to weaken all associations, unions and alliances amongst them. He aimed to increase resistance to the Indirect Rule Policy of conscripting young men in the chiefdom.

On his address to the bereaved community, Aguelet Agei told the mourners gathered for untimely death of their chiefs that: "We are here to pay tribute to Chief Malek, Sub-chief Ayuel Baak, and to all the gallant warriors who fought alongside the leaders and laid their lives on the line so that we can live in this Apuk that we claim to be ours today!"

"This new war must have a multi-dimensional line of attack, because wherever we go the young people are conscripted by alien forces as if they have no role at all to our civilization. We, as fathers and mothers cannot tolerate this! We all know why we are where we are today. So, the test is that we must defend our young people because my survival will remain a fantasy if Apuk is not under our firm control. We cannot remain content with my survival. My survival does not describe or convey meaning to the hundreds of Apuk people who perished. My survival does not give good reason for the lives that were sacrificed through battles fought. My survival does not give good reason for the blood that was shed to water our freedom. The slaughter of our chiefs and gallant warriors was not in vain. Young Agei has now taken over the chieftaincy throne for the next generation; one that wants to carry the Apuk forward."

Our great grandfathers were patriots who united the Apuk warriors under successive chieftaincies to overcome the history of decades of foreign raiding, the hostility between populations that resulted, and the memory of atrocities still fresh in the minds of the people.

The Dynasty Founded by Rum

1940s-1950s: *Agei Malek on the Throne*

Modern traditional administration emerged during the reign of Chief Agei Malek. The dangers of a chieftaincy based on loyalty and belonging based on blood and soil were amply demonstrated in recent history. The revolt to dislodge Aguelet Agei began at the Manyiel Cattle Camp. Family members who were opposed to the responsibility of collecting the payment for *apuk* for crime that Aguelet Agei committed went to him at Mangar Agaach village at midnight.

Payable *apuk* was non-monetary which was estimated in numbering around 5 cows for the opponent clan victims who were injured or severely injured and thirty cows for victims killed during inter-clan and inter sub-clan fights.

When Chief Agei received information that his maternal uncle was leading groups conspiring with the colonial administration to take his throne, he requested an urgent meeting with the council of elders from Apuk Lith to discuss these new developments. Agei Aguelet Agei Malek Rum and Chief Agei Malek Agei Malek Rum met with members of their families and agreed to find a solution regarding conspiracy against them. Their elder uncle Agei Malek Ngoth, who was the direct advisor on behalf of the family of Rum Wol, persuaded them and the elders that Agei Malek had done enough and should retire due to old age (he was 70). He then stated Mathok must be ordered to come and take over chieftaincy throne, regardless of being a son of the last wife and both Agei Aguelet and Agei Malek agreed on this. His mother was Ajak Ayom Arou, daughter of a Paramount Chief from the Abuok clans.

Agei Malek resigned voluntarily and handed over the throne to his half-brother Mathok Malek peacefully. He then took him to the British Commissioner of Tonj District, Mr. Wilson, and introduced them to each other. Agei Malek stated that he must step down because of age and Mathok is the Chief of the Apuk Lith from this day forward. Mr. Wilson accepted the decision but asked Agei Malek to continue working alongside Mathok Malek to train him on the job. Agei Malek then retired to lead a normal life at Kongdeer Machuet village.

1960s to 2006: Accession of Malek Mathok Malek to the Throne

When Malek Mathok Malek Agei ascended to the chieftaincy throne in January 1960 after the death of his father Paramount Chief Mathok Malek Agei in December 1959, the Chiefdom of Apuk was stable. Most cases encountered were issues affecting individual members of the community across divisional sections of clans and sub-clans. Traditional conflict occurring between clans or tribes in the Apuk Chiefdom and neighbouring clans was reduced through enforcement of laws and an effective justice system. Chief's courts and traditional courts were instrumental in the reduction of violent tribal conflicts, domestic disputes, and petty crimes.

During his reign, the Maluil division of Apuk clans split from the Chieftaincy in 1976 to create the Southern Chiefdom of the Apuk under Chief Akot Makuac Akot of the Pabuor Clan. The Maluil division is composed of the Tarweng, Manging, Malony, and Angol clans and subsections. Chief Akot belongs to Manging section within the Apuk clans in Tonj State.

2006 to Present

Paramount Chief Malek Mathok Malek was on the throne until he died from sickness caused by a complication from a diarrhea descendaria in December 2006. His son Kur Malek Mathok succeeded him in January 2007.

The Chieftaincy Factor

It should be noted the desire for the chieftaincy among different subclans and the antagonistic attitudes shown are not the root causes of the current chiefdom divisions between the Maluil clans on one side and the Machuet and Aliai clans on another. The rift between

The Dynasty Founded by Rum

them is deeper and more complicated with historical, political, and most importantly, ideological dimensions.

When, in 1976, the Apuk divided into two parallel chiefdoms, Paramount Chief Malek Mathok was on one side and newly selected Chief Akot Makuach on the other. Akot Makuach is from the Pabuor clan possessing spiritual supernatural powers and Malek Mathok is from Parum clan possessing spiritual supernatural powers. Bol Ciirial originated from the Pabuor clan among the first migrants and settlers at Apuk Lith known as Apuk today. Malek Mathok is the descendant of Rum Atany from Wundior descended from Rum Wenkook and of a lineage I have explained in detail earlier.

On the accession of Akot Makuach from Bol's clan to the new chieftaincy throne in southern Apuk. This new Chiefdom was composed of the following sections:

1. The Tarweng Maluil Section
2. The Angol Maluil Section
3. The Manging Maluil Section
4. The Malony Section

Traditional courts including customary cases were still one and shared between the two Chiefdoms within the whole of Apuk Juwiir.

Malek Mathok maintained the leadership and senior chieftaincy in northern Apuk with the Chiefdom comprising the following sections:

1. The Kongdeer Machuet Section
2. The Agurping Machuet Section
3. The Maluach Machuet Section
4. The Aremrap Aliai Section
5. The Buong Aliai Section

The history of this Chiefdom is uncompromising in its low opinion of its larger and richer neighbour to the south and its understanding of how it was conquered by traditional enemies in the ancient period and

APUK : A STATE IN WAITING

by the Lwalla in the early Bol Mel dynastic era as divine retribution for Rum Atany's Chiefdom's return to idolatry worship.

When large numbers of immigrant clans arrived, residual tribal affiliations were strengthened, probably because of the possibility of re-establishing current Apuk tribal land-holdings. However, the special religious roles decreed for the ancestors and divinities were preserved. The shrine centres (or *Yiek*) became the sole place of worship and sacrifice among the settling migrants.

APPENDICES

APPENDIX 1

Mourning Rituals and Practices for the Burial of a Priest Chief

Convoy Carrying the Body in Tonj State in South Sudan

The ambulance in the convoy of vehicles arriving at Tonj Town on March 21, 2012 is seen here carrying the body of Late Deng Malek, Deputy Judge and heir to the Unknown Sacred Spear. It was on the way to Malou Cattle Camp in Machuet of Apuk.

Near Tonj Bridge

The convoy is waiting for people sacrificing a ritual bull on the main road.

APPENDIX 1

Crowd Receiving the Body

The people came out in large numbers to welcome the body of Deng with the bull donated by Madhel Malek to be sacrificed in front of the vehicle. There the ritual blood of the bull will pour on the ground to allow the body to pass over it to wash away the evil spirit and transmit guardians from clan divinities to reconcile and allow for a safe funeral.

Government officials and the population in Tonj Town came out in numbers. They included members of the Judiciary Court of Tonj South County where Deng was serving as the Deputy of the Magistrate Judge. All were there to welcome the body. Among the people seen above were Lt. Colonel Fidele Majok Mabior, Director for the Prison Service, Makuer Tiau, RRC Officer, Magistrate Judge. Rual Deng Malek is seen in the middle of the crowd.

March 21, 2012 A Bull Slaughtered for Ritual Ceremony

This picture shows the first bull that was slaughtered for welcoming the high priest-chief Deng Malek home in a procession with the ceremony of the ritual bull sacrificed on the main Road on Tonj Bridge. Mador Malek is seen here slaughtering the sacrificial bull with a spear of Malek Agei for blood to pour down on the main road on Tonj Bridge in honour of the spear master. The bull was the first donation from Madhel Malek Agei.

Mourning Rituals and Practices for the Burial of a Priest Chief

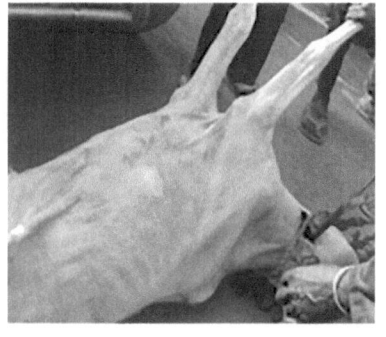

Ritual Bull before Slaughtering

After the body of Spiritual Master Deng arrived at his house, the son of his sister is here seen pulling a sacrificial bull. He is followed by Wol Aguelet Agei and Manyual Mathok Malek.

Present were many family and community members who heard the news of the arrival of the body. People are reciting traditional hymns of ritual sacrifice circling counter-clockwise three times before sacrificing the bull in front of the vehicle.

The blood is a sign of welcoming the living spirit *agolong*, the life spirit *akuic*, and the body spirit *atiep* that were away with the deceased Deng. Among the people pulling the thong of the ritual bull are Wol Aguelet Agei holding the shield behind the bull, Manyual Mathok Malek in the white dress with bag, Deng Aguok Athulueth Agei on behalf of the sisters. There were also other members of the clan family and the public who joined the ritual procession of their leader and heir to the Unknown Sacred Spear which predates back hundreds of years.

Invocation Hymns for the Slaughtering are Being Sung

The Bull is Slaughtered and Cut into Pieces for Mourning Practices

Onlookers included Madhel Malek, Mador Malek, Lt. Colonel Fidele Majok, Commissioner, Deputy Governor, Magistrate of Tonj South County, and other Government officials.

APPENDIX 1

The sacrificial bull is now being cut up for removal on the road, so the body may pass over the blood to drive evil spirits away in the belief that there must have been wrongdoers behind the death of Deng and this blood can purify the body before it reaches the house. The body will be open to viewings for family members and the public later in the house. This is the first time a body arrived in a coffin in this village since as it is in an isolated spot. The area was a former sanctuary for the SLPA.

People Watching the Ritual Sacrifice taking Place

Out of the picture a bull is being slaughtered to pour blood on the ground as a sign of welcoming the living spirit and body spirit back home to integrate with the family members.

Ayak Ngor is standing next to the vehicle that brought the body of Deng to the house in Malou village. It was joined in Tonj Town by over 15 cars to accompany the body.

The Body Passing Over Blood

Here we see the body about to pass on the blood. Ritual offering with animal sacrifice is based on the belief that blood is living with body spirit (*atiep*), life spirit (*akuic*) and living spirit (*agolong*) which do not die with the physical body. Living-blood has power that guides a person from danger and washes away sins, wrongdoings or any bewitching suspicion against

Mourning Rituals and Practices for the Burial of a Priest Chief

members of the clan and clan divinities. Some masters of the fishing spear are descended from Parum Atany Wun-Dior that worships ring (flesh). They do not eat blood and the heart that houses blood for that reason. They do not eat the heart of any beast, whether from wild or domesticated animals. The tongue cannot be given to a spiritual master present to eat because it is believed that masters of the fishing spear use their tongue to pass people messages of the Clan Divinities and it will disobey the powers of wisdom. The tongue has major responsibilities regarding the messages the spear master passes out on behalf of divinities and the people he serves.

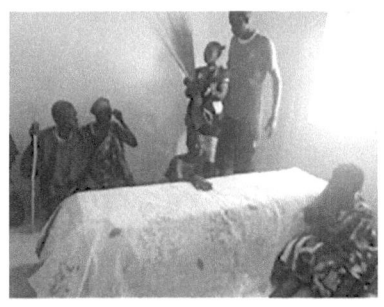

The Body Covered with Sheets

The body is finally brought into the house and put inside a room. There, relatives and family members come to view the Late Deng Malek, Spiritual Master of the Parum Clan in Apuk. He has had five wives and is survived by three wives and fifteen children at the time of writing. Standing near the body is Wol Deng, Arek Arual Agei the wife of the maternal uncle, Bol Apach Mabuoch, the son of the brother of Ajok Mabuoch who is the mother of Deng, Madhel and Mador, Adeng Aguelet Agei. Adhel Akeen who has a hand on the coffin is a wife of Deng. A woman is holding a grum, and another woman is sitting next to the coffin.

Burial Arrangements Being Made

The image shows a meeting of family members regarding the ritual burial, March 21, 2012. They are discussing the burial arrangement under the tree on the property of Deng. They aim to agree on the burial site and arrange the funeral according to traditional burial principles of

APPENDIX 1

the master of the fishing spear's family. Madhel Malek stated that Deng died as spiritual clan leader of the wider society in Apuk and heir to the Unknown Sacred Spear of ancient spiritual grandfathers who produce the spear for Parum clan Divinities and must be buried alongside his father and grandfather's tombs who were the heirs to the Unknown Sacred Spear before him.

Seated on the chair is Madhel Malek and his wife. The Hon. Ayak Ngor Athian is behind listening, Hon. Augustino Agei Dut, sitting on the left, Brigadier Aguelet Malek, half-brother from the second wife of Chief Malek Agei, Manyual Mathok Malek on the extreme right, followed by Malek Deng Agei, Wol Aguelet Agei, Deng Aguelet Agei, Mador Malek Agei among others. All have accepted the decision of Madhel Malek Agei to have his brother buried in Malou Cattle Camp next to his father and grandfather Agei Aguelet Agei Malek, who inherited the Unknown Sacred Spear as senior children along the line of heirs in the family that continued for centuries. The first person who produced this holy spear is unknown by family members that found themselves holders of the inherited spear of this specific Parum clan lineage family. I asked my father about this in November 1981, when I was awarded a scholarship to go to Cuttington University in Liberia. His reply to me was: "I do not remember who manufactured this spear, and who came up with the idea of a spear that has become the power of authority, spirituality, and the control of clans".

The Five Spears

When Deng, was far away for treatment in Kenya, clan spirits remained with the sacred spears for guardianship and life-giving to the society. When he was returned, they were rushed to the body by a woman who placed them next to it to welcome the body spirit, life spirit and physical body back home and to reunite them with the ancestry spirit in the fatherland.

Mourning Rituals and Practices for the Burial of a Priest Chief

(1) Unknown Sacred Fishing Spear, bith kuuc ee wun;
(2) Ritual sacrifice spear, tong koc (addressed as tong Aguelet Dit),
(3) Oath service Spear, alol ee kueeng or alol ee meel tier ku meel jony and Oath Services for Truth and only as the Truth and Divinity is my witness, presided over in the society by Chief Malek Agei, Chief Deng and today by Mador Malek Agei.
(4) Spear for homicide penalty for blood wealth in reconciliation and forgiveness between the victim and guilty clans and concerned members of the two families, tony tem ee tier apuk ku kueeny ku adoor dhieth ci teir looi ee kam keen,
(5) Spear of life, tony ee wei.

The spear for offering beasts of ritual sacrifices to clan spirits, atiip, jak, agoloong and divinity for peacemaking, rainmaking, guardianship and oath taking, are believed to have powers that forward the intended invocation through to guide the body spirit, life spirit and living spirit of the heir from evils wanting to intrude to take away those powers from strong spiritual descendants. Spiritual spears must be transported forward by women members of the spiritual clan family. Ayak Ngor is seen above standing next to sacred spears which she brought from the house and put there to welcome the body spirit, life spirit, and the physical body, and to guard them from evil. She assists family members viewing the body and regulates the flow of viewers to the room. She is the wife of Madhel Malek and mother to Achan Madhel, Deng Madhel, Ajok Madhel, Malek Madhel, Agei Madhel and Angau Madhel respectively. Madhel Malek is the second son of Malek Agei who was the master of the fishing spear, chief of Traditional Appeal Court, and the oath maker spiritual priest in

APPENDIX 1

southwestern Apuk. The spears will follow the body up to the burial site and will be kept near the grave for three days before they are taken back to the house. They will be taken out for the next funeral rite and moved by a designated clanswoman to the gravesite. The spears will be put on shrines throughout the time of prayers in the celebration to remove fencing from the grave. They will then be put on the shrine of his father Malek who passed the spears to his son Deng as the successor by birthright. When the fence is removed, and more bulls sacrificed, there will be one bull for Madhel Malek and maternal uncle, Aguok Bol, to return the living spirit, life spirit and body spirit of Deng to the house to reunite them with clan spirits and the spirits of children and surviving wives, to reconcile and remain united as the guardian of life in the family.

Family Elders Viewing Body

This is the first time the village has seen a coffin for burial. Spiritual master burial traditionally was undertaken with the hide of bull slaughtered for the occasion.

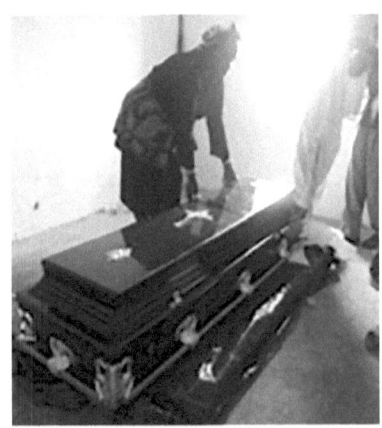

Elders from Family Viewing Body

Elders led by Awien Agei, sister of Malek Agei have entered with two old women to view the body.

Mourning Rituals and Practices for the Burial of a Priest Chief

More Viewers

Madhel Malek, Wol Aguelet and four girls viewing body to be taken to the Holy Shrine Site in Malou Cattle Camp on March 21, 2012.

Malou Burial Ground

In this picture are drums called Angau Apiok, a ram tethered on the peg with a thong under the shrine and near the tomb of Agei Aguelet on the left-hand side. The white bull will be a sacrifice, and the hide will make ropes to tie the wooden branches of the bridge on top of the body with a living ram inside the grave. The people preparing the spear master burial are called from the Padiangbaar clan for attending to the master of the spear on the occasion of his death, and ritual burial funerals and ceremonies like this. They are hired at an agreed fee, usually in cows, which is determined according to the status of the spiritual master in the community he served.

Deng's Son

The son of the spiritual master is shown here wearing the crown, which is plaited with the black feathers of ostrich, Ajom Nok Wut. Sitting on the chair wearing it symbolizes spiritual leadership and continuation of clan lineage. Ajom or ajom-nhom is a tradi-

APPENDIX 1

tional hand-made headdress designed by utilizing natural feathers and a hollow oval helmet. It, Akup also serves to protect the head in club fights when plaited from the leaves of the coconut tree. The leaves of the coconut tree are used to thatch roofs and to make hats, helmets, baskets, and fans called ayikol or akuetha. When decorated with the black feathers of the ostrich they form Ajom nhom, a symbol of prestige and pride worn as a traditional crown in social functions and more importantly, during engagement processes. The long stick next to him on the chair belongs to Malek Agei and was inherited by Deng Malek. Sons of sisters are seen cutting wooden branches of a tree traditionally accepted for burial bridges for spiritual masters of the Parum clan. On the left are people helping in the burial preparation at Malou Cattle Camp. Cow dung is scattered around by herders in the cattle camp, where there are high priest tombs with sacred shrines and decorated pegs to tether ritual sacrifice bulls and rams with thongs. They pour milk on the pegs, under the shrines and on the tombs in the ensuing ritual invocations, libations and sacrifices.

Crafting the Burial Cover

Here, people are helping the sons of Deng's sisters arrange branches of a tree that will cover the grave while the burial preparations are being finished. Kur Deng is seen here sitting on the chair with the stick described above.

Bull blood ritual sacrifice for burial

This picture shows Mador Malek sacrificing a bull for blood which is tethered near the shrine and tomb of Malek Agei.

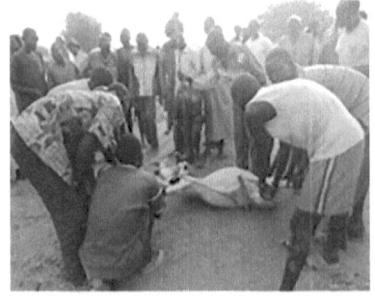

Mourning Rituals and Practices for the Burial of a Priest Chief

Tethering the ram beside the body in the grave.

Paramount Chief, Kur Malek Mathok Malek Agei is shown here inspecting and directing the process of burial to follow Parum principles. He holds a long stick which he inherited from his father Paramount Chief Malek Mathok. Kur Malek is the sixth Traditional Chief since the British came and established the chieftaincy of the Apuk Chiefdom. The British Administration saw Malek Rum as a political, war and spiritual leader, then confirmed him as the First Traditional Chief. Malek, was injured in battle and died. He was then succeeded by his son Chief Agei Malek Rum Wol Rum as the Second Traditional Chief. Agei, was again injured in battle at Thon Gai. He was succeeded by his son Chief Malek Agei Malek as the Third Traditional Chief, who in turn was killed in cold blood by British Admin-istration representatives.

The Fourth Chief Agei Malek Agei then succeeded his father. Fourth Chief Agei handed the chieftaincy over to the Fifth Chief Mathok Malek, his half-brother from the second wife of his father Chief Malek because of old age and pressure from the British Administration. Chief Mathok Malek died in 1959, succeeded by his son Chief Malek Mathok as the Sixth Chief of the Apuk Chiefdom.

APPENDIX 1

The body laid to rest

The image shows the body of Deng Malek as it is finally lowered into the grave. The wooden platform is then put on top of the body and the living ram. This is a donation on his behalf to take along to the ancestors in the spirit world he is about to join. It is believed his spirit is living and communicating with ancestry spirits in the spirit world, and to inform them that their children are doing well.
According to clan tradition, body spirits and life spirits never die. Therefore, he came to join them because they asked him to.

Representatives of Warrap State at the burial.

Shown here are Akec Tong Aleu, Commissioner of Tonj South County, Makuer Tiau, Director of RRC for Tonj South County, Lt. Col. Fidele Majok Mabior, Director of Prison Service for Tonj South County, Brig. Gen. Yol Mayar Marek, Deputy Governor for Warrap State. They were joined by bodyguards and other State Government officials.

Most of the people came from Wau, Kuajok and Tonj to take part in the burial procession of the late Deng Malek. Peter Makuok came from Juba along with Ayak Ngor, Brigadier General Aguelet Malek, and friends. Brigadier General Yol Mayar Marek, Deputy Governor of Warrap State, Police Service officers, Prison Service officers, Wildlife officers and Military officers came in numbers to participate in the funeral of their spiritual master.

Mourning Rituals and Practices for the Burial of a Priest Chief

Wooden platform being affixed to the top of the grave.

This picture shows witnesses seeing how the Spiritual master of the Parum clan is buried with a platform on top of the body and ram.

Deputy Governor yol Mayar and Hon. Augustino Agei is inspecting the platform to make sure there is no space left open to allow mud to drop down after closing the grave. From right to left, Bol Gai Kook, Yelek Athulueth Agei (one of the sons of Deng's sister), Chol Machar Baak, Hon. Agei Dut Aguet, Peter Makuok, Deputy Governor, and Brig. Gen. Yol Mayar Marek.

Security guards

Shown are the bodyguards deployed for the dignitaries attending the funeral. Tonj State had just been created at the time of writing. The old shrine on the tomb of Chief Agei is seen between the bodyguards and the vehicle to the right.

APPENDIX 1

The representatives present were:

1. Brig. Gen. Yol Mayar Marek, Deputy Governor, Warrap State,
2. Hon. Prof. Madhel Malek Agei, State Minister, General Education, Warrap State.
3. Hon. Ayak Ngor Malek Agei, MP, National Legislative Assembly of the Republic of South Sudan, Juba
4. Hon. Akech Tong Aleu, Commissioner of Tonj South County, Warrap State (now Governor of Tonj State)
5. Hon. Augustino Agei Dut Aguet, MP, State Legislative Assembly, Warrap State (now Tonj State Legislative Assembly).
6. Brig. Gen. Paul Aguelet Malek Agei, Deputy Director of Prison Service, Tonj, Tonj State
7. Lt. Col. Fidele Majok Mabior, Assistant Director, Tonj State
8. Hon. Makuer Tiau Anyuon, Commissioner of Wanhalel County, Tonj State (former Director for RRC of Tonj South).

DAY TWO

Public gifts

Community donations are freely given by donor families and the entire community following the departure of their spiritual master or priest to join ancestors in the spirit world. They believe these donations will reach their ancestors and clan spirits when the departing master reaches the spirit world.

Ritual Prayers

From left to right: Peter Makuok, Hon. Agei Dut, Paramount Chief Kur Malek, Wol Malek.

Mourning Rituals and Practices for the Burial of a Priest Chief

Women in mourning ritual prayers

The death of priest-chief is usually mourned with celebrations, donations and warfare songs and games. Many people sleep near the tomb for three days after burial. More ritual prayers are recited and led by elderly family members. They are assisted by volunteers that know hymns that should be sung during spiritual priest burials.

Shown here is Awien Agei, sister of Malek Agei (with grey hair) in front of women attending the funeral.
From left to right, Malek Deng Agei, Madhel Malek, Aguelet Malek, Peter Makuok, Augustino Agei Dut. Those standing behind include Malek Madut Deng, two bodyguards for Madhel Malek and three young boys attending the mourning prayers.

From left to right, Mador Malek holding a spear for sacrificing animals in his right hand. It was made by Aguelet Agei and it is addressed as tong Aguelet Dit. Madut Malek is holding a spear. Other mourners are sitting behind him reciting ritual hymns and invoking ritual prayers.

APPENDIX 1

The woman in front on the left is Arek Arual Agei, wife of the maternal uncle, Bol Apach Mabuoch, the brother of Ajok Mabuoch. Next to her is Wol Aguelet Agei Thii. Kur Deng Malek is holding a shield and wearing the Ajom as symbol of honor for leading the ceremonial procession of a deceased master of the spear. Deng Aguelet Agei is wearing a black jacket. Atany Madut, nicknamed Marial Madut or Marial Deng, is holding a shield and is the half-brother of Kur Deng in the union of Atik Dhur Machar. Two elders in white dress from the Machuet Apuk section are shown attending the ritual procession. Madut Malek is in a grey dress with a spear. He is the half-brother of Deng from the union of the second wife Yikor Kok and Malek Agei. Wol Manyiel Monybith Wol Malek is wearing black cloth with a spear in the right hand. Standing behind Kur Deng is Matik Madut Matik, maternal uncle of the descended brother of Adut Ngor Matik, nicknamed as Adut De Malek. Many more were present during the first ritual sacrifice for the bull of grandfathers, thon yik.

Here we see bits of smoke coming up from burning cow dung mixed with the waste entrails of the bull sacrificed the previous day

Mourning Rituals and Practices for the Burial of a Priest Chief

for the burial ritual. It is believed the smoke will purify evil spirits Blood sacrifice is valued in Parum clan and Wundior beliefs, and the spiritual master is usually associated with meat-flesh (ring) in living-blood which is considered life. The physical body dies with flesh, but the life spirit and body spirit do not  die. Other items are a mattress, bags, hoes, mattocks and other items which were used for grave digging. Spears put on shrine include the Unknown Sacred Spear. There is also a sacrificial spear called Aguelet Dit, a spear for blood wealth for crime acts of homicide, a life spear or lifesaving spear, an oath services spear (alol kueeng jony), a plaited grass winnowing-tray (atac, atany or ateny). It is mostly used by women for winnowing grains in a mortar made from a hollowed-out tree trunk (the Dong hat), set in the ground. The grain is pounded with a long pestle (lek hat) for making flour in the house.

The plaited grass winnowing-tray is the symbol of the Parum clan and widely believed to be the main source of clan spirits. It is associated with the deity and founding father and is called Atany Wun Dior or Atany Wundior, meaning a group of women.

People standing are singing hymns for prayers and appealing to divinities for forgiveness and reconciliation for sins and wrongdoings. The hymns mainly focus on the causes of the death of their leader and heir to the Unknown Sacred Spear and for supplication from clan and ancestry spirits.

The grandfather spirit bull pictured was tethered on a peg with a thong and sacrificed. The living blood poured on the tomb of Malek is believed be passed on to ancestry spirits to welcome their son home in the spirit world.

Below right we see the first bull sacrificed for clan spirits from Rum and Atany to Aguelet Agei and Malek to welcome their son and his spirit to the spiritual world they established. The next bull seen standing tethered via peg and thong is the donation from the children of the last wife of Agei, Achol Bol. All donated bulls are tethered on pegs in order of the line of birth in the lineage and according to the order of wives. No mistakes are to be made from this clan line as it may cause consequences of divinity punishment for disobedient children. People attend the burial of the chief of the spiritual clan in great numbers, sometimes thousands.

APPENDIX 1

One young man carrying a spear in the right hand and a shield on the left hand can be seen displaying actions of war while singing a war song. The people behind are reciting hymns of Rum Wenkook and Atany Wundior.

Showing are 2 mattocks, a shovel, a plastic bucket, mosquito net poles, a mosquito net, shoes, two white chickens sacrificed, a white bull sacrificed, and burned cow dung ashes. The mourning group is facing to the eastern side of tomb while reciting ritual songs. It is a belief the death of spiritual master must be celebrated to thank the divinity for giving them their spiritual master and that they must sing ritual songs of invocation for Divine clan Divinity frequently. It must be frequently echoed to give it more power.

Cam yai, war songs and prayers

The Machuet Apuk section is seen in this picture with one of the three ritual bulls donated from the Aguurpiny, Maluach and Kong-deer. Machuet of Apuk. It is usually regarded as the first place where Apuk developed and expanded wider to Aliai Apuk,
Malony Apuk, Angol Apuk, Manging Apuk and Tarweng Apuk respectively. This picture shows people of all ages at the holy tombs and shrines singing invocation songs for what has happened to the family. As I said earlier, bulls are donated by sons of sisters as cultural practices in Apuk and in lineage families, especially spiritual powers clans. The ritual bull pictured tethered on the peg with a thong was donated by the Kongdeer section.

The invocation order came to Manyual Mathok Malek on this occasion and he is standing in front invoking on behalf of the second wife Ajok Mathiang, the mother of Chief Malek Agei Malek Wol Rum and the half-brother of Aguelet Agei Malek Wol Rum. Standing next to Manyual Mathok wearing black trousers and holding a spear and club is a descendant of Malek Junior, brother of Malek Senior in the union of Athiech Mathiang and Wol Rum Agei. Each family wife and child invoke in a specific order along the lineage line so that everyone appeals to the mother and father that had begotten them down to the present generation. They ask for forgiveness, reconciliation, and a peaceful family with a brighter future ahead for their offspring in ongoing generations.

Mourning Rituals and Practices for the Burial of a Priest Chief

Donations of the Apuk Malony with war songs

This picture shows the Malony Apuk donation arriving with a group of people singing ritual songs going around tombs and shrines. The young man is carrying a shield as other people carrying spears chant traditional spiritual and war songs.

Malony Apuk group reciting ritual songs

The songs are sung in honour of their spear master with their Chief Manut Baak Athian. The white ram they donated is seen in picture tethered on the decorated peg with a thong. Donations can be bulls or rams

Malony Apuk group reciting ritual hymns

Here, the Malony Apuk group and chief are singing more ritual songs in honour of their spear master.

APPENDIX 1

Ritual prayers and hymns reciting by Agei descendants

From left to right are descendants of Rum, the founder of Parum clan to the current Agei Malek Rum offspring. Madhel Malek started the on the left and has doubled behind according to family positioning in the ritual burial ceremony on the final day.

Seen in front from left to right: Kur Deng, Atany (Marial) Deng, Malek Deng Agei, Manyual Mathok Malek, Paramount Chief Kur Malek, Dut Anyar Mayen as maternal uncle from Abuk Anyar Mayen, mother of Malek Agei, father of Deng Malek. Behind one can see the faces of Akok Wol Agei, Agei Aguelet Agei, and Agei Deng Malek and others. The final burial ceremony is usually crowded since many cultural mourning rituals and practices are made to mark the beginning of the end for cleansing appeals and thanksgiving for supplication of prosperity from ancestors after receiving their son in the spirit world.

Ritual Bulls in an Orderly Sacrifice

This picture shows a bull of the deceased master of spear, Deng, which he selected with twenty cows from among the marriage cows for the dowry of the daughter of his brother, Mador Malek. Because he is the first son in the union of Malek Agei and Ajok Mabuoch, this bull is going to remain tethered under the Agei shrine to indicate his presence here among the people celebrating the death of the physical body. Life spirit, body spirit and living spirit are all in this bull, which is why it must be tethered before any other bulls are brought forward and tethered on pegs in a specific order in line with birthrights according to tradition. Put on the Agei shrine are the clothes of the deceased master of a spear; a cooking pot, a club, the bedsheet of the deceased, and the Angau Dit Drum. Sitting next to them is Adut Aguelet Agei.

Mourning Rituals and Practices for the Burial of a Priest Chief

Ritual invocation songs for sacrifices

Amel Deng Malek brought water, milk and atany or atac to put under the shrines. The ash of burned dung, slaughtered white chickens, bulls, a black female calf, and drums are pictured. As well, the hides of slaughtered sheep for rituals are hanging on top of the two shrines. Lastly, there is equipment for digging, spears on the shrine, and decorated pegs.

Priest chiefs and offspring of the deceased member take opportunities to appeal to the deceased member to take their concerns to their grandfathers present in the spirit world as he is now going to join them. They ask him to appeal to the ancestors to provide them with full protection from evil spirits. Priest chiefs, family members speaking and praying in the burial ceremony, and elderly members of the community in the village all mention the need for guidance and spiritual protection to be conveyed to ancestors by the deceased.

Funeral Rites

The picture shows a man jumping high off the ground.

People sing songs of prayer, peacemaking, war and prosperity after the tragic death of a priest chief.

355

APPENDIX 1

Mourning ritual celebrations

The woman is displaying warfare poses with other women and holding a spear in her right hand. She is near the old shrine on the tomb of Paramount Chief Agei Malek Agei buried next to the tomb of Agei Aguelet Agei Malek Rum. Agei Aguelet Agei and Agei Malek Agei love one another and were buried here at Malou Camp

The mourning day for the priest-chief was attended by people of Apuk in numbers estimated at over 10,000 people. Donation in the form of rams and bulls was 36 animals including one black calf. Women lead the celebration here hoping to get a spiritual blessing. They came to comfort the widows of the priest.

Here we see the second wife of the spiritual master wearing plaits displaying warfare stances in honour of her husband while wearing a headdress of ostrich black feathers, Ajom Wut. She is joined by several women charging behind her displaying the same stances. A bull called mading thon is their target. They are pressing mading thon to fight the war well and defeat adversaries, which in this case is the evil which brought death the spiritual leader at a time

of need. Mading Thon, from the marriage of the daughter of the brother of the deceased, has been offered to the life spirit and body spirit of Deng Malek to guide the families and the entire clan away from danger after reaching the ancestry world of spirits. It was donated by a maternal uncle and is

Mourning Rituals and Practices for the Burial of a Priest Chief

going to be sacrificed on the third and final day of mourning and ritual sacrifices.

The donation of a female black heifer from the Kongdeer Apuk is tethered on a peg under the shrine of Malek Agei near the tomb facing in a counter-clockwise direction following the order of lineage. It was donated by Agei Malek Ngoth Malek Junior, brother of Malek Senior in the union of Wol Rum and Athiech Mathiang. Their two sons Malek senior and Malek junior have the same name, because Wol was the only son, juol, in the union of Amel and Rum, and Rum himself was also an only son, juol, in the union of Agei and Awien who was juol as well. There were not enough records gathered from the unknown period to the known generation of Atany (Ateny), his son Agei, his Rum (or Wol) son of Rum to explain the origin of the Unknown Sacred Spear, which they inherited and passed on to Malek Wol, Agei Malek Wol, Aguelet Agei Malek, Agei Aguelet Agei, Malek Agei Aguelet, then to Deng Malek Agei.

Individual prayer time for relatives to reflect

This picture shows a bull to be sacrificed welcoming the late Deng who passed away in Kenya. The body was transported from there through Juba to Tonj State in South Sudan. Madhel Malek officiated the sacrifice rituals. He authorized younger brother Mador Malek to carry them out following the traditional principles of a high priest or deity funeral of the Parum clan for this specific occasion.

APPENDIX 1

Family History

Deng is the first son in the union of Malek Agei and Ajok Mabuoch Jang, who was mortally struck by lightning in 1955 thunderstorm at the Rual May Adult Education School being attended at the time by Malek Agei, high priest chief and Chief of the Traditional Court of Appeal for the Apuk in Thiet. The school was opened by the British Government, two kilometres away from Thiet Town for the children of chiefs and influential leaders of clans in the former Tonj District.

Deng inherited the Unknown Sacred Spear as the elder brother of Madhel Malek and Mador Malek from Malek Agei and Ajok Mabuoch. It was passed on to Malek from Agei Aguelet who inherited it from Aguelet Agei.

However, Aguelet Agei Malek Rum did not marry another wife after his only wife Adut Ngor Bak Matik. He was known for the wars he fought, the people he killed, the apuk paid to the families of victims killed and for the many injuries he sustained and survived. Aguelet exhausted clan family member's herds due to killing enemies who were compensated with payable apuk with cows collected through the collective responsibilities of the guilty clan to be given to the clan victims.

As covered earlier in the book, they wanted to take the life of Aguelet away as the only solution to stop payable apuk for victims killed by a family member. Aguelet survived the attack launched against him in his house at Mangar Agaach, three kilometers (two miles) from Manyiel Cattle Camp because he was a gigantic man and good fighter. He was rescued by the children of his sister Amel Agei, who travelled from Pachien in Kuach Akeen Koor up to Mangar Agaach and took Aguelet with them to the Pachien homestead.

Malek was the first son in the union of Agei Aguelet and Abuk Anyar. Agei married his second wife Achol Bol and be gotten Wol Agei, Aguelet Agei, Amel Agei, and Athulueth Agei as their children in their union.

Aguelet Agei was the only son, Juol among two girls: Amel and Awien Agei, in the union of Agei Malek Rum and his first wife, Athulueth Deng Thou. Agei Malek Rum married four more wives after Athulueth and they are as follows:

Athulueth Deng Thou, the first wife of Chief Agei Malek Rum, is from the Padiangbaar Clan. The first son is juol Aguelet Agei, (two daughters: Amel and Awien). He immediately inherited the Unknown Sacred Spear of Ancestors.

Mourning Rituals and Practices for the Burial of a Priest Chief

Ajok Mathiang, the second wife of Chief Agei Malek Rum, is from the Pakuieth Clan. The first son is Malek Agei Malek Rum who ascended to the throne of Apuk Chiefdom to replace Chief Agei Malek Rum, who died from injuries.

Athieng Mayom, the third wife of Chief Agei Malek Rum, is from the Pagong Clan in Muok Clan of Dinka Rek. The first son is Adiar Agei Malek Rum. He has other brother Jiel Agei Malek Rum and sister Abak Agei Malek Rum settled in Lou Ariik of Dinka Rek

Adut Malek Yor, the fourth wife of Chief Agei Malek Rum, is from Nyang Clan in Kuanythii section, where her specific sub-clan is not recoded. The first son is Akook Agei Malek Rum, who was born without brother and sister. Akook Agei Malek Rum got married and has children.

Ayak Kuach, the fifth wife of Chief Agei Malek Rum, is not recorded with her clan. The first son is Deng Agei Malek Rum, who died infant and second son Dhel Agei Malek Rum took over the responsibility assisted his brother Kok Agei Malek Rum in the family.

(Some wives do not have recorded information about their clans.)

APPENDIX 2

The Reunion with Body Spirits after the Burial of a Priest Chief

In November of 2012 the ceremony for the installation of a shrine on the tomb of a spear master or priest chief after burial was undertaken for Deng Malek (the deceased). This was followed by the reunification of the body spirit with his children and wives. This occurred on the last day as shrine was raised on the tomb. Seven bulls were slaughtered during the rituals and sacrificial ceremony.

The body spirit of priest chief Deng Malek was taken from burial site in Malou Camp to the house by using bulls provided by his brother Madhel Malek and maternal Uncle Aguok Bol (the descendant brother of Angau (Aluat) Anei Akol Kuot). The ritual prayer for reunification between the body spirit of Deng and family members (children and wives) was performed for the living spirit, life spirit, body spirit, ancestry spirits, jaak, yieth, agoloong, and maternal spirits to return to the house after the burial shrine is raised up in the day of ceremony. The Unknown Spear (or Unknown fishing Spear), the Spear of Aguelet, an oath spear, and personal spears taken to the burial site are usually returned to the house following reunion prayer in ritual ceremonial bulls using sacrificial bulls and rams slaughtered under shrines at the house.

Below are pictures of rituals and practices after the burial shrine ceremony conducted at the Tombs site at Malou Camp and at the house of high priest chief Deng Malek. Two bulls offered for ritual sacrifice for reuniting spirits in the house were slaughtered through the supervision of hired spear masters from the Pagong and Padhieu clan respectively.

The Reunion with Body Spirits after the Burial of a Priest Chief

After Burial Rituals and Shrine Ceremony

A group of youths and women carrying spears and umbrella parrying shields. They are wearing celebration clothes, ornaments and accessories.

They have entered around the tomb moving clockwise, from left the rounding the tomb, the shrines and decorated pegs. They rotate three times walking in lines singing war songs, prayer songs, and the Parum clan song,

People have come to the burial place, charging with shields, displaying war practices.

Young people are at the mourning burial place. Many spend night near the tomb for the ritual celebration days. There are people seen on a mat where they spent the night.

Those arriving from their village are currently displaying warfare games.

One charges another, and the opponent responds in the same way. They do this while waiting for people who went to the bush to carry shrine about to arrive to Malou Camp. They continue

charging while carrying spears, sticks, cubs, and shields sing to one another with ritual songs, war songs. They get very excited during the celebration. It is a tradition to circle the shrines, tombs and pegs in a particular order to seek every spirit's blessing.

APPENDIX 2

The Parum clan has spiritual powers and its clansmen claimed to have been chosen by the spirits of clan divinity to be contact between human and god of divinity spirit through powers communicated with pointing spears dedicated for the function and prayers in the ritual services. The shrine is a symbol to the spirits which sit on  top to listen to prayers and wash away where evil spirits may emerge to fight them before descending on people etc. to inflict damage, severe or minor, and alert clansman of danger. They are expected to respond by offering sheep or prayers according to the culture and to call for forgiveness or evil destruction.

The new shrine for the tomb of priest chief Deng Malek was brought to the mourning burial tomb from the bush where it was cut by the son of a sister, who is now seen wearing green cloth in the middle of young people carrying the shrine around tomb to be submerged on the hole made at the graveside.

Youths are singing songs of war, songs of the clan of the deceased, ritual songs and ceremonial songs appealing to the divinity to provide continuous life, to abandon prosperity after the death of high priest chief of the land and bring peace between enemies and sub-clans. They also sang appeal songs reciting refusal for hatred, evil, and hatred as they celebrate and pray.

The shrine is put down near the hole made on the side of the tomb and people have gathered for ritual prayer before it is put on the hole

The Reunion with Body Spirits after the Burial of a Priest Chief

and raised up in accordance with traditional practices for the burial of a priest chief in the Parum Clan.

A flag is being tied on the shrine prior to raising. This is a fairly recent practise adapted during the contemporary period.

The shrine is raised up with ritual prayer songs being sung while the shrine is being raised up. Community members are there celebrating the shrine inauguration near tombs and shrines of Malek Agei, Agei Aguelet Agei and Paramount Chief Agei Malek Agei Malek. They are the founders of the holy burial place of Malou Cattle Camp.

After raising the new shrine, youths are celebrating by singing songs.

The young people are seen celebrating after raising the shrine. They began songs of war and clan for the cleansing ceremonial celebration on tombs and continued moving around shrines, tombs and pegs for spirit rewards for good health and prosperity in the country.

Ceremony, Celebration and Games with Warfare Actions

The mourning burial and ritual practices ceremony continued the next morning after the shrine was raised. You can see people sleeping at the mourning and burial place on mats. New arrivals are displaying warfare games and others are there facing the tomb and shrines with prayer songs in praises for Agei Aguelet, Malek Agei, Agei Malek and Deng Malek, while beseeching their body spirits, ancestry spirits, and world spirits to guide the nation.

APPENDIX 2

Ceremony and Ritual Sacrifices for Slaughtering Bulls

Here we see mourning rituals with bulls being slaughtered according to their family lineage. Bulls for slaughter are donated from direct family members.

Final Rituals with Bulls Left to Reunite Spirits in Houses

Bull for Uniting Spirits and Ritual Prayers of Appeal

Shown are mourning ritual performances for the completion of the ceremony. Bull Mayen, which is seen here cannot be slaughtered here. It is left over to carry back to houses and cattle camps the living spirit, body spirit and ancestry spirits which have come to participate in the burial back to houses so that they unite with children and wives. Mayen and Madok are

The Reunion with Body Spirits after the Burial of a Priest Chief

two bulls to carry along them the spirits to unite both spirits and family spirits in houses after completion of mourning burial and raising of shrines. The shrine raised is believed to be the seat of spirits where they sit during ritual sacrifices and prayers of appeals for their intervention on the disasters be falling on the people at large. A man reciting warfare and ritual songs is seen running in the middle of people, holding club and shield made of buffalo hide.

Madut Malek Charging in Warfare Actions

Madut Malek and Malek Deng Agei

The brother of priest chief Madut Malek Agei and son Malek Deng Agei charging against each other in celebration honoring their high priest chief. This was practiced quite often during the burial ceremony of ritual celebrations and in the time of raising shrines for spiritual priest chiefs. Looking around are people who gathered for the ceremony. Warfare actions are usually displayed on this occasion in a vigorous way. They can cause incidences ending with death or severe injuries. Youths celebrating are always call to exercise restraint. Fortunately, this ceremony ended without harm.

APPENDIX 2

Aguelet Malek Warfare Action on Agei Malek Shrine

Here is Aguelet Malek Agei, displaying warfare on the last day. He is displaying next to the shrine and tomb of Agei Malek Agei, Paramount Chief, after bulls have been slaughtered according to family lineage. The two bulls were donated by Aguok Bol Wol Anei, maternal brother of Angau Anei Akol Akot. Angau Anei Akol Akot was the mother of Agei Malek Rum Wol Rum, the first traditional chief who was founding leader of Dinka Apuk to start working with Anglo-Egyptian Sudan Government.

Aguelet and Wol Angau Malek Agei Celebrating with Oxen

This is the afternoon after the cattle have returned and been tethered on pegs on the left-hand side. The big drum called Angau Apiok was bought by Malek Agei in 1971. There is a small drum next to it under the shrine of Malek Agei. Both big and small drums are called Angau Apiok drums. The big drum is called loor, and the small drum leng. The shrine is now seen erect on the tomb.

The Reunion with Body Spirits after the Burial of a Priest Chief

Celebration with Oxen

On the final day, the oxen celebration is the next activity for traditional practices in the ceremony of the priest chief. Women are carrying spears, branches of trees, stems of sorghums and clubs while moving round the shrines, tombs and decorated pegs. Drums are seen also lying on the ground or hanging on pegs. It marks the last day of nights spent sleeping on the grave side in Malou cattle Camp.

Majok Deng Malek Displaying His Oxen in the Final Day of the Reunion Ceremony

Majok Deng Malek (Majok Madut Atany) is seen carrying a spear on his right-hand and shield made of buffalo hide. Another young clansman carries drum over his shoulder on the left. Women behind them are sharing in the celebration. Majok staved bulls along the way when the cows returned to their camp within Malou, at 100 yards away from the burial place. It a cultural practice in Apuk Juwiir.

APPENDIX 2

Marial (Atany) Deng Malek and Majok Deng Malek in the Ceremony

Atany is the first son in the union of Deng Malek and Atik Dhur Macar. He is displaying his oxen after the burial shrine was raised and spiritual cleansing was perceived as accomplished to celebrate ceremonially.

Majok Deng seen here holding a shield in the left hand and a spear in the right hand after killing a bull on the way for the honour of his father. All his adult children killed one bull each before the arrival of cattle to the site of burial. This is a tradition followed by children of priest chiefs from lineage clans with spiritual powers.

Shrines, tombs, decorated pegs and two drums are seen around the site of tombs in Malou Cattle Camp. This marked the end of the second stage conducted nine months after the burial.

Agei Deng Malek Agei is displaying oxen. Young people staved bulls as many as they can along the way for cleansing the cattle.

The Reunion with Body Spirits after the Burial of a Priest Chief

Taking oxen around shrines and tombs on the left side is part of the ritual practices. They stave as many as they can on the way after burial of priest chief ceremony to receive spiritual blessing. This is perceived to increase numbers for both cattle births and lifespans for the oxen owners celebrating. They will also receive prosperity for appearing at the ceremonies for the death of a priest chief.

The Union of the Body Spirit and Family Members a Year after the Death

Deng's Body Spirit Returns to Houses with Bulls

Standing with a stick is Aguok Bol. Aguelet Agei is sitting and two bulls are tethered on pegs. Spears have been put on the shrine. There is water for libation on the calabash.

Priest Chief Deng Malek's body spirit has been brought back after the burial shrine ceremony was concluded. The Unknown spear measuring 185 cm long; the Aguelet Spear measuring 180 cm long, the Oath spear made by Malek Agei and measuring 130 cm long, and other personal things have been returned to the house at the same time with the body spirit.

APPENDIX 2

Ritual Prayer for Reuniting Spirits, Children and Wives in the House

Relatives of the spear master gathered to perform ritual prayers and sacrifices with bulls for the reunion. From left to right- Madut Deng Agei, Agei Kuom Agei, Machar Dhur, Deng Aguok Athulueth Agei (son of the sister responsible for shrine raising, pegs, tethering bulls on pegs etc.). Agei senior Deng Malek, Madhel Malek Agei, Aguelet Malek Agei, and other three persons behind them are family members.

Agei Deng Malek standing with stick, wearing T-shirt with picture of his late father Deng Malek, is considered the heir in the family according to the position of his mother, Yar Guran Ador. He is the only child (juol) in their union. He has lived in Canada since 2001.

370

The Reunion with Body Spirits after the Burial of a Priest Chief

Spiritual Priests Supervising Rituals and Practices of the Reunion of Spirits

The high priest seen directing the elder Aguelet Agei to go and slaughter the second bull after the first bull was slaughtered by Mador Malek on behalf of the family. The first bull was issued by Madhel Malek on behalf of the family and the second bull was issued by Aguok Bol on behalf of maternal uncles.

Aguelet Agei seen holding the special spear for ritual bull sacrifices to slaughter the second bull. It is ritual tradition practice for women to cover the private parts of bulls for ritual sacrifices. Women are here seen busy with aprons used for covering.

Types of Spears for High Priest Chief

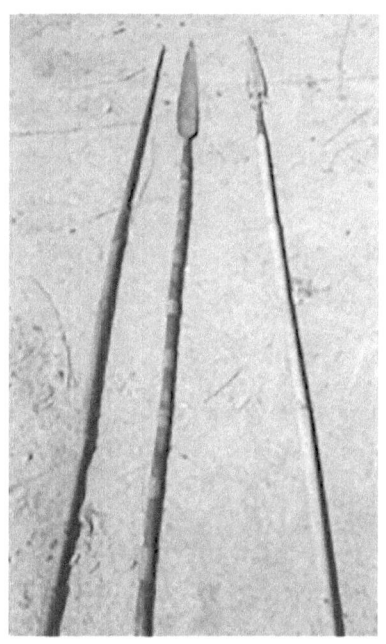

The spears used by the Jaang Apuk Lith in Machuet Apuk were obtained in trade. Traditionally in the past they were considered of superior quality when produced by the 'Jur Luo' smiths in the Jur River District areas. It is not clear which century period and types these three spears should relate to. The people using them are from Machuet Apuk in Jak village, where spiritual leaders emerged centuries ago, and continue through heirs.

APPENDIX 2

These spears have general similarities to the ancient Jur Luo spears and the newly crafted Jaang smiths made spears, but the form seems to be more complex and the shaft circular for the first oath spear on top. It has a further 2 barbs on either side, one curving down, and the other curving upwards. It is of better quality made and by Jaang smiths (Dinka smiths) to suit their situational applications with a slightly lighter type of wood.

The Jaang (Dinka) term for this type of spear is given as tong and bith. This is usually combined with a second term to describe its appearance. Popularly known as follows:

Tong alol: The top spear above is a Tong alol. However, there are different types of tong alol design with barbs curving down and others curving upwards. They come in many styles. Priest Chief Malek Agei was appointed Chief of the Traditional Court of Appeal in 1949 and tasked to perform oath services between enemies in disputes without any reliable witnesses to ascertain the offences and solicit the truth with judiciary skill. He therefore made a tong alol for oath services as an alternative resolution of clan disputes.

Tong abanban: The spear in the middle, is a tong abanban, which is different from tong alol, tong achokwey, or tong aroldok.

Bith laak: The bottom spear, is a bith laak (binh laak). There are different types of bith, such as binh laak, binh nyueth, binh yuay, binh anerich, makuen bith, binh achokwey, etc.

Tong Alol for Oath Services

Alol kueeng was in use since 1949 by priest Chief Malek Agei. It was inherited by his elder son Deng Malek. It was then transferred to Brother Madhel Malek, who transferred it to Mador Malek the youngest brother. This spear was to be inherited by the child of Deng Malek designated as the senior family son from the senior wife Yar Guran Ador. His son Agei Deng would have taken over the responsibility of oath taking if he was at home in Apuk Juwiir

Tony Alol is a traditional spear consisting of an iron point with a short triangular blade ending in 2 elongated barbs that extend downwards from the shoulders. It has a rounded central midrib running down the length

The Reunion with Body Spirits after the Burial of a Priest Chief

on both sides. The rounded body thickens below the blade to form a solid section with a flat pointing upper and lower face pointing downwards and has curved sides. Two small downward curving barbs extend from alternate sides. At its base, it joins with a solid circular shank, with two barbs on either side. One curves down and the other upwards.

At its base, the shank expands to form a cylindrical socket with a seam running up one side and is slightly open at its base. This has been fitted over the top of an oval bamboo shaft, the surface of which has been stained dark brown. It has a blackened color along its length, where it looks as if branches have been burnt off. The surface is smooth and polished. It tapers to its base, which has been fitted with a long iron spear butt with a

APPENDIX 2

socketed top and a slightly open seam running down the side. This tapers to a solid oval sectioned body that ends in a flat base. The iron elements are a metallic grey colour, with some surface rust over the socket. It has been fitted onto a long, narrow bamboo shaft with a circular section that tapers to a flat base. The spear is complete and intact, with a few minor scratches across the bamboo. The tony alol spearhead is 80 cm long and its bamboo length is 104 cm long; the spear blade length, width, and thickness at the midrib have not been measured. The shank diameter and the socket diameter, shaft diameter, socket diameter and base diameter were not measured.

Spear Aguelet Dit for Ritual Sacrifices -*Tong abanban*

The Aguelet Spear is used for special sacrifices offered for ritual prayers and libation. It consists of an iron spear-head with a narrow leaf shaped blade ending in rounded shoulders and is thickened down the centre on both sides to give a slightly lozenge shaped section with a midrib running in to a solid round sectioned shank. This joins with a round sectioned shank becoming more prominent towards the base. The spear-head ends with a cylindrical socket that expands towards its base, with a closed seam running up the front. This has been fitted over a lightweight bamboo shank with a slightly oval section over the surface. This tapers towards a slightly rounded butt and is a yellow coloured bamboo. The surface of the bamboo has been decorated with iron flatted with a hammer to be thinner in order to coil itself flexibly and easily when tied around bamboo or any wooden shaft being decorated. There are yellow and grey colours with some surface rust over the socket of iron. They are used for decoration consisting of a series of short rounded lines running upwards framed on one side by tying along the yellow bamboo body that has created a row of 8 upwards pointing decorations to the ending bamboo part. The end part of bamboo has been fitted over the coiled iron flatted slightly thicker for such spears. It makes spear heavy when in use and it protects the shaft at the join to the head. The spear is complete and has rust over some of the iron surface. Its weight, total width and blade length have not been measured. The spear alone is 85 cm long, and the wooden shaft is 80 cm long. The spear shank diameter and thickness have not been measured. The place of production was not specified.

The Reunion with Body Spirits after the Burial of a Priest Chief

The following spear is of Jur Luo manufacture, and is known as tong abanban, tong yar, or tong Ajuong. It is different from others like the tong ajokwei, toong for plural, like spear or spears in English.

The Unknown Fishing Spear – Bith Bany

This spear is over three centuries old and may be over six centuries old. It is not known who made it. Bith bany is meant to be kept only by descended clansman from a clan with spiritual power. Bith, according to the culture, is the centre of power to prophesize, to guide, to pray and to create awareness for any dangers among the community.

Bith and bany bith were and still are sources for the development of dynasty era, war control and leader, political authority and social unity in the Dinka Apuk culture.

This is true according to history of the family of Agei Malek Rum in the Dinka Apuk homeland. Bol Mel emerged through bith and bany bith. Rum also was believed to have been freed from captivity because he was the descendant from a clan with spiritual power, the Parum clan.

A Bith

A fishing spear consisting of an iron spearhead on a bamboo or wooden shaft. The Unknown Spear above has been fitted over light-weight bamboo shank with slightly oval section. There are some scorch marks rounded over the neck. It has a smooth surface with a rounded elongated body and a slightly rounded butt. It has a rusted surface of a grey-white colour with thinner pointed tip. The spearhead has a plain, round-sectioned tip

APPENDIX 2

that widens into a narrow elongated, rounded smooth long pointing body. The sides of this spear-bith have been worked to form a smooth section with the thinner and pointing tip which was created by obliquely struck chisel blows down the upper face and the underside. The flat upper and lower surfaces between long body have been smoothened with a hammer to appear round running downwards to the lower part of the long body section.

The spearhead is complete and intact but has rusted areas on its lower part and is a metallic grey colour when cleaned up. It has been set into a narrow bamboo shaft with a slightly irregular, knotted body that tapers in to a flat pointing end. It has light whitish colours and is complete. There are two rings for decoration. They are crafted of steel or iron flatted with a hammer made to be thinner for passing it round the bamboo on the upper part. There is iron fitted to the end of the bamboo to protect it. The spear has a length of 85 cm. The spearhead, body width, thickness and socket diameters all have not been measured.

The Unknown Spear has continued in existence since the dynasty era and has been passed down to the next generations of hereditary masters of the fishing spear (the priest chief, or members of the Parum clan of masters of the fishing spear, whose clan religious convictions are now thought to have much more power than those of other spiritual clans).

The Reunion with Body Spirits after the Burial of a Priest Chief

*STATE MINISTRY OF EDUCATION,
WARRAP STATE. SOUTH SUDAN.*

Awarding of Secondary School Certificates

State Minister of Education, Madhel Malek Agei, Professor.

APPENDIX 2

Cattle grazing ground in Malou. January 2011

January 2011, Madhel Malek Agei. Malou and Ahoom with cattle grazing nearby at Kongdeer Machuet, Dinka Apuk Juwiir, Tonj State.

Marial Achot grazing at Malou

The Reunion with Body Spirits after the Burial of a Priest Chief

Ayihou Lake in Maluac village and savannah forest at Machuet Apuk

LEFT: Lake Ayihoou is located in Machuet west near Maluach village.
ABOVE: Adeech Jook Lake is between Atongkamiir and Anoch villages.

Marial Achot and Mabil.

Ahoom Lake

Ahoom Lake is located in Machuet Apuk. It is is two kilometers away from Malou Camp. It is commonly known as Toch Agei's, Paramount Chief Agei Malek Agei's and Agei Aguelet Agei's place. All of them have been buried in Malou Cattle Camp along with Priest Chiefs Malek Agei Aguelet Agei and his son Deng Malek Agei Aguelet Agei.

APPENDIX 2

Wanhalel River

Wanhalel River Bank of the western site of Apuk Juwiir is where the historical conference was held that begat the popular Wanhalel Dinka Customary Law in 1927.

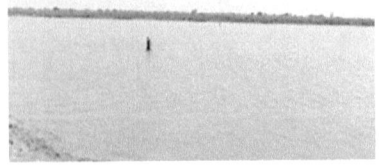

Fisherman in the Wanhalel River

Wanhalel River is useful in many ways. People drink water there and can also bathe. January 2011, by Dr. Madhel Malek Agei

The Reunion with Body Spirits after the Burial of a Priest Chief

Wanhalel River shore

The Wanhalel River is shared by Apuk Juwiir on the western bank, including Yar to the southwestern bank. The Thony share Wanhalel River in the eastern bank. The Muok share Wanhalel River in the west at the south of Yar and a small enclave at the eastern Bank at the western part of Thony.

Dinka Apuk Villages: Machuet, Aliai and Maluil Apuk

January 2011, by Madhel Agei, PhD.

One storage house wall is not completed.

A storage house in traditional style is seen from far behind big house

APPENDIX 2

Traditional spears for Madhel Malek Agei, Ayak Ngor. March 2013.

APPENDIX 3

Erection of a Shrine to Deng and Enactments of Warfare from the Past

Madut Malek Agei, sub-chief of the Apuk Kongdeer sub-clans is seen here in action. He is holding a spear in his right hand and a shield on the left side. He is charging towards his opponent to stab him in hand to hand combat. This was on display at the Malou Camp shrine during a ceremony of the high priest chief at the Jak holy shrine ground.

Madut is now displaying war tactics during the ceremony after the death two month's previously of his senior step-brother Deng from his first wife Ajok Mabuoch Jang. This style of combat is to charge the enemy and then stab closely while retreating. In times past, you killed the enemy; he killed you, or it ended on a stalemate. At the end, in mock battle, you kneel down watching each other and then retreat victoriously.

APPENDIX 3

Aguelet Malek Agei, the Brigadier and Deputy Director of the South Sudan Prison Service of Tonj State is displaying standing combat of in this situation. He is demonstrating how to act when fighting is intense and throwing a spear at the enemy close at hand is the only option. This enactment was in November 2012, during a ceremony at the Malou Camp shrines of the Paramount Chief Agei Malek Agei. The traditional Chief of the Appeal Court, high priest Chief Malek Agei Aguelet Agei and Deputy Judge and priest Chief Deng Malek Agei are pictured respectively. The Brigadier is displaying war-style in celebration for the raising of a shrine on the grave of Deputy Judge and priest Chief Deng Malek Agei. In this kind of fight, one must be vigilant to knock away incoming spears. This is indicated by the positioning of the shield.

Here, Aguelet Malek is displaying combat manoeuvres and shows shield positioning when an enemy casts spears at you. Women were often shielded together with the person holding the shield from spears.

Erection of a Shrine to Deng and Enactments of Warfare from the Past

A group of Apuk youths at the burial celebration at the Malou Cattle Camp shrines are carrying spears and protective shields. They are wearing traditional dress, ornaments and accessories while marching towards the holy shrines. They are in warfare mode practising combat movements in the ceremony with war songs and ritual songs combined. They are ready to respond right away if they are provoked.

www.ingramcontent.com/pod-product-compliance
Lightning Source LLC
Chambersburg PA
CBHW030250010526
44107CB00053B/1657